CLOUD

SHORT CIRCUITS

Mladen Dolar, Alenka Zupančič, and Slavoj Žižek, editors

The Puppet and the Dwarf: The Perverse Core of Christianity, by Slavoj Žižek

The Shortest Shadow: Nietzsche's Philosophy of the Two, by Alenka Zupančič

Is Oedipus Online? Siting Freud after Freud, by Jerry Aline Flieger

Interrogation Machine: Laibach and NSK, by Alexei Monroe

The Parallax View, by Slavoj Žižek

A Voice and Nothing More, by Mladen Dolar

Subjectivity and Otherness: A Philosophical Reading of Lacan, by Lorenzo Chiesa

The Odd One In: On Comedy, by Alenka Zupančič

The Monstrosity of Christ: Paradox or Dialectic?, by Slavoj Žižek and John Milbank, edited by Creston Davis

Interface Fantasy: A Lacanian Cyborg Ontology, by André Nusselder

Lacan at the Scene, by Henry Bond

Laughter: Notes on a Passion, by Anca Parvulescu

All for Nothing: Hamlet's Negativity, by Andrew Cutrofello

The Trouble with Pleasure: Deleuze and Psychoanalysis, by Aaron Schuster

The Not-Two: Logic and God in Lacan, by Lorenzo Chiesa

What IS Sex?, by Alenka Zupančič

Liquidation World: On the Art of Living Absently, by Alexi Kukuljevic

Incontinence of the Void: Economical-Philosophical Spandrels, by Slavoj Žižek

The Dash—The Other Side of Absolute Knowing, by Rebecca Comay and Frank Ruda

Subject Matter: The Anaesthetics of Habit and the Logic of Breakdown, by Aron Vinegar

What's That Smell? A Philosophy of the Olfactory, by Simon Hajdini

How to Research Like a Dog: Kafka's New Science, by Aaron Schuster

The Emperor's New Nudity: The Return of Authoritarianism and the Digital Obscene, by Yuval Kremnitzer

Cloud: Between Paris and Tehran: Kiarostami/Corbin/Lacan, by Joan Copjec

CLOUD: BETWEEN PARIS AND TEHRAN

KIAROSTAMI/CORBIN/LACAN

Joan Copjec

THE MIT PRESS   CAMBRIDGE, MASSACHUSETTS   LONDON, ENGLAND

The MIT Press
Massachusetts Institute of Technology
77 Massachusetts Avenue, Cambridge, MA 02139
mitpress.mit.edu

© 2025 Massachusetts Institute of Technology

All rights reserved. No part of this book may be used to train artificial intelligence systems or reproduced in any form by any electronic or mechanical means (including photocopying, recording, or information storage and retrieval) without permission in writing from the publisher.

This book was set in Copperplate Gothic Std and Joanna MT Pro by New Best-set Typesetters Ltd. Printed and bound in the United States of America.

Library of Congress Cataloging-in-Publication Data

Names: Copjec, Joan, author.
Title: Cloud : between Paris and Tehran : Kiarostami/Corbin/Lacan / Joan Copjec.
Description: Cambridge : The MIT Press, 2025. | Series: Short circuits | Includes bibliographical references and index.
Identifiers: LCCN 2024049522 (print) | LCCN 2024049523 (ebook) | ISBN 9780262552394 (paperback) | ISBN 9780262383271 (pdf) | ISBN 9780262383288 (epub)
Subjects: LCSH: Kiarostami, Abbas—Criticism and interpretation. | Women in motion pictures. | Muslims in motion pictures. | Islam in motion pictures. | Motion pictures—Philosophy.
Classification: LCC PN1998.3.K58 C67 2025 (print) | LCC PN1998.3.K58 (ebook) | DDC 791.4302/33092—dc23/eng/20241025
LC record available at https://lccn.loc.gov/2024049522
LC ebook record available at https://lccn.loc.gov/2024049523

10 9 8 7 6 5 4 3 2 1

EU product safety and compliance information contact is: mitp-eu-gpsr@mit.edu

To Michael and his memory, with love

CONTENTS

Series Foreword ... ix
Acknowledgments ... xi

INTRODUCTION: A CINEMA OF SUBTRACTION ... 1

PART I: STRAIGHT SHOTS

1   **THE IMAGINAL WORLD AND MODERN OBLIVION: KIAROSTAMI'S ZIGZAG** ... 17

2   **THE VERTIGO OF ORIGINS** ... 45

3   **FROM THE CLOUD TO THE RESISTANCE** ... 59

4   **BATTLE FATIGUE: BODIES AND RESURRECTION** ... 79

PART II: PILLOW SHOTS

5   **MAY '68, THE EMOTIONAL MONTH** ... 101

6   **THE CENSORSHIP OF INTERIORITY** ... 121

7   **THE SEXUAL COMPACT** ... 145

Notes ... 169
Index ... 191

SERIES FOREWORD

A short circuit occurs when there is a faulty connection in the network—faulty, of course, from the standpoint of the network's smooth functioning. Is not the shock of short-circuiting, therefore, one of the best metaphors for a critical reading? Is not one of the most effective critical procedures to cross wires that do not usually touch: to take a major classic (text, author, notion) and read it in a short-circuiting way, through the lens of a "minor" author, text, or conceptual apparatus ("minor" should be understood here in Deleuze's sense: not "of lesser quality," but marginalized, disavowed by the hegemonic ideology, or dealing with a "lower," less dignified topic)? If the minor reference is well chosen, such a procedure can lead to insights which completely shatter and undermine our common perceptions. This is what Marx, among others, did with philosophy and religion (short-circuiting philosophical speculation through the lens of political economy, that is to say, economic speculation); this is what Freud and Nietzsche did with morality (short-circuiting the highest ethical notions through the lens of the unconscious libidinal economy). What such a reading achieves is not a simple "desublimation," a reduction of the higher intellectual content to its lower economic or libidinal cause; the aim of such an approach is, rather, the inherent decentering of the interpreted text, which brings to light its "unthought," its disavowed presuppositions and consequences.

And this is what "Short Circuits" wants to do, again and again. The underlying premise of the series is that Lacanian psychoanalysis is a privileged instrument of such an approach, whose purpose is to illuminate a standard text or ideological formation, making it readable in a totally new way—the long history of Lacanian interventions in philosophy, religion, the arts (from the visual arts to the cinema, music, and literature), ideology, and politics justifies this premise. This, then, is not a new series of books on psychoanalysis, but a series of "connections in the Freudian field"—of short Lacanian interventions in art, philosophy, theology, and ideology.

"Short Circuits" intends to revive a practice of reading which confronts a classic text, author, or notion with its own hidden presuppositions, and thus reveals its disavowed truth. The basic criterion for the texts that will be published is that they effectuate such a theoretical short circuit. After reading a book in this series, the reader should not simply have learned something new: the point is, rather, to make them aware of another—disturbing—side of something they knew all the time.

Slavoj Žižek

ACKNOWLEDGMENTS

This project, evolving as it did over a long time in fits and starts, would never have come to light without the quizzical tolerance, good sportsmanship, and sound advice of those whom I dragged into it and others who pointed me in the right direction while standing back. Unable to name them all, I will mention only a few whose assistance was particularly timely. A fellowship from Harvard's Radcliffe Institute was indispensable for launching my research and clarifying its direction. It was there that I met, among other inspiring fellows, Sari Nusseibeh, who suggested that I take a look at the work of Henry Corbin. Graduate students from Buffalo with whom I cofounded and edited the journal Umbr(a), and Sigi Jottkandt, a Buffalo alum who went on to found the online journal S, worked tirelessly with me to produce in record time two separate volumes on the unlikely topic of Islam and psychoanalysis. My search for potential authors led me to the groundbreaking work of Stefanio Pandolfo, who was persuaded to contribute an essay to one of the issues despite other pressing commitments that might have excused her. Most recently, I was pleased to discover the innovative work of Hadi Fakhoury, whose investigation into the theoretical relations between Corbin and Schelling has renewed interest in both philosophers. The fellowship of these and other generous thinkers has been sustaining and inspiring.

I also wish to thank the editors, past and present, at the MIT Press for the care they took with this book. The editors of the Short Circuits series—Slavoj Žižek, Mladen Dolar, and Alenka Zupančič—are longtime friends and colleagues and know, I hope, that they have my profound thanks. Urvi Vora, the most recent member of the publishing team, is responsible for restoring order to countless drafts of individual chapters and for calming the frenzy of their author.

My profoundest debt and deepest thanks belong to Michael, through whom I became and will ever remain palpable to myself. My orbit around the sun of his unique generosity, will not break.

INTRODUCTION

A CINEMA OF SUBTRACTION

Bread and Alley (1970), Abbas Kiarostami's first film, was made under the auspices of Kanun (the Center for the Intellectual Development of Children and Young Adults), a cultural organization founded in 1965 by the wife of Mohamad Reza Shah, later deposed by the Iranian Revolution. A short, ten-minute black-and-white film, it features a young boy who must negotiate his way past a menacing-looking dog. The film is devoid of dialogue, its only sound that of the extra-diegetic Beatles song, "Ob-La-Di, Ob-La-Da," which accompanies the boy's carefree, pre-dog-sighting stride, only to disappear and resume again after the canine threat has been deflected. It is a sweet film, simple and straightforward on its surface. Yet it bears a heavy burden, not only because Kiarostami referred to it as "the mother of all [his] films." For others, too, it heralded—or so it has been effectively argued—the Kiarostami aesthetic and paradigm: realistic in the sense that it presents a pristine, uncluttered vision of the world, modestly focused on a minor incident involving a protagonist, solitary and single-minded, who relies solely on his own stubborn will and an ingenuity that allows him to overcome the challenges confronting him.

While it is acknowledged that in later films the protagonists are not always young, nor in each case male, and often tend to be less irresistibly likable or capable of resolving the problems they confront, these exceptions do nothing to address the larger misconceptions embedded in the above account. There is, I will argue, a considerable distance between Bread and Alley's intent and the intent given to it by others less thoughtful about—and sometimes very critical of—what they take to be the basic paradigm of the director's work. Critics claim that Kiarostami is a humanist or a realist in the ordinary sense, that he was indifferent to the plight of women, or turned his back on his own culture and countrymen by making films for export to satisfy a touristic gaze. They also argue that he failed to acknowledge, let alone confront, the stifling political circumstances that were choking the country or take Iran's leaders and policies to task, as other filmmakers did. That these criticisms are unfounded can only be refuted through rigorous readings of the films themselves.

This is not to deny that there exist many fine analyses of the films capable of parrying misguided charges such as these. One might begin, for example, with the acute observations made by Youssef Ishaghpour in his still, inexplicably, untranslated book *Le reel, face et pile: Le cinema d'Abbas Kiarostami*. In a single clipped but insightful passage, Ishaghpour puts his finger on what he sees as a significant turning point in Kiarostami's filmmaking, where others are more inclined to observe only the continuities, which are also there. He identifies this consequential insight by offering a brief but detailed comparison of an early film, *The Traveller* (1974), to a later one, *Where Is the Friend's House?* (1987), which established Kiarostami's reputation worldwide. Both films were at Kanun. Both—like *Bread and Alley*—feature a resourceful and resolute young schoolboy who will stop at nothing to accomplish his task and are set—as in his first film—in an Iranian village with narrow, winding paths littered with obstacles to be overcome. Yet, the estimation of Ishaghpour, these two films are literally worlds apart. Here is how he describes the differences between them:

> In *The Traveller* the places—the streets of the small village, the house, the school—serve as the setting of the story, while in *Where Is the Friend's House?* they become through their repetition, "states"; there, the world is the site of an action, here, "the action" takes place in a world. This [shift] distinguishes occidental mimesis from the Persian miniature: in the occidental tradition, a universe is dominated by man and by his action, which determines the meaning of the world; while in the Persian miniature, there is a world more important than man, in which his actions and drama are not determining, and "history" is of little importance, and . . . things, details and their rhythmic-ornamental organization manifest another dimension: [call it] "paradisical."[1]

The distinctions Ishaghpour draws between the films suggest that Kiarostami adopts in the later work refined his "oriental" aesthetic, an aesthetic that may have evaded not only the perception of Western audiences but of Iranians as well. We must, however, be careful not to lose Ishaghpour's point by "orientalizing" the meaning of "oriental." In other words, we must avoid falling prey to a cliched understanding of this "other" aesthetic.

It has been noted, for example, that Kiarostami had a penchant for "philosophical long shots" in which the actors and their actions are visually diminished in scale as the camera pulls back to regard them from afar.[2] These shots can be seen to invoke Persian miniatures. But what does this mean? An average orientalist reading of these miniatures would contrast an occidental privileging of the individual with an oriental absorption of individuals into a larger whole. This precipitous opposition breezes past without bothering to note the complications that ought to deflect it. The distinction Ishaghpour makes is precise; it contrasts "the world [le monde]" of *The Traveller*, which serves as the setting of the story, with "a world [un monde]," that is to say, an indeterminate world, which appears in *Where Is the Friend's House?* In the first case, the world is closed, finite, and the human drama must thus either be contained within it (a historicist reading) or heroically, ruggedly alone, the hero faces off against it by transcending its limits (a humanist reading).

Kiarostami's films, however, occur in an indeterminate world and conform to neither of these alternatives. Thus, while it would not be incorrect to detect in *Where Is the Friend's House?* a kind of Persian miniaturization of the human drama that unfolds in it, it is imperative that we understand this correctly. Here is what the film is not asking us to believe: while young Ahmad may, through persistence and cleverness, manage to dodge various obstacles to save his schoolmate from censure by their teacher, his victories are small beer in the larger scheme of things. The orientalist error resides in the assumption that the "other dimension" is a place from which human actions may be judged and/or measured as relatively trivial.

Here is the problem with this interpretation: the world of the film—as Ishaghpour intedicates—is indeterminate; the other dimension at issue cannot be located at a measurable distance from the human drama, nor can it be regarded as a seat of judgment. True, Ishaghpour speaks of "a world more important than man," but his argument makes no sense unless one takes him to mean "more important than man conceived in isolation from this dimension." The salient point is not that the other dimension bears witness to the impotence of human action, which is incapable of intervening in the world in any significant way. The point is, rather, that this other indeterminate dimension, this outside, falls within man—it is buried, occulted there. It thus falls to him to dis-occultate it, make it known. The great advance of *Where Is the Friend's House?* lies in the fact that it makes this indeterminate vastness of the world evident in and through the actions of young Ahmad.

A simple synopsis of each film, *The Traveller* and *Where Is the Friend's House?*, exposes the way their overt parallels are rendered by formal divergences as Kiarostami's cinema takes shape. In the earlier film, Qassem sneaks out in the dead of night and heads to Tehran to attend a live soccer match. Although he finds his way to the stadium without any trouble, the arduous journey tires him; he falls asleep and thus misses the match. In the later film, Ahmad slips away from his village to look for a neighboring one in order to return a notebook to his friend, who lives there. While he arrives at the destination where an elderly guide tells him he will find the house of his friend, Ahmad declines to knock at the door and deliver the notebook to its owner.

The differences that set the films apart are far from slight. For example, we are only shown Qassem's one-way journey from his village to the stadium, while Ahmad is shown crossing back and forth between his and the neighboring village twice, without any narrative motivation.³ This repetition opens within the abstract temporality of the narrative, a time—or dimension of time—that does not clock the progress of the narrative. The forward propulsion toward the goal slackens as events begin to transpire less on the level of the narrative than somewhere beyond it. It is as if another dimension had opened up, a surplus elsewhere created via repetition. The central "action"—Ishaghpour places this term in quotations marks to distinguish it, one surmises, from narrative actions—of the film ceases to belong to the order of (narrative) facts and opens some other fictive order. The failure of Qassem to fulfill his desire to see a live football match is explicable in terms provided by the narrative: the exhausting journey takes a physiological toll on the young boy causing him to fall asleep and miss the game; while his dream of being beaten up provides a psychological alibi, a haunting sense of guilt prevents him from allowing himself to enjoy the game. The hesitation that prevents Ahmad from accomplishing his objective, on the other hand, is given no physiological, psychological, or any other alibi.

How, then, to understand the retreat of Ahmad from his thus far obsessively pursued goal? It is clear that the flat, horizontal logic of narrative cause and effect loses much of its fascination—here and henceforth in Kiarostami's films generally—as the other dimension, produced via repetition, emerges in it. The act of friendship Ahmad wishes to perform cannot and will not be accomplished by returning the book he acquired in error. Nor will he come face to face with his friend on the threshold of the latter's door. If these solutions are ruled out by the film, it is because it defines the accomplishment of the act in terms other than those of simple reciprocity or the making good on a prior loss. But what strikes us as uncommonly curious, I will add, is the stubbornness of a negativity that seems to attach itself to the image of the house at which Ahmad arrives not once but twice as if to mark it as twice wrong, or wrong in more than one sense. That it is not the right house is clear, for we discover, during the first arrival, along with Ahmad, that it belongs to another boy, one whose pants, visibly different from his friend's, are hanging on the clothesline.

The second arrival does not dispute through additional narrative or visual information the correctness of our former conclusion, and thus the house's unimpeached wrongness stands out as simply inexplicable—unless we conclude that "this is not the house" is in this second time marked, or, better, unmarked, in some more fundamental way. Everything *seems* to transpire as if—along with the forward thrust toward the goal—the image itself has lost steam, gone weak-kneed in the face of its deictic function. And yet, this is not it. What is astonishing about the scene is that it makes us witnesses of the image's failure to declare "this is the friend's house." Film theorists will recall that Christian Metz, in an attempt to clarify the way cinema could be said to function as a language, insisted that individual images ought to be regarded not as words but as statements. An image of a revolver, for example, should be taken as a declaration: "This is a revolver."[4] My point—you will detect the irony—is that this scene in particular, and Kiarostami's work generally, utters a retort: "Thus I refute Metz." For far from implying that the image fails in its task, that it is weak or unreliable, the image in the films of Kiarostami refuses to bow down or make itself subservient to reality. In brief, the primary aim of the image in his cinema is not denotative; it is not propelled by a deictic intention.

My argument runs parallel to, and takes some cues from, the one elaborated by Jean-Luc Nancy in his book on Kiarostami, *The Evidence of Film*, where "evidence" is credited with resisting reduction to any probative or documentary enterprise and the notions of language and the image are no longer charged with the task of making themselves transparent to facts.[5] Rather than pointing to objects existing in the world, evidence indicates or manifests an unseen.[6] The strongest, overall confirmation of this central thesis can be found in Kiarostami's frequently offered description of his film practice as an engagement in the "art of subtraction." "We create," the director said in an interview, "not by adding but by subtracting."[7]

The radical significance of this statement is at risk of getting lost in the fact that it is so obviously accurate that we think no further about it. In all of Kiarostami's films, narrative actions are pared down to a rare minimum, their motivations in short supply and conversations riddled with silences. Additionally, there are all those unignorable holes in the ground: a plethora of sculpted, underground spaces, which periodically recur in his films. Up to this point, Kiarostami's attempt to "wash out our eyes" can be confused with the minimalist projects of modernism in general, which had also become fed up with the piled-up density of denotation. We must dig deeper if we want to understand the way subtraction relates to the strong definition of the image with which Kiarostami composes his films. It helps to recall that the term with which Kiarostami characterizes his work reaches back to a premodern distinction made by Leonardo da Vinci between two contrasting ways of making art: via addition (*via di porre*) or via subtraction (*via di levare*).

This avenue of investigation will lead us—inevitably, in my estimation—to Freud, who evoked the distinction several times at the beginning of his career with the expressed purpose of aligning his new psychoanalytic method emphatically with the latter term. In "On Psychotherapy," for example, Freud imports the distinction to set psychoanalysis apart from the technique of suggestion, which psychoanalysis was intent on displacing:

> Painting, says Leonardo, works *per via di porre*, for it applies a substance—particles of colour—where there was nothing before, on the colourless

canvas; sculpture, however, proceeds *via di levare*, since it takes away from the block of stone all that hides the surface of the statue contained in it. . . . [While] the technique of suggestion aims at proceeding *per via di porre*; it is not concerned with the origin, strength and meaning of the morbid symptoms but . . . superposes something—a suggestion—in the expectation that it will be strong enough to restrain the pathogenic idea from coming to expression. Analytic therapy, on the other hand, does not seek to add . . . anything new, but to take away something, to bring something out; and to this end concerns itself with the genesis of the morbid symptoms . . . which it seeks to remove.[8]

Freud might have said this better later in his career, but we can make out what he means to say from our knowledge of where these fledgling insights would eventually lead him. While his reproach to previous methods of treatment sounds mild, it cuts to the quick. For he accuses them of covering up, or concealing, the unconscious. He states this almost in these very words. What he actually says is that the suggestive technique "conceals from us all insight into mental forces; it does not permit us, for example, to recognize the resistance to which the patient clings to his disease and thus even fights against his own recovery."[9] If I insist on pointing out that he almost states his position in the way I do, it is because he does not explicitly mention the unconscious at this point of his argument and even appears to dodge it in his characterization of the *via di porre* as operating on a "nothing before," on a blank canvas.

This depiction is, unfortunately, misleading, for—from the perspective of the *via di levera*—this prior nothing is far from trivial (it is not a mere nothing) or benign (insofar as it is the site of a resistance to recovery). The "nothing" at issue here is what Freud would name the unconscious. If the exposition of his argument is less clear than it should be, it is because he begins descriptively, thus seeming to lend credence to the proposition that there are two ways of making art, while he actually ends up invalidating the first, the art of addition, as less than useless. The polemical argument places larger issues at stake—not only the means of obtaining therapeutic effects, but also, inevitably, sublimation and the function of the symbolic by which the therapeutic effect is procured.

We cannot pursue this whorl of consequences in depth, but must linger awhile on a point that stands out almost immediately: if the art of addition is an art of covering up, the opposing art—of subtraction or psychoanalysis—cannot be said to be an art of exposure. This is so, once again, because what is at issue is the unconscious, which cannot be exposed or dragged out of hiding. There is nothing to expose since the unconscious is hiddenness itself and thus, by definition, not susceptible to unconcealment. That there is an unconscious is a founding fact of psychoanalysis; it posits an original negativity and an attendant impossibility and requires the art of psychoanalysis to adopt a negative stategy. Its primary aim is to put a stop to the privation of being. Lacan formulates propositions that help clarify this last point. He defines impossibility as "that which does not stop not writing itself." This is what I am calling psychoanalysis's founding fact, which can be dealt with solely negatively, by "stopping to not write itself." The task to which the art of subtraction is called is double. It must not only put an end to the obscurantist agenda of covering up the unconscious, of a recalcitrant wanting to know nothing about it, while avoiding the foolish error of trying to expose it. The art of subtraction is tasked with drawing attention to the subtraction that is the unconscious, without sacrificing the subtraction—its hiddenness—itself. To stop not writing it is the equivalent of Nancy's formulation: the art of subtraction is the art of evidencing of what is not. All is not given or spelled out.

Kiarostami's art, I will argue, in the chapters that follow, is not a minimalist art but an art of *plenitude*, of *expansion*. It attempts to restore to the world the fullness evidenced in its valorization of contingency. I will develop my arguments through explications of the films, the Islamic philosophy that I—like Ishaghpour—take to underpin Kiarostami's aesthetic, and ideas formulated within psychoanalysis. Some will be perplexed by the proposal of such a path and particularly by what may be regarded as psychoanalysis's intrusion into it. The defense of my approach will rely on local arguments offered in individual chapters. Here, I will stress a single point, made throughout the book: the essential commonalities between Islamic philosophy and psychoanalysis stem primarily from: (1) the centrality in each of a permanently subtracted element—God, in one case, and the unconscious in the other; and (2) an insistence on bearing witness to this subtraction or withdrawal from being and sight. It is the relation between these two points that is responsible for the fact that in Islamic philosophy and psychoanalysis, images and language are conceived in positive terms, as efficacious in themselves rather than subservient to reality. Rather than colorlessly abstract, images and language are regard as having powers of illumination and embodiment. The emphasis I place on the subtracted element and the imperative to safeguard it dictate my readings of Kiarostami's work. That this causes my path to veer from, or collide with, other approaches is inevitable. I will now flag some of these deviations and my justifications for them.

Veiling. A first approach, taken by some feminists interested in Iranian cinema in general, was to regard the veiling of women and the entire modesty system, which dictated what could be shown on screen, as a positive turn, inasmuch as it provided women a safe harbor from the objectifying look of leering men. It was argued that their removal from the field of vision, their veiling, freed women for action by allowing them to pass freely—that is, unseen—in society where they could work comfortably alongside men. While many insightful analyses of Iranian films were born of this impulse, there is to my mind a serious weakness to the wider argument: it fails to acknowledge the nontrivial difference between a veiling that aims to occult or completely efface what lies beneath and one that alerts us to its restless vivacity . That the draconian modesty system—which punished a woman for allowing a lock of hair to peek out from under her hijab, or for dancing because her movements would indicate the shape of her body under her clothes—was not designed to empower women or allow her to pass freely through society—is, to my mind, clear.

Nor am I persuaded by the argument that this system had in itself the unintended consequence of empowering women by allowing them to participate in the larger society. Its intention and actual effect is the cloistering of women, cutting them off from society. What the opaque form of veiling aims to occult is sexuality itself—which is, in any case, invisible, known only through its effects and never in itself. For from psychoanalysis we learn that sexuated being is that being which opens onto social being or a being entangled within a social apparatus. Nevertheless, I do take seriously the feminist criticisms of the objectification of the image of women and will thus address that concern by turning back to the question of the image, its function in film and in reality.

The image. Kiarostami dwells on this question of the image, which is a constant in his cinema—thematically and aesthetically—beginning with *The Traveller*. To raise money to attend the soccer match, Qassem hits on a scheme: he offers to photograph the other boys in the neighborhood for a bit of cash. Never mind that his camera is defunct and there is no film in it; the offer proves irresistible. All the boys line up to pay for an image of themselves—smiling into Kiarostami's functional and obliging camera, which grants them the wish Qassem's cannot. In *Close-Up* (1990), the Ahankhah family is so eager to see themselves on a film screen that they allow themselves to be bamboozled by Sabzian, a man who pretends to be the famous film director, Makhmalbaf. Once again, Kiarostami's camera takes over the task of fulfilling the family's wish, after it is discovered that Sabzian is ill-equipped to accomplish the task.

Even the villagers in *The Wind Will Carry Us* (1999), having spent the entire screen time dodging the TV film crew that arrived to film them, end up looking into Kiarostami's camera near the film's close, as if their resistance to being filmed were no match for their desire. As Ishaghpour puts it in his essay "The True and False in Art," "It would be fair to say that, according to Kiarostami, the whole world has just one wish: being photographed, appearing in a film, being on the screen. So much so, that it would be necessary to change Descartes's formula into 'I have an image, [therefore] I [am].'"[10] Why should women be exempt from this elemental desire to have an image—a desire so elemental that even the God of Islam is acknowledged to have pined for one. For want of an image he was hidden even from Himself.

Those who protest against the assimilation of women to an image are right to do so, though it needs to be acknowledged that there is a critical difference between an image that assimilates what it depicts (or: reduces it to an object) and an epiphanic image. The latter—or "incorruptible"—form of the image performs an epiphanic function. It directs us to attend not merely to what it shows on its surface but also to what nestles in its shadow. One of the most famous illustrations of such an image is the painting of a veil by Parrhasios, which prompted those who looked at it to wonder what lay beneath it. The function of the image in this case is not merely to draw our attention to what is visible but also to what is not. Here I feel compelled to recall Ibn 'Arabi's conception of love as a nearness which is so excessive that "it acts at first like a veil."[11]

Earlier, I offered a negative claim regarding Kiarostami's cinema, insisting that it does not function deictically. It is now possible to offer a positive, inverse claim in its stead. Rather than pointing to a referent, a reality already out there in the world, the image, in its strong sense, manifests something that exceeds the jurisdiction of the visible for two reasons: it is excessively close, too close to objectify, and, at the same time, inexistent. Kiarostami's *Like Someone in Love* (2012), filmed in Japan, advertises in the first word of the title its engagement with this conception of the image. The notion of likeness, of resemblance, is interrogated throughout the film and no more pointedly than when the supremely enigmatic female character, Akiko, blurts out, "Not a day goes by that I'm not told that I look like someone." The oblique reference to "someone" cancels itself out. Or, better said, it assigns to resemblance a peculiar, intransitive sense. For what it says about Akiko is that she resembles no one, no one to whom we can point or designate, least of all herself. If she resembles or is like herself, it is only insofar as she is not identical to herself. She holds together as a subject only on the condition that she is irreducible to a set of traits that objectify her. To be a subject, one has to be possessed by an excess that escapes capture by being.

At one point in the film, Akiko lets out a screech of protest against her pimp, who is pressuring her to go out on a job. Or, this is what we surmise, for she is not on screen when the screech is heard, and when the camera returns to her again in a reverse shot, her face is empty of any sign of emotion. A similar disruption of the field/reverse logic in *First Case, Second Case* will be examined in my fourth chapter. Here, as there, the obviousness of the mismatch—which holds back from identifying the sound of shriek with its perpetrator—forces us to take notice of it. *Like Someone in Love* continues to flaunt its trickery through its use of windows, especially in the long cab ride that takes Akiko from the bar, around and past her grandmother, to her appointment. In earlier films, car windows served as apertures through which characters looked out; in this film, they appear as surfaces that seem like "a

Mobius strip, to have two faces, one internal and the other external, while in fact it has only one."[12]

In *Avicenna and the Visionary Recital*, Corbin analyzes a specific literary form referred to as a "recital." His analysis confirms many of the insights Ishaghpour offers in his analysis of Kiarostami's films. Corbin's claim is that the recital form presents the world not as an abstract magnitude but as a lived reality. It does so by making itself the "the repository of the Image" each of us carries as our unique expression.[13] The image singularizes the subject by according the latter a surplus that cannot be found in the abstract universe of rationally constructed systems, where it remains concealed "beneath didactic demonstrations and impersonal developments."[14] What leaps out at us is the claim that the image "precedes all perception" and "transcends all expression."[15] If this captures our attention, it is because it reminds us that abstract systems do not need to expend a lot effort to hide or cover over perceptions that do not emerge in the first place. These systems need only to continue to obscure what is already occulted, what is not available to sight and can thus remain forever unthought.

It is from this realization that the recital's distinction as a symbolic form comes to light. For all we need do is locate the operation that makes what transcends or evades perception. Kiarostami does this for us in film after film: to make what does not appear appear, one must deploy a bit of flimflam. Some contraption or apparatus of dissimulation, some feint, is necessary to make what is unavailable to sight visible. The recital form, as defined by Corbin and invented by Avicenna and Sohravardi, relies on linguistic devices to accomplish this feat. Is it too obvious to point out that this was the same conclusion Freud came to, when at the end of his essay on the uncanny, he explains that his nearly exclusive recourse to literature throughout the essay was mandated by the fact that literature has at its disposal devices for making visible what is otherwise invisible?

Throughout history, the apparatus most often deployed in the service of this demonstrative deception has undoubtably been the mirror, and one of the best-known instances of this particular use of the mirror is the one deployed in paintings rendered in Renaissance perspective. In *The Origin of Renaissance Perspective*, Hubert Damisch underscores Fillipo Brunelleschi's description of perspective as "a structure of exclusion," that is, as a rule of construction that functioned only "on condition that everything escaping its jurisdiction be excluded from its field." Damisch argues that this meant that a vast "unmasterable background" could not enter paintings in perspective except via some apparatus or ruse—or, more precisely, by "the use of a mirror"—that would allow what was heterogeneous to the space, and therefore unfigurable in it, to appear in the "form of a reflection."[16]

The films of Kiarostami do not present themselves as an apparatus-free zone. Far from pretending to be innocent of technological intervention, they place cameras, camera crews, and the entire cinematic apparatus in plain sight; they flaunt the dissimulation in which they engage. In his final film, *24 Frames* (2017), for example, still images are visibly manipulated by digital, CGI (computer-generated images), and other means to animate them or cause movement to appear in them. None of this overt meddling is employed as a means of unveiling a hoax. Instead, Kiarostami operates in a distinctly Shakespearian-Freudian manner: he deploys the bait of falsehood to snag a carp of truth. Artifice is visible throughout his film not as devices bared, or scams revealed, but as ploys that are necessary to give evidence of truths that cannot be exposed. Here, once again, with a slightly different but compatible rationale, the image in his films is irreducible to a duplicitous double or diminished copy of an original. Instead, his image responds to an imperative: what cannot be shown must be shown to be unshowable. The image manifests an inaccessible proximity that de-completes what is made visible. It is a rigged device that introduces an oblique angle of incidence, that permits what is not tin front of us to come into view. I have already invoked Parrhasios's painted veil. To that example we can now add this account of its operation: the excess comes into view not directly but obliquely, as a shadow cast by the image itself.

Documentary/fiction, certainty/uncertainty, *agnosticism/Gnosticism*. That Kiarostami's films weave together documentaries and fiction is a truism in need of examination. My arguments above attempt to respond to this need, but other observations can be made about the apparent tension between the two impulses. Sometimes, it seems, as in *First Case/Second Case* (1979), that real life events, such as the Iranian Revolution, hijack the film Kiarostami is in the midst of making. At other times—*Close-Up* is the best example of this—the film seeks to hijack actual events unfolding in the news. But in these and in all others, fiction and reality are so subtly intertwined that it is impossible to say where one begins and the other leaves off. The influential essay "Kiarostami's Uncertainty Principle" by Laura Mulvey deals deftly with this implication of each in the other. Mulvey argues and shows through analyses of several films that spectators are compelled to assume a "conscious sense of uncertainty about . . . the truth or reality of what seems to be happening."[17] I do not disagree agree with this description, but my argument differs from hers in that it sees the primary principle of Kiarostami's cinema as a certainty principle. The reason for this stems from my sense of his cinema as being one of subtraction. This is to say that the films proceed from a certainty—a knowledge of subtraction—which assigns itself the task of manifesting it rather than denying it through procedures of obnubilation or unveiling. While the *trompe l'oeil* (which Mulvey in fact mentions in her essay), the painted veil, or angled mirror devices required to accomplish this feat do themselves create situations that skirt categorization as true or false, the films are driven, in my estimation, by a certainty.

The most ambitious aim of my project is to align not only Kiarostami's cinema, but psychoanalysis as well, to the Gnostic tradition that informs the visionary recitals of Avicenna and Sohravardi and begins with Ibn 'Arabi, the revered father of philosophical Gnosticism. Earlier, I referred to the fact that Ibn 'Arabi linked the experience of love with an excessive nearness. He further described this nearness as measureless; rather than figuring a path to an adjacent (or exoteric) object, it marks a pure (or esoteric) distance. In the case of *Like Someone in Love*'s Akiko, it is her self-love on which the film focuses, that is to say her inadequation to (or pure distance from) herself.

My return to Akiko via Ibn 'Arabi is meant to flag a couple of points that will underlie the whole of my argument. First, I suggest that what may appear as merely a formal or aesthetic question of the image has both sexual and political dimensions, which I will attempt to develop in separate chapters. Second, while Gnosticism is generally assumed to be a theory of man's "fallenness" from grace and his inability to attain higher knowledge as a result of his remaining incarcerated in his body, the Muslim Gnosticism on which I rely views the body differently, not as an anchor that drags one down, but as the site of pleasure. This revision of an earlier Gnosticism depends on an extensive contemplation of the relation between God and man. Rather than a simple retreat from the world, these Gnostics regard His withdrawal as a retreat into its interior. In this way they eroticize the non-relation that binds man to Him. Similar in many respects to F. W. J. Schelling's concept of a "non-unilateralist monotheism," the Muslim mystics define the relationship between God and man, their mutual constitution as an intimate link.

From the many cracks opened in the Kiarostami universe, evidence of sexuality seeps through in various forms: sadistic, humorous, sly, troubling, importune. Yet, despite the general out-of-placeness of its appearances, it does not surprise me that it does appear and does so in these forms. What does surprise me is the fact that they are often met with censure by some who accuse Kiarostami of betraying the culture that nourished him. Persia's rich literary culture is far from innocent of sexuality. Tutored by the exquisite libidinal tortures of Muslim mystics, Persian poetry espouses the erotic.

The first part of the book is a straightforward attempt to establish convincing links between Kiarostami's cinema (which was my starting point, the enigma I wanted to unwind), the new Gnosticism invented by Islamic philosophers, and psychoanalysis. It would not be correct to presume that these links are mere backward projections of my psychoanalytic perspective into areas that have nothing to do with it. Oftentimes my dawning knowledge of Gnosticism or a scene in a Kiarostami film caused me to rethink what I thought I had learned from Freud and Lacan. The second part contains "pillow shots," a term borrowed from Noel Burch's study of Japanese cinema. Pillow shots are cutaways or non sequiturs that shift the perspective away from the narrative thread that preceded it. These shots are regarded as "poetic" insofar as they expose a passion that has undergirded the narrative. In this part I focus on the affects of anxiety and shame and their relation to sexuality generally. Present by implication in the first section, they are here given their own space.

The various chapters were written as independent essays over a number of years. While their gathering here results in overlaps and variations—certain films, for example, are revisited and examined from a different perspective in different chapters, certain concepts are revealed to have different implications in different chapters—they seek to work together to present a complex thesis.

Finally, a word about the Cloud, which is one of a cluster of terms given by Islamic philosophers a to a nonexistent or "imaginal" place that operates, nevertheless, in the actual world. Cloud was chosen for my title over its synonyms because it has once again become the name of a nonplace that significantly impacts our daily lives. An argument that runs throughout the book is that this nonplace, Cloud, is pivotal to understanding the way individual beings relate to others. In two chapters, one devoted to the Iranian Revolution and the other to May '68, the political dimension of this relation is brought to the fore. In the first case, I focus on what Khomeini called the "sensorium of the Iranian people," which he credited with having the capacity to unite Iranians, to allow them to throw off foreign influences and thus move together as one. The problem: Khomeini's understanding of the sensorium is "unclouded." Sight simply sees what it is given to see. This simplistic notion strips the organs of sense of their negative dimension to which the Cloud draws our attention. The chapter on May '68 turns to *Seminar SVII*, in which Lacan reprimands the students for neglecting this very dimension, while offering us a picture of the modern form of Cloud or, as he calls it, the "alethosphere." This is the Cloud with which we are familiar: a nonplace where technological gadgets and prosthetic devices enhance our perceptions and put us in touch with the rest of the world. Lacan warns the students to be careful, for these gadgets siphon off jouissance and offer us a fake pleasure in its place. And, we must add: they offer a fake Cloud.

1
STRAIGHT SHOTS

1

THE IMAGINAL WORLD AND MODERN OBLIVION:
KIAROSTAMI'S ZIGZAG

A zigzag path carved into a hill winds from base to crest, where it is crowned by a lushly leafed tree standing solitary and upright like a kind of hieratic bouquet. This image recurs throughout the films of Abbas Kiarostami, but most prominently in three films—*Where Is the Friend's House?* (1987), *Life and Nothing More* (1992), and *Through the Olive Trees* (1994)—which critics refer to as "the Koker trilogy," simply because they are all set in the same location, the village of Koker in Northern Iran.[1] Easily mistaken for a "found" image, part of the natural geography of the films' actual setting, the recurrence of the image would seem to raise no questions nor require explanation. And yet there can be no confusing this image with natural geography, for as we learn from interviews, the films' director, did not simply stumble upon this peculiar landscape while scouting locations. He had his film crew carve the pronounced zigzag path into the hill.

An artificial landscape, then, inserted by Kiarostami into the natural setting, replicates, as it turns out, a miniature found in a manuscript executed at Shiraz in southern Persia at the end of the fourteenth century.[2] In the miniature, just as in the Koker trilogy, a sinuous path curls up the side of a hill atop, which sprouts a single, flowering tree. This miniature graces the cover of *Spiritual Body and Celestial Earth*, a book devoted to Islamic philosophy in which the book's author, the influential Iranologist Henry Corbin, praises the miniature as "the best illustration . . . which has come down to us today" of what he calls "visionary geography."[3] Distinct from natural geography or physically "situated space," which is organized according to preestablished coordinates, visionary geography is instead "situative." Neither purely abstract nor purely concrete and sensible, visionary geography is a "third" or intermediary realm between the abstract and the sensible; it functions as the threshold of reality, as "the origin of [actual] spatial references and [that which] determines their structure."[4] In this realm, the sense-perceptible is raised and pure intelligibility lowered to the same level; matter is immaterialized and spirit corporealized, or, "to use a term currently in favor," Corbin adds, "an anamorphosis is produced."[5] In Arabic this intermediate space is called *alam-al-mithal*; Corbin translated it as *monde imaginal*, the imaginal world.

Theorized under different names by different philosophers or left unnamed, the imaginal world only became visible as a fundamental concept of Islamic philosophy thanks to Corbin's decision to gather the disparate reflections on its function under this one term. In the words of Christian Jambet, Corbin's most famous follower, this felicitous translation "opened a new path" in the study of Islam and gave us "nothing less than a master signifier with which to decipher the meaning and destiny of [the Islamic] soul."[6]

Corbin did more, however, than restore the concept to its central place in Islamic thought; he became its vigorous advocate and bemoaned the consequences, into the present, of its regrettable loss. In his estimation, the year 869 CE, that is, the year of the Fourth Council of Constantinople, was a decisive turning point, for from this moment on, the *mundus imaginalis* fell permanently under the penumbra of its anathematization. During the fourth century, a series of Councils were convened to hammer out Church dogma to establish the Church as a central, unified authority. If it was specifically the Fourth Council that inspired Corbin's lament, this is no doubt because it was at this Council that Photios I, Patriarch of Constantinople, was deposed in retaliation for his condemnation of the *filioque* clause.

A Latin addition to the earlier Greek creed, the filioque clause stated that the Holy Spirit proceeds from both God, the Father, and "from the Son." That is, it accorded Christ equal divinity with the Father and thus "abolishe[d] once and for all the tripartite anthropology of spirit, soul, and body in favor of the simple duality of body and soul." By deposing the most powerful critic of the filioque, the Council signaled its embrace of the double procession of the Holy Spirit. And from this moment on, according to Corbin's stinging denunciation, "the way was open [to] the Cartesian dualism of thought and extension. For from this moment it became impossible to conceive of Spiritual Forms in the plastic sense of the term [as having a capacity for change] or of true substances that were fully real and had extension even though they were separated from the dense matter of the world."[7] In other words, what was at risk of being discarded was a materialism that was not founded in matter.

What was anathematized—and so thoroughly so that we have since come to associate its execration not just with the Council but also with the triumph of secularism—what was anathematized is the world of "subtle matter" (a matter that was neither purely spiritual nor purely material) and an organ of knowledge, the imagination, distinct from both the intellect and the senses. The impoverishment of the status of the prophetic imagination and the images formed there—which would henceforth come to be regarded as simply unreal, mere fantasy—went hand in glove with an impoverishment of reality itself, which, too, began to lose its dignity.[8] The dualistic thinking of Western metaphysics is then in Corbin's estimation, the direct issue of the fundamental dogma of Christianity: God's incarnation in the person of Christ.

OSTENTATIO CORPUS

Corbin objected vehemently to the Church's decision to view God's appearance as Christ as a unique historical occurrence located at a precise and irreversible moment of chronological time, rather than as an event that happens repeatedly at different moments in time and uniquely to each of the faithful. The latter position is the one adopted and collectively defended by the *falasifa*, those the Islamic philosophers who took their inspiration from Avicenna, who asserted that the soul expresses itself in an aspiration toward the still unrealized and not, as Averroes held, in an intellectual desire to know God.[9] For the *falasifa*, the uncreated, the divine, had to be returned to repeatedly and ceaselessly created, for theirs was a world whose ends were not already given. It was this belief that set them in direct conflict with Church dogma, which maintained that the godhead passed over into or became incarnated in esoteric matter, in a single finite Being, and that this fact was publicly and universally attestable.

Broadly construed, the dogma of incarnation concerns a central paradox not just of Christianity but of monotheism in general. Far more than a simple reduction of the polytheistic pantheon to a single God, monotheism was a "revolution of cosmic proportions" in that it introduced a new, previously unthinkable being into the world.[10] Instead of merely reducing the many to one, monotheism—in its striving to make the One-God the God of all—radically rethought the One, conceiving it not as self-identical but as always more or less than itself. One and yet plural, one only through its plurality. Christ offered a perfect illustration of this conception, for He was at once God and not identical to Him, different but inseparable from Him, the second person of God.

Still, the precise statement of this paradox entailed a protracted debate, one that lasted centuries and began even before the First Council of Nicea (326 CE), when the doctrine was first asserted. It should be noted that Corbin aims at a specific, literal conception of the dogma of incarnation, one that tended to congeal rather that multiply the One. We can approach his argument by clarifying a possible confusion that may result from his precise dating of the theophilosophical disaster that excised the imaginal world in favor of a human/divine duality. The synod of 869 CE is notable not only for having thrown its support on the side of the *filioque* clause but also for reaffirming support for the iconophiles, who had battled the iconoclasts in two long and bitter wars (730–787 CE and 813–842 CE) over the status of the image.

(While these bloody image wars have often been viewed as a doctrinal disguise for mundane struggles for political power, it can be demonstrated that the reverse was true. We will return to this point later.) Now, that the Church embraced both the image and the *filioque* in the same breath would seem to cast doubt on Corbin's linkage of a reductive dualism with the devaluation of the image—but only if the questions is, "Who won the wars?" the detractors or defenders of images? The real question is, "Which definition of the image prevailed?" The answer to this is: not the one for which the iconophiles fought.

The question the iconophiles had to confront was, "How can material man-made images be conceived as images of a limitless, immaterial God?" St. John of Damascus (676–749 CE) disarmed the iconoclasts of their single most powerful weapon, the prohibition against "graven images," by arguing that God Himself suspended the prohibition when He instituted a new world order by incarnating Himself in Christ, who is—significantly referred to—in 2 Corinthians 4:4 as "the image of the invisible God." Violating/fulfilling His own law, God lifted its custodianship when He moved out of Himself, as it were, becoming Christ while remaining God at the same time. This act of procession, which defines the plural unity of God, makes Him an image of Himself, led John continuously to pose questions about the nature of images and what it means to "depict" God. An image, he explains, is "a likeness and pattern and impression of something, showing itself in what is depicted; however . . . the image is one thing and what is depicted is another—and certainly a difference is seen between them, since they are not identical."[11]

It should be noted that John did not endorse the *filioque* clause, for he did not regard "Christ the image" as consubstantial with God. Immaterial, infinite, God is by definition without image in the material, finite sense. Images cannot give us "direct knowledge" of what they depict but instead allow us to see that "the depicted" lay hidden.[12] For John and other iconophiles, the primary function of the image was to bore a hole, an opening, in the visible world through which the invisible could shine through.

However, the Fourth Council of Constantinople abandoned the terms of the original debate. Up to this point, the debate had centered not on the difficult question of *God's* image—how can there be images of God?—but the simpler issue of *Christ's* image. Not Christ as an image of God (as it was formerly posed) but Christ's image as a pedagogical tool. That is, in 869 CE, a pedagogical imperative took over the earlier debate and was responsible for elevating the image to the status of the Word. Images of Christ were now revalued for their ability to depict for the skeptical illiterates who made up a large portion of the Church's membership, the historical events of Christ's life on earth, his unique status as the image of God. Not only did this shift dissolve the Trinitarian conception of the divine, but it also dissolved the entire tissue of relations between God and man which the image conceived as icon had opened. No longer epiphanized in the variegated likenesses of men, no longer a multiplier of images, the One-God was now congealed as a result of His instantiation in the single image of Christ. Images began to be accepted by the Church on the grounds that they performed the function of representing the unique historical events of the life and death of Christ, as embodiment of God.

The effect of this was epoch-making; for all at once, images lost their translucency and became opaque. Iconophiles distinguished icons from idolatrous images on the grounds that the former opened onto a dimension that would otherwise remain absolutely invisible. They valued icons for the way they allowed the light of the hidden, the withdrawn, to shine through them. What this light illuminated was our intimate relation to the divine, not the divine itself, whose privileged obscurity was preserved. Once images were revalued for their illustrative rather than illuminating function, they were no longer conceived as portals, passageways, between the invisible and the visible and came to be regarded instead as if they "were [themselves] the light that reveal[ed them] and [made them] visible."[13]

At the moment it ceased to shine through images from an invisible source, the meaning of light itself shifted. Once conceived as the phenomenon designated by the Latin *lumen*, light was now reconceived as *lux*.[14] The difference can be stated in the following way. *Lumen* was attributed to an invisible source; the dazzling brilliance with which it became manifest at each image-locus was such that it rendered that image unique, singular. In contrast, the point from which *lux* emanated was no longer real (understood here as the point of an encounter not with an ultimate but a withdrawn ground) but abstract.[15] When Corbin complains that the dogma of incarnation commits a grievous error by turning God's appearance, his image, into a publicly and universally attestable fact instantiated in an object, or in "exoteric matter," he is objecting to the way that dogma "de-luminated" the world, bathing it in an abstract source of light that shone "indiscriminately on every object."[16] Lux lights a world with no hidden dimensions, a world in which all can be revealed, for when no distance separates what is seen from the invisible source of illumination, everything can come into the light or "become objective to itself in reflection."[17] Islamic philosophy is a philosophy, then, of illumination, that is, of lumen. The locus of illumination was said to be the "soul," the inwardness unique to each individual who maintains a relation to another dimension. These terms will lead you astray if the peculiar topology of the *falasifa*, according to which what is most "internal" or "esoteric" turns out to be external to the subject. We will come back to this later.

Now, if these historical alterations of the conception of images and light did occur after the Fourth Council, we should be able to provide evidence of the shift and thus demonstrate what was lost. As it happens, we do not have far to look. We find it in the very place one would expect to: in the changing iconography of Christ. Art historians have long observed that in the early centuries, Christ was often depicted as a *puer aeternus*, an eternally youthful boy in whose form the light of divinity seemed to shine through. In later centuries, after the concept of the incarnation had been more fully established as the centerpiece of Christian orthodoxy, the earlier manner of depicting him was abandoned in favor of images in which he was pictured—Corbin states the observation discreetly—as a "mature man with signs of a differentiated virility."[18]

This very point is made much less obliquely in a book-length study of representations of Christ in Renaissance art, in which the art historian, Leo Steinberg, reproduces hundreds of images that persuasively show that Christ's fully rendered genitalia were insistently placed on display in the art of the period.[19] It seems that it had become necessary by about 1260, the time the broad movement of the Renaissance began, to show that the son of God was "complete in all the parts of a man." This meant that even when the subject of a woodcut or painting was not a man but happened instead to be the infant Jesus, it was not his glowing heart but the unmistakable and ostentatiously displayed presence of his penis, his publicly confessed "flesh," that greeted the spectator's eye.

Around the 246 images reproduced in *The Sexuality of Christ in Renaissance Art and in Modern Oblivion*, Steinberg weaves a scholarly and visually astute argument that, among other things, covers much of the same ground as Corbin does in this part of his argument. Steinberg, too, makes a point of distinguishing the Renaissance depiction of Christ from earlier Byzantine and medieval images of the Christ Child, in which Christ's body disappears under ceremonial robes that come down to his feet and he "remains an 'image,' a Holy Icon, without any admixture of earthly realism."[20] Like Corbin, Steinberg ascribes the distinctive gesture of these Renaissance representations—namely the *ostentatio genitalium*—to the dogma of incarnation, which had become a dominant pictorial subject during the period.

In brief, Steinberg clearly demonstrates that Renaissance art assumed as one of its most important tasks the visualization and proof of the dogma of incarnation. The Iranologist, Corbin, and the art historian, Steinberg, concur on this point: the fervor behind these later representations of Christ was fueled by a need to quash a principled doubt that still threatened incarnationist theology. Here is Steinberg:

> Since the Incarnation draws its effectiveness from responsive faith, it would have forfeited that effectiveness, had it been open to legitimate doubt: without proof of blood, the flesh assumed by the godhead might have been thought merely simulated, phantom, deceptive. Such indeed w[as]

the pestiferous doctrine advanced more than a thousand years earlier by Docetists . . . those who held Christ's assumed body to have been spiritual, not carnal, so that he only appeared to be suffering.[21]

Now, here is precisely where the art historian and the Iranologist part ways. For, as Corbin tells us, the "pestiferous doctrine" against which the Quattrocento orators "discharge[d] the full spleen of their rhetoric" in order to fervently embrace the dogma that the godhead had incarnated Himself in the oozing, bleeding, suffering flesh of His son, this "pestiferous doctrine" was never anything more than a feature or tendency of a disorganized mass of Christologies that flourished before the great Church schism. Corbin, however, defends this tendency and transforms it into a resolute feature of the philosophy of illumination, which vigorously challenged the idea that the divinity made merely one appearance at one moment in time. From the Greek noun *dokhema* (a vision or fantasy but also opinion or expectation) and the verb *dokeo* (to appear or show itself but also to think, imagine, credit, admit, or expect), Docetism was denounced by the church for the reasons Steinberg gives. Let us examine a passage from the Qur'an (4:157), chosen by Corbin to demonstrate the "resolute docetism" that subtends it.[22] The passage, which unequivocally denies that the Jews killed Christ Jesus, reads like this: "They neither killed nor crucified him, though it so appeared to them. Those who disagree in the matter are only lost in doubt. They have no knowledge of it other than conjecture."

No matter that its doctrinal status and affiliation with a school are disputed, this docetist assertion still struck believers as pestiferous. For that Christ could not have been killed nor crucified because he never actually existed—that what witnesses saw was not a divine reality but a mere "phantom," "simulated"—is a claim that seems to have touched on a core Christian belief and thus still risks being read as a religious and political insult on a grand scale.[23] Fully aware that this passage and his defense of it have the capacity grievously to offend, Corbin nevertheless insists that it is not the passage itself, but the monotonous and misguided derision of docetism that is the source of the problem, for this derision is responsible for the misreading of the passage's intent.

The Qur'an does not deny the existence of Christ, his divine reality, nor the reality of his suffering. What it does forcefully deny is that (1) man has the capacity to kill or eradicate the divine and (2) the divine enters into or incarnates itself in a body or a world, as in a container or tomb. In the docetic conception, the divine does not enter into the world but comes to the level of the world and thus displaces it from itself. No longer an enclosure, a container, the world is now out of line with itself, spread out indefinitely without perimeter. This is to say, the Islamic philosophers who exhibit a docetic tendency adamantly maintain that "the other world already exists in this world."[24] A far cry from the "other world" of dogmatic religion, theirs "has no beginning or end" but is instead "perpetually engendered in this world."[25] While the world is "existentiated," or comes ceaselessly into existence, there is no Creator, solitary and outside of time, who brings it into existence out of nothing. From this, it is possible to see that "far from degrading 'reality' by making it an 'appearance'; [as its detractors charge, docetism] on the contrary, transform[s] reality into 'appearance,' makes [it] transparent to the transcendent . . . manifested in it. Thus docetism attaches no value to a material fact unless it is appearance, that is, unless it is apparition."[26] In brief, docetism argues for the existence of a material apparition.

We will need to say more, however, to elucidate this notion of "material apparition," of a materialism that challenges much of what goes by that name. We can begin by noting that what is at issue for Steinberg stands in stark contrast to apparition: the visualization of the material fact of Christ's body, or, as he puts it, much too precipitously, the *sexuality* of Christ. Steinberg asserts that "by harnessing its theological impulse to the attestation of the utter carnality of God's humanation, Renaissance artists confronted the incarnation entire, upper and lower body together, not excluding even the Body's sexual component."[27] But is it correct to say that by exposing Christ's genitalia, his "sexual parts," Renaissance artists exposed his sexuality?[28] Did they not, rather, inadvertently bring into focus a crucial distinction between the body in its material density and the body as "material apparition," that is, the sexualized body? Corbin described the doctrine of incarnation as "the great sin of literalist theologians," and nothing justifies his claim better than the work of these Renaissance artists who attempted to give visual proof of the doctrine. The sin of the literalists consisted in their "assimilation of . . . dissimulation to what it dissimulates."[29]

"Dissimulation" refers to the "epiphanic form" or "apparition" or "image" through which God becomes manifest, but if the image dissimulates, it cannot be by pretending to be what it is not. For how can that which has no image be assimilated to its image? How can that which is withdrawn from the world be incarnated there? The error of assimilation is equivalent to that of conflating an object that appears in a mirror with the mirror's substrate. In this case the object is no longer suspended in the place of its appearance but collapsed with it. Assimilation reduces, destroys, that which it manifests as hidden by claiming to unveil it.

Again, the question comes back to the meaning of "epiphanic form," "material apparition, and "image." What can it mean to say that the divine appears in the world without being collapsible with it, that divine being is "suspended" in the world as image? How can something be fully real and have extension without being reducible to the dense matter of the world?

What appears in the world, without being of the same substance, is a radical elsewhere, an other scene, which turns our heads, orients, or magnetizes us such that we turn away from the world. What suspends itself in the finite world is not flimsy fantasy but precisely the fully real extension of the ego through its relation to this other place. Extension in this sense characterizes not some thing (res extensa) but relation; ego extends itself beyond itself and toward what is other to it. Docetism maintains that God appears in the world as our singular relation to Him. He is not made flesh, not incarnated in a finite body, as the literalists would have it. Rather, it is the finite bodies of individual beings that are "made flesh," though in a different sense now. Through their relation to the unliquidatable otherness of the Divine, they are "subtilized," rendered capable of an infinity of real acts and irreducible to their vulnerabilities, diseases, and death. Since the term flesh strikes us as too irrevocably tainted by the dogma of incarnation to take on the new meaning we want to give it, we prefer instead to speak not of the finite subject's becoming flesh but rather of its sexualization. But this will require that we continue to stress the impropriety of Steinberg's confusion of sexuality with incarnation. As developed by Freud, and the discourse he founded, sexuality is, we would argue, resolutely anti-incarnationist. It is no coincidence that a docetic concept of the image survived in notions such as imago and archetype to play a role in the theorization of sexuality, even though the notions were often poorly understood.

Although we cannot fully develop this line of argument here, we can sketch its parameters by reflecting a bit on the response of later artists to Renaissance representations of Christ's sexual organ. We have not yet examined the full title of Steinberg's study, which goes on to take note of the subsequent consignment of the sexuality of Christ to modern oblivion. Post-Renaissance artists abruptly reversed course by refraining recoiling, even—from picturing the private parts of the Savior, going so far as to overpaint earlier representations of Christ's genitalia to veil their indecent exposure in Renaissance paintings. Steinberg draws attention to the unique nature of the Renaissance period, which would enjoy no sequel, in stark terms: "Renaissance artists, committed for the first time since the birth of Christ to naturalistic modes of representation, [they] were the only group within Christendom whose métier required them to plot every inch of Christ's body."[30]

He attributes this explicit mapping of Christ's body to the historically isolated synthesis of the Christological dogma of incarnation and a naturalistic mode of representation, and accounts for the recoil of later artists and audiences from this pictorial fusion of nature and divinity only briefly and in a flat, historicist way. Characterizing the style of Renaissance artists as "incarnational realism," Steinberg implies that the time would come when realist representation would divest itself of the dogma to which it sought during the Renaissance to give visual proof and would become realism, simply. In a later moment the fusion of realism and religion would come to seem distasteful, and realism would no longer seem an appropriate style for rendering images of Christ, whose corporality ceased to be considered a proper subject of representation.

In short, outside of a few scandal-provoking works by modern artists, the practice of depicting Christ's genitals was abandoned after the Renaissance because it came to be seen as pornographic. I state this more bluntly than Steinberg does, partially in order to insert Kiarostami into the discussion of the phenomenon of "modern oblivion." Kiarostami insisted more than once that showing too much, or giving too much information, is "pornographic." How should we understand this? In Steinberg's argument, the phrase "modern oblivion" designates the effacement of any representation of Christ's genitalia not only from artistic practice but also from post-Renaissance, or modern, consciousness. We would argue, however, that rather than abandoning or betraying the doctrine of incarnation, a certain "naturalistic mode of representation" continues in modern consciousness to instantiate the doctrine even though the subject of Christ's incarnated body is no longer the subject of most art. That is, it was precisely through the effacement of epiphanic forms, or appearance in the strong sense, and in the depiction of Christ's genitals that a "modern oblivion" began to manifest itself; and the later recoil from this depiction was itself proof of this effacement/oblivion. That is, contra Steinberg, what we see in the reactive reluctance of post-Renaissance artists to merge Christ with the human order is evidence of their continued—if compensatory—adherence to the tenets of incarnational realism.

Recall that Corbin's attacks on the doctrine of incarnation targets its reduction of the tripartite division of divinity in favor of a simple duality: divine versus finite being, pure spirit versus matter. The problem with simple dualities is the inevitability with which one of the terms usurps the other to produce a hierarchy. Officially, the doctrine of incarnation was supposed to benefit humanity; the utter carnality of God's humanation in Christ was said to save man by elevating him above other creatures. On the contrary, Corbin argues, this doctrine resulted in the demotion of man to finite being, to the status of opaque matter.

In support of Corbin's argument, one might enlist an observation made by Hegel regarding a modern form of the opposition between faith and knowledge. Hegel proposed that it was for fear of "reducing the sacred Grove to mere timber," that modern subjectivity denied itself God intellectually in order that it might still pine for Him in sighs and prayers.[31] Translating this observation into the terms of our argument, we are emboldened to propose a theory that runs counter to Steinberg's. If later artists ceased to render the Son of God as fully incarnate, it was less out of fear of blasphemy, than of losing the real God of their faith.

Corbin called attention to Hegel's diagnosis while putting his own spin on it: modern consciousness, he insisted, built a "rigid and insurmountable opposition between subjectivity . . . and the eternal itself." This rigid opposition was the result of a modern obliviousness to, or total obliteration of, all mediation between God and empirical reality. This, in turn, threatened empirical reality with utter "ineffectuality" and "absolute solitude and aloneness."[32] The point underscored by Hegel and Corbin is that at a certain point the symbolic and the intellect lost their dignity. What was needed to overturn this devaluation was an elevation of the symbolic.

This argument does not figure in the account Steinberg gives of the rejection of incarnational realism by post-Renaissance artist, yet the argument's validity is nevertheless made plain in an observation he makes regarding the actual depiction of Christ's genitalia in Renaissance art: "the sexual member exhibited by the Christ Child, so far from asserting aggressive virility, conceded instead God's assumption of human weakness; it is an affirmation not of superior prowess but of . . . the Creator's self-abasement to his creature's condition. And instead of symbolizing . . . the generative power of nature, Christ's sexual organ . . . yields . . . not seed, but . . . the first fruits of [his] growing death.'"[33]

Corbin makes a strikingly similar observation: "Incarnated, [Christ] is buried in the flesh until the time comes for him to be buried in the grave."[34] And in terms that echo Hegel's, while supplementing it with a further point, Corbin goes on the say, "The Burning Bush is only a brushwood fire if it is merely perceived by the sensory organs. For Moses to perceive the Burning Bush and hear the Voice [of God] calling him," we must suppose an organ of trans-sensory perception, the creative imagination, and credit the existence of an imaginal world.[35] While the sacred Grove rises up, fully transcendent and inaccessible, to offer a merely false hope to the pining world it abandons, the Burning Bush provides radiant testimony of the incorruptibility of finite existence. The insurmountable duality, which tilts in favor of the transcendent Grove, is transformed, becomes passable, by the addition of the imaginal world. The introduction of the imaginal, it seems, reorders earthly existence in the following ways: it disrupts the hierarchy of dualist oppositions; fortifies, or vivifies, the dimension of the symbolic; and (this is the surprising, new point) alters the way in which we conceive bodily organs.

In my third chapter, "From the Cloud to the Resistance," I will devote further attention to these organs—or what Imam Khomeini spoke of as the "sensorium" of the Iranian people. Here, prompted by the term "trans-sensory perception," I will make a few brief points. What work does "trans" perform here? The term *side-long glance* leaps to mind, no doubt because it conjures up an indeterminate space we do not perceive directly. One's eyes may be focused on what is in front of them, but not fully, because one suspects something else is going on elsewhere. Avid readers and committed critics of Aristotle, Islamic philosophers must have rolled their eyes as they read "On the Soul." Aristotle begins with a distinction between an organ and an object and the space between them. His argument should have proceeded easily from here, for everyone would agree with him that if you were to place a coin on your eye, you would not be able to see the coin. Some space is necessary to separate an organ from its object. One sees across this space. But when it came to touch, which seemed by definition to eliminate the distance between organ and object, his argument threatened to unravel. Aristotle responded by (1) insisting that this distance must be there, however imperceptible it might be and (2) pushing the organ of touch from the surface into the interior of the body.

What Aristotle stumbled upon, without recognizing it as such, is the esoteric dimension of bodily organs. Islamic philosophers seized upon it, realizing that it meant that sensory organs were not merely passive receivers of stimuli coming from outside, but that these stimuli activated an unknown interior, which had the power to act in turn on the outside. Indeed, a very famous thought experiment confirmed this idea and pushed it further. Avicenna imagined throwing a man into an empty space where he would encounter no other object, no turbulence, or parts of his own body. Avicenna concluded from his experiment that his "flying man" would come away from this exercise with one certainty—that he existed.

The "I am" is a trans-sensory certainty of touching an otherness that emerges not from the world outside, but from within myself. The distinction Lacan makes between the eye and the gaze buttresses the Avicennian argument. Human subjects do not sense without sensing themselves. One cannot see, for example, without sensing that we are looked at by an Other. All humans senses are trans-senses, even if it is possible to deny this to ourselves.

Let us return, finally, to the discussion of Renaissance paintings that led to this detour, to the ostentatious depictions of Christ's genital organ, from which later artists recoiled. The problem, as Steinberg himself acknowledges, is that the depiction of this organ in an attempt to prove that Christ entered fully into the esoteric world of empirical reality merely exposed the weakness of Christ's carnal nature. Fully actualized, he became part of a decaying reality. What was effaced in this sorry episode was the esoteric dimension, the indivisible remainder that evaded depiction. The organs of trans-sensory perception do not merely relieve the body of an exclusive reliance on impressions received from the external, empirical world; they forestall corruption by originating new perceptions. On further point to tie up: when Kiarostami bemoans the pornographic impulse to show too much, he is not sanctioning taboos against of sexuality but bemoaning the burial of sexuality in incarnate substance.

DOCETIC REALISM

The cinema of Kiarostami is a realist cinema compared early on to that of postwar Italian neorealism or—in part because several of his films are (simulated or semi-simulated) documentaries—to *cinéma vérité*. I will continue to propose that the realist or documentary impulse behind the work is docetic, that what Kiarostami tries to make appear or show itself in his films is an illuminated reality. It is a gamble, I realize, to state my thesis in esoteric terms since it runs the risk of blocking recognition of the contemporary significance of the arguments they once and still serve. Fortunately, Kiarostami has preceded us in the translation of these terms into the language of everyday, contemporary reality, and we will thus rely on these translations to state our arguments.

One way of introducing the work of Kiarostami is through the only apparently slight 1983 film, *Fellow Citizen*. Set in an area of Tehran that has recently been closed to traffic, it consists entirely of a string of special pleadings, convoluted excuses, and (most likely) outright lies with which desperate motorists hope to be able to convince the traffic officer on duty to allow them to pass through the barrier. None of the motorists displays any disrespect for the officer or the law. Indeed, what is striking is the way a kind of respect, or at least a faith in her pact with the law, seems to invite the endearing ingenuity with which each attempts to skirt it. The consistency of the responses—not one fails to engage in ruse—in combination with the demeanor of the drivers leads us to understand that what we are witnessing does not go under the name of exception. None of these citizens (the title defines them as such and thus links them to the law and to state power) considers himself to be above or outside the law. Rather, each seems to take it for granted that the law does not cover all circumstances, that there is in the law itself something that is not decided by law and that this emancipates those subject to it from having to take a straight path. Their eyes are on the lookout for loopholes.

One by one, the cars pull up from the back of the screen to the foreground, where the traffic official stands guard, and one by one, each driver spins some simple or elaborate tale to persuade the guard to let them pass through, before being finally turned back, obliged to find another route. The fellowship of the motorists depends not on their being able to enter an inner sanctum but precisely in their displays of guile—and their ultimate dispersal in different directions. Is this entire film not a re-inscription of Kiarostami's signature image, the solitary tree replaced by a law that plants its sinuous root in the very real world of traffic and construction, only to send each of its subjects off on their own path?

Recall a point briefly made earlier regarding the long drawn-out Byzantine wars, fought with enormous historical consequences, over the nature of the image: the warring factions, we insisted, sought not simply to grab political power but, more fundamentally, to determine what constituted it. That is, the wars were a bloody struggle over the very definition of the symbolic function of political authority. The iconoclasts held a position known as *akribeia*, which is basically what we think of as strict constructionism; it favors exactitude, the rigorous application of the "original intent" of laws without concern for changing circumstances. The iconophiles took a different view: they held that there was an economy of political power, where *economy* referred to an act of dispensation, of arranging or ordering wherein divine authority disposed or distributed itself in history, in relation to the whole of creation, including the Church and its fathers. Economy concerns thus the nature of the link between spiritual and temporal power, law and everyday reality, the visible and the invisible. Among the many meanings of the term *economy*—dispensation, plan, arrangement, providence—others just as fundamental stick out in the context of our discussion: guile, lie, ruse.[36]

Throughout his films and in several published statements, Kiarostami insisted on the importance of the lie, which he claimed is the only means we have of getting at the truth. But what meaning can truth have if lies are our only access to it? And what can truth mean in the (after all) realist film world of Kiarostami, which makes no reference to an "other world" in the dogmatic, hierarchical sense, no reference to a first principle or final cause to which this world would be subservient? Without these, there can be no measure of truth and thus, it would seem, no truth.

But if the realist principle subtending his films obliges Kiarostami to admit of no world but this finite one here, it does not oblige him to embrace the nominalist contention that this world consists only of finite things in themselves and absolutely disqualifies notions such as infinity and truth. Kiarostami would be the first to admit that there are only things in themselves except—he would want to clarify—there is the imaginal world, hence truths. In this context, *except* clearly does not mean to say that the imaginal world is set outside and above this one; the imaginal world names the "other world" within this one. But although it appears among the things of this world, it is not one of them, for, simply put, the imaginal world does not exist. It is not another existing thing but what inexists between them. It is conceived, above all, as the power of constraint and separation. Through the intervention of the imaginal world, law is constrained or held back from unfolding all at once, and the things of this world are separated such that they are prevented from forming a continuous block, one phenomenon becoming the cause of another that in turn causes another, inexorably. This last is the definition of determinism, law that is applied irrespective of the reality it confronts. It is also the definition of iconoclasm, which, in being a rejection of the icon, was at the same time a rejection of the economy of power.[37]

Kiarostami's films constitute reflections on the ontological status of the image; they reintroduce us to the power of the imaginal dimension. In a world increasingly controlled by imaging techniques, where images proliferate and command a growing share of our attention, his films are remarkable for diagnosing the problem confronting the modern world as a dearth of images.[38] The glut of images accounts for a scarcity of icons. One of the main maladies of his frenetic characters is their want of an image.

The extraordinary 1990 film *Close-Up* is the clearest illustration of the problem. In the film, Hossein Sabzian, a mostly unemployed printer and Turkish-speaking member of the *mostazafin*—the downtrodden class that the Islamic Revolution was supposed to have lifted up but did not, the dispossessed betrayed yet again, this time by the regime that replaced the Shah—finds himself in an intolerable situation. Having fallen through all the cracks in the system into near-total obscurity, Sabzian longs to have an image, to gain some foothold in the visible world. And yet, because he seems to have a less-than-clear sense of how to acquire an image, he commits a crime that has no chance of succeeding: image theft. To have an image means to be singular or— as we argued earlier—to have a unique relation to the "elsewhere" or otherness to which we are each exposed.

Sabzian does, however, seem to be clear on one point: an image is something primary. To have an image is to have a capacity; it is a fundamental corporeal and not merely abstract matter. Thus, he decides to snatch not the image of some matinee idol, a movie star, but that of a movie or image maker. In an act of desperation he attempts to pass himself off as Makhmalbaf, the famous Iranian filmmaker beloved for his film *The Cyclist*, which is about a similarly dispossessed person, this time an Afghani refugee. Momentarily mistaken for Makhmalbaf by a woman sitting next to him on a bus, Sabzian slips into the role of famous director and is eventually caught trying to dupe this woman and her family, the equally film-struck Ahankhahs. He has been thrown in jail and is awaiting trial when Kiarostami reads about the case in a newspaper and decides to film the trial and a reenactment of the crime in which the principal characters are all persuaded to play themselves.

Close-Up does not spring ex nihilo from the head of its director but from reality itself; yet nor does the film attempt merely to replicate the preexisting reality of the situation. Not content to lag behind the story reported in the newspaper, to permit reality to continue to preexist it, the film looks, we might say, for a *rent* in reality that allows it to outdistance the actual situation. In the end it intervenes in, and brings about, an alteration of the real-life circumstances: the procedure and outcome of the trial are positively affected by the very filming of Kiarostami's film.

The primary function of the opening sequence is manifestly one of delay. This is not to suggest that the film has not yet "caught up" with reality, as I put it just now, but that it has already found its place in it. In this first sequence the police and reporter from the newspaper that broke the story pull up at the home of the Ahankhahs to arrest Sabzian. While we in the audience fully expect to enter the home along with the police and to witness the arrest, we are denied access both to the home and the scene. We remain outside with the camera in the cul-de-sac of a street in front of the home, where there is nothing to see other than the ill-equipped reporter, who has forgotten to bring a tape recorder, running around door-to-door trying to borrow one from the neighbors and the taxi driver, biding his time as he waits for his fare by picking flowers out of a dump and inadvertently dislodging an aerosol that rolls down the street.

This tactic of delay has the effect of putting off the appearance of Sabzian, as if to emphasize the problem of his image deficit. But this is not all. It will be the task of the film to allow him to acquire an image, not the pilfered image of a look-alike but his own self-likeness. To accomplish this task, the film will have to turn us into witnesses to his appearing, to his emergence in the visible. The first sequence partially empties the screen so that the here of what is visible to us will be able to resonate in a there that is not. To forestall misunderstanding, we must again stress that the creative work of imagination implied by the film's task does not produce "images free of all sensible restraint."[39] Imagination does not create something from nothing. Rather, the active imagination has, first of all, a negative aspect; "it puts an end to the privation of being that holds things in their occultation."[40]

What does this mean? If there is something that is not, if there is an opacity that cannot be brought to light, we are faced with an absolute impossibility. Every positive action is by definition doomed, reduced to impotency. "Putting an end to" is an act of a different, negative order. It restrains, holds back the overwhelming flood of impossibility. Of the imaginary world we could say that it forestalls the impossibility of relating matter and thought, God and man. It stops not writing a relation and opens instead a new dimension—of contingency.[41]

Imagination does not create new, unfounded visions (this is what distinguishes it from illusion or mere fantasy); it imagines nothing or, put differently, it "gives form to absolute nonexistence, to that which, according to rational demonstration, can't possibly have form."[42] This implies that there is a difference between the absolute nothing out of which some absolute Creator fashions the world, and a "relative nothing" fashioned by imagination. Although it stops short of creating illusions or fantasies—"daydreams," as Freud would say, imagination, in the sense Islamic philosophers used it, gives form, as creative writers do, to nonexistence. Creation is not the province of a primary cause outside the finite world but takes place within this world.

In addition to being described as a power of limitation, the imagination was also defined as a power of linking. Ordinarily, to link means to bring two or more things together, make them converge in a space. The imaginal world is not such a space; it is instead empty and the terms do not preexist their being put in relation to each other.

Lacan somewhere describes the real as "teeming with emptiness." This phrase suggests a way of thinking the linkage at stake in the imaginal space as an articulation of movements: as a vibration, teetering, or oscillation—as, perhaps, an empty instability. The flutter of a heart or an eyelash, a sigh or breath; do not these movements, which manifest a passion, suggest relation, articulation, linkage? In fact, these sorts of movements—paramount among them, the sigh—are significant concepts of Islamic philosophy; they name the "vibration of [divine Being] in [our] being."[43] Passionate sites of relation, they transform what would otherwise be a negative theology, in which God remains totally unknown, into a unique, personal God, in which human being has access to divine pathos and God is relieved of the solitude of His unknownness. The imagination empties the human soul of the things of the world to submit it not to divine or any other sort of being but rather to submit it to what is not, to the passionate wavering of "being-in-suspense," that is: unfinished.

With this, we are brought back to *Close-Up* and Sabzian's specific, self-declared passion for cinema. While this passion places cinema at the film's center, *Close-Up* does not become a film about cinema, in the self-reflexive modern sense, but remains focused on everyday reality. More precisely, it is a film about reality's current state of impoverishment and the role the cinematic image might play in restoring its luminous dimension. To accomplish this task, Kiarostami sets out to fulfill the request of Sabzian that the director make a film that shows his passion. The film has to feed the lust of the eye. At the same time, one might argue that *Close-Up* gives evidence of the link, posited earlier, between the icon and the economy. That Sabzian's image deficit is connected to a deficit of political economy is apparent in the film's opening sequence, for the delay inserted by the imaginary serves a double role. It not only prevents us from witnessing the arrest but also gives us an opportunity to observe a malignancy of the political function. The active force of delay exposes to the spectator a kind of laxity or informality that turns out to be much less benign than it might first appear.

Before meeting Sabzian or hearing his complaint, we learn in this sequence that his suffering is not isolated. The taxi driver is a former airplane pilot in the army who lost his job when the Iran–Iraq war ended; the police drive up not in an official van but in a taxi, and we will learn later that the sons of the well-to-do Ahankhahs are, like Sabzian, underemployed. These are all signs of the failed revolution and of the state's retreat, which has abandoned its citizens, leaving them alone to improvise as best they can without the aid of formal structures of support. As we know, the laxity of the law does not mean it is not in force; its very retreat exposes its citizens to harm.

The primary function of the opening delay is, however—as we began to argue—one of disoccultation. The narrative is stalled to give time to what would have otherwise been occulted to appear. To understand this strategy, one need only ask oneself the following question: had Sabzian's arrest been filmed at this point, in what light would the scene have been lit? Lumen or lux? As noted earlier, lumen is the light that illuminates the threshold where the unique, passionate encounter between each subject and Divine otherness takes place. Lux, on the other hand, is associated not with passion but with abstract reason; it spreads itself homogenously over all that is known and appears not as a threshold but as a medium of vision and understanding, that is, of rational clarity. While lumen reveals itself at the point of encounter with another dimension, lux is thought to be solely at the disposal of rational man, who reveals the truth by its means.

In recent years, however, Hans Blumenberg has argued that the rationalist conception of light has undergone modification. The process of elucidation now occurs less and less in the general, public light of reason and more and more against a background of darkness into which a sharply focused, directed light is cast. Vision is less often permitted to roam freely in the clean, well-lighted space of reason and is increasingly coerced by a beam of light that picks objects out of the darkness. In short, the possibilities for the sovereign "manipulation of light" by man, originally introduced by the shift from lumen to lux, has reached a new level of violence in which, Blumenberg claims, the modern, "technological light of 'lighting' has imposed [on man] an 'optics' that goes against his will" and his very freedom.[44]

Rather than a space of unfreedom, however, I will argue that this new space of light is more usefully described, and especially in the context of our discussion, as forensic. Had the opening sequence included the scene of arrest, the first appearance of Sabzian would have been a mug shot, the shot of a suspect who had been nabbed, a fraud who had been unmasked. Lux, the light of scientific and juridical exactitude, by switching off the translucent light that comes to us from elsewhere, sequesters us in a totally opaque world. And yet, viewed in its own terms, lux is driven by a principle of transparency. According to this principle, everything can and must be made visible by means of light's penetrating rays, which is able see through and disperse the mist of illusions, lies, and obfuscation. This principle knows no limit; it regards whatever is not or cannot be made visible as simply nonexistent.

If the violence of this principle of transparency has intensified, as per Blumenberg's claim, this is because it is now in the hands of a state that exercises its powers through retreat. What we mean when we speak of a retreat of the state is that it has defaulted on its duty to provide the protections it is called upon to grant its citizens. To protect them from what, exactly? The intrusions of an all-seeing Other, and thus the destruction of the *sens intime* necessary for subjectivity itself.[45] At one time, the all-seeing gaze belonged to the God of dogmatic religion, but in modernity it has come into the possession of the abstract principle of lux, the immanent, unsleeping, 24/7, eye of lux, which reduces everything to the opacity of a visible object, which sees everything and eviscerates singularity. The obligations of the state are commonly viewed as the protection of the privacy, freedom, and the right to assembly of its citizens, but these notions have been so thoroughly corrupted by the principle of lux, which reduces its citizens to their visibility, that we now need to unearth the primary obligation, which underwrites the others: the protection of each citizen's self-intimacy, her secrecy or modesty.

In this context the matter takes on an additional layer of complexity given that the authoritarian state of the Islamic Republic of Iran bills itself as the enforcer of the subject's modesty. The question comes back to this: do its laws' countless prohibitions function to protect what is truly invisible, or do they sacrifice it by chaining citizens to their utter carnality?

Kiarostami eventually interpolates into the trial proceedings at the film's center a scene in which Sabzian's arrest is reenacted; this delayed reenactment has, however, a dramatically different effect than it would have had it been filmed during the opening sequence. Rather than entering the house alongside the police and intruding on a scene already in process, this time the camera is positioned inside the house before the police arrive. This will not be a scene of forensics in which the culprit is surprised, caught off guard and exposed to the categorizing gaze of an abstract authority. The image of Sabzian with which we are presented is not a frozen mug shot but a moving image in the most fundamental sense, the scene one of pathos. Sabzian plays himself once again, but this time something is visibly askew. He appears to be out of sync with his role, which is to say, with himself. He has a knowledge of too much.

As we watch the reenactment, we are aware that Sabzian is aware that he is being filmed; he knows that he is being looked at. The "fourth wall" is not broken, however, as is in the modernist gesture of self-reflexive cinema. We do not occupy the same space as Sabzian, nor does he sense our presence, an audience watching him. And yet does appear to be captured by another gaze. The scene becomes slanted, slightly off center, as though Sabzian were listening a little less to what is being said, focused a little less on what is going on around him, distracted by an elsewhere invisible except for the magnetic pull it exerts on him. In brief, Sabzian seems to regard himself with a kind of hesitancy, as if he were unfamiliar with his own motivations, visibly affected by himself. Rather than being turned into a passive object of vision, Sabzian is here both patient and agent of his being seen.[46]

The postponement of the scene of arrest, was itself an arrest of impossibility that had come to define Sabzian's life. It created a space for the trial and the contingency of it outcome. To film the trial, Kiarostami adopted a novel technological strategy; he used two different cameras, one a distance and the second a close-up camera. The first recorded what was admissible as evidence by the court, the second what was inadmissible, Sabzian's passion. The temptation—to be avoided at all cost—is to see the first as objective, the second as offering access to the inner core of Sabzian's being. Kiarostami once made a general remark that is especially relevant to *Close-Up*: "We have a saying in Persian, when somebody is looking at something with real intensity: 'he had two eyes and he borrowed two more.' Those borrowed eyes are what I want to capture—the eyes that will be borrowed by the viewer to see what's outside the scene he's looking at."[47] What is "outside the scene" is so in a radical sense: it is invisible not merely temporarily but by virtue of *not* being, or of its being a suspension of the impossible. This second pair of eyes is the esoteric pair; they "document" what is invisible while safeguarding its invisibility.

The Persian saying Kiarostami invokes is less quaint than it sounds, for behind it lies the distinctive economy of Islamic philosophy, the elaborate theophanic dimension that sets it apart from every form of "unilateral monotheism."[48] This theophany begins with the retreat of God, which operates—as we want to show—in marked contrast to the retreat of the modern state. To begin drawing this contrast, we turn to the hadith that is perhaps the most intensely contemplated by Islamic philosophers, foremost among them, the great Ibn 'Arabi: "I was a hidden Treasure and I yearned to be known. Then I created creatures in order to be known by them."[49] The subject of this yearning is God Himself, an emphatically apophatic God, as the phrase "hidden Treasure" indicates. An apophatic or negative theology posits a God who is nondelimited, indeterminate, without feature or image.

For this form of theology the question of the image is particularly delicate. How to conceive an image of that which is incorporeal, invisible, immaterial, without form or limit? We have seen how intensely this question was debated during the Byzantine period. What strikes one as new in this hadith, however, is how profoundly the question of the image concerns God Himself, who depends on it. He is unable to create to creatures in His image. This is so even though a different hadith seems to suggest otherwise: "God created Adam according to His own Form."[50] If there is a Form of God, it cannot exist before Adam but must come about through the latter.

Islamic philosophy is a philosophy not of the multiple but of the One. Its first principle is that of the Oneness of God, the only necessary being in the universe, the only one who cannot not be.[51] And yet this One could not be counted as one were left to Himself. This seeming contradiction led the Muslim mystics, and most notably Ibn 'Arabi, "the great expositor of 'Unity,' [to] devote most of his attention to affirming the reality of the principle of multiplicity and explaining its relationship to the Oneness of God.... God in His Essence is absolutely one from every point of view. But as soon as this is said, someone has said it, so in effect the reality of the other has to be affirmed."[52] In brief, the multiplicity of others, their plural reality is what attests to God's oneness. This reemphasizes the crucial difference to which we drew attention earlier between docetism and incarnationism: Christ cannot be the image of God, who cannot appear "in person," in any universally attestable form. Rather, God manifests Himself in a multiplicity of forms, none of which can claim to be the image of God.

The position of the Islamic philosophers dispels the commonplace "Orientalist" assumption that non-Western societies have a less developed sense of the individual than do societies in the West. "Iranian metaphysicians of the Avicennian tradition" regarded individuation as the positing of a being and not as a mere negativity.[53] While Western thinkers often oppose the individual and the universal, the *falasifa* did not conceive individuation, the profusion of the multiple, as occurring in a second stage through the negation of the One, but rather as initially occurring within the One. Individuals proceed out of the One without exiting from it and thereby attest to His oneness. Still, Ibn 'Arabi, author of *The Book of Unity*, did not hesitate to insist that "unity ignores and refuses you."[54] Why? Because while it remains true that the One is that which is common to the multiplicity of beings, it is also true that it eludes each and every one of them. The One escapes capture by each of the multiplicity.

Corbin's warnings against the "literalist sin" of assimilating the dissimulation to what it dissimulates is here graspable from another angle. The multiplicity of images that manifest God do not expose the "hidden Treasure"; on the contrary, they permit Him to remain hidden. The icon-image attests not to His presence but to His withdrawal, to the retreat of His oppressive, all-seeing presence in favor of His relation to us. Rather than leaving individual beings bereft, abandoned, His retreat opens a salutary separation from Him and sets a limit to His necessity. Thus, while Ibn 'Arabi constantly emphasized the solitary nature of human existence—solitary precisely due to God's withdrawal from us—he repeatedly linked his notion of the solitary with that of proximity.[55]

In the wake of Divine withdrawal, we acquire a feeling of proximity—of being "alone with" a retreated God—far stronger than any such feeling we might have with an actual neighbor. A sense of closeness to something closer to us than our "jugular vein" follows on the heels of God's abandonment of us.[56] Unlike the feeling of intimacy experienced between "two heterogeneous beings," this feeling of proximity, of a superlative intimacy, is of "*one* being encountering himself (at once one and two, a bi-unity)."[57] What seems to be indicated here is a separation that is not pushed all the way to a division into two. That which is brought close is not conceived as another fully present being but rather a being that is held back, suspended: potential being. The feeling of intimacy obtains not between two heterogeneous persons or things, therefore, but between two distinct modes of existence.

Ironically, in his otherwise useful essay on light's historical relations to truth, Blumenberg associates the cinematic close-up to the penetrating light of lux, particularly as its logic has been transformed by modern lighting technology, which spotlights specific objects and features, picking them out of the darkness as if to indict them. The contrast between this view of the close-up and that proposed by Deleuze could not be sharper. Deleuze reads the close-up not as a technique for extracting a detail from a scene to enlarge and scrutinize it, as if under a microscope, but as a luminous technique that "abstracts [what it shows] from all spatio-temporal co-ordinates." The close-up, says Deleuze quoting Béla Balazs, "opens a dimension of another order."[58] We have tried to show that this other dimension comes to the fore through the imaginal world in which suspended or virtual being "reside." This other "situative" space has no place in the "situated world" of actual being.

One of the ethical questions haunting Kiarostami's cinema concerns the "proper distance" to be taken by a filmmaker toward his subjects. In this context his fondness for long shots is often said to be the measure of that distance, to be an indication of the principled reluctance of Kiarostami to trespass the barrier of intimacy. Without disputing this reading of his long shots, I would argue that the close-up addresses this question of proper distance no less clearly. For, when it comes to intimacy, the distance fundamentally at issue is that minimal one that separates a subject from herself, the distance within which her passionate attachment to her own otherness, her own "radical diversity," lodges itself. The close-up aims at showing "what . . . is not there, qua represented," as suspended being; or—to cite Deleuze, again, this time quoting Eisenstein's views on the close-up—it aims at "the 'pathetic' which . . . is apprehended in . . . affect."[59] Far from transgressing a barrier, the close-up exposes a threshold, an opening, through which the light of an invisible world shines. This threshold is the very abode of intimacy.

We noted earlier the simple fact that Sabzian chose to adopt as his own the image of a filmmaker rather than a film star. This fact becomes more interesting when considered in light of the early religious opposition to cinema in Iran. Among the list of reasons for this opposition is "the religious belief that any act of creation which simulates the original creation of God is blasphemous."[60] Because God was supposed to be the sole maker of images, the creation of human images by man was deemed an usurpation of His divine power. But if this reason could be overcome and cinema allowed to flourish in Iran, it may be in part because this reading of God's powers was spectacularly challenged within Islamic philosophy. This challenge is centered on an interpretation of an important Qur'anic verse that reads thus: "It is not you who killed them, but God did so. You did not throw what you threw [sand in the eyes of the enemy at Badr], but God [did]" (8:17).

At times, Corbin interprets this verse by drawing a parallel to Luther's flash of insight regarding a psalm with a similar structure. In contrast to Aristotle's Unmoved Mover, who works *through* us to guide us toward a final cause, Luther contends that the psalm did not define our relation to God unilaterally, as His appropriation of our will, but as a matter of mutual passion.[61] At other times, however, Corbin contrasts the reading of this verse offered by the *falasifa* with that offered by their philosophical contemporaries, the Ash'arites. The Ash'arites argued that the Qur'anic verse identified God as the secret agent of all our acts, meaning that all the organs of our bodies are mere instruments of His will. While the *falasifa* agreed that there was a secret behind our acts, something unknowable to us, they insisted further that there was a secret of this secret. More paradoxically still, Ibn Arabi insisted that the secret of the secret was that there was no secret. We can presume that he wanted in this way to forestall an infinitely regressive search for the ultimate cause of our actions.

The secret of the secret is not locatable at a terminal point; it resides, on the contrary, in the fact that neither God in sovereign isolation from us, nor we in our self-enclosed isolation from Him, is capable of any real act. God, alone, is necessary, but alone He is without capacity, for capacity emerges only as a bilateral or joint affair. In opposition to the Ash'arites, then, the mystics conceived the organs of the body not as tools or instruments of God but as bodily organs that belonged neither to God or man in. Thus, when we read that "the soul gains awareness that it 'sees' God not through itself but through Him; . . . it contemplates God in all other beings not through its own gaze, but because it is the same gaze by which God sees them," we must not make the mistake of understanding this in the perverse sense, as stating that we identify with, and see through the gaze of, the Other.[62] How else to read it? What does the Qur'anic verse, "You did not throw . . . God did" mean? Corbin often claims to have discovered the key to understanding this verse in Luther's concept of *significatio passiva*, which brings together a passion with an action. It is only by opening oneself up to, or making oneself passive before, what is alien in us, that we are able to act, not automatically, but in the real sense.

Am I able to say more about this? Yes. Psychoanalysts have long observed a condition they refer to as the "hospital phenomenon," which plagues young children who, upon experiencing even a momentary absence of their mothers, are menaced by a profound sense of destitution. Overcome by a feeling of total abandonment, these children behave as if they had been stranded on the precipice of an absolute void. It is this phenomenon that occasioned the little game of fort/da, on which Freud famously reflected. Freud hypothesized that the game was designed to conquer the debilitating experience of the void—of "the ever-open gap," or "ditch," as Lacan refers to it—left by his mother's exit.[63] It is noteworthy that in his discussion of this game of throwing, Lacan urges us to look for the game's "true secret," without, however, uncovering any easy answer.[64] Lacan rejects the proposal that the game is one of mastery in which the boy, through his own agency, tries to control of his mother's comings and goings rather than being passively submitted to them. He also rejects the notion that the bobbin that is thrown back and forth represents the mother, for the game, he claims, precedes, or, constitutes the very origin of, representation. The secret does not lie in any object or person. It relies, Lacan insists, in the "radical diversity" captured by the repetition, the repeated concomitance of the primitively opposed fort and *da*.

In brief, there is no simple agent of the bobbin's throw. In a later variation of the game, the boy leaps up to see his image reflected in a mirror, then dives below it to disappear. This demonstrates effectively the game's revelation of the subject's division. This mirror does not, then, reflect back to the boy an ideal image of himself. It instead shows that his *Da-sein* stands out against the retreat of any foundation. If this retreat does not leave the boy helpless, destitute of capacity it is because, as Lacan puts it, the game succeeds in detaching from the subject "a small part" or "small object a" (gaze, voice, breast, and so on) whose salient function seems eerily similar to Corbin's "trans-sensory organ." Each of these organs are passive not in the merely exoteric sense of being bombarded and potentially worn down by stimuli, but also in the fundamental, esoteric sense: being receptive to one's own otherness.

THE BODY AND THE BARZAKH

"This is the place to say, in imitation of Aristotle, that man thinks with his object."[65] Lacan drops this sentence, without further elaboration, into the middle of his reinterpretation of the *fort/da* game. We are thus left to figure out why. "Object" seems to refer to the small part of Ernst that detaches itself from him while remaining inalienable. With this object/organ, the boy "leaps the frontiers of his domain" (i.e., the gap or absolute nothing introduced by his mother's absence), which is thereby "transformed into a well" (i.e., the absolute nothing now transformed into the unthinkable source of thought).[66] Lacan does not bother to tell us where Aristotle makes this claim or what he thinks it means. So, let us put it aside for now and return to our own research.

The concept of the image is inseparable from that of the limit. This limit is often thought to define the image's perimeter, its borders. Iconoclasts objected to the image on this ground; the image limits, freezes in a form. Iconophiles regard the limit as that which divides and links, rather than circumscribes and isolates objects from each other. We find the second definition at work in the following well-known Qur'anic verses (55:19–20): "He has set two seas in motion that flow side by side together / With an interstice between them which they cannot cross." The term *interstice* translates the Arabic term *barzakh*, which is not only a fundamental concept for the followers of Avicenna but also—significantly—that place the imaginal world. Listen to Ibn 'Arabi's definition:

> A *barzakh* is something that separates . . . two things while never going to one side . . . , as for example, the line that separates shadow from sunlight. [In the Qur'anic verses about the two seas] the one sea does not mix with the other. . . . Any two adjacent things are in need of a *barzakh*, which is neither the one nor the other but possesses the power of both. The *barzakh* . . . separates a known from an unknown, an existent from a nonexistent, a negated from an affirmed, an intelligible from a nonintelligible."[67]

The *barzakh* is a limit that—instead of circumscribing an object in order thus to define it as a bounded whole—divides, separates the object from itself. It is precisely because the *barzakh* does not circumscribe what it limits that Ibn 'Arabi ceases to speak of a separation between things, and turns around to speak of a separation between a known and an unknown, an existent and a nonexistent, and so on. The limit joins something to an indeterminate surplus. This is what is meant by "never going to one side": the limit does not posit a second, contradictory term. The concept of the "Supreme *Barzakh*" names a specific separation, of God from Himself, a separation of the nothing He is as nondelimited form from His theophanic forms. The ordinary *barzakh* separates the intelligible from the sensible in the sublunary world. It is the *barzakh* that raises the principled objection to the dogma of incarnation inasmuch as it denies to the flesh of Christ any toleration of admixture. Human and divine do not meet in the flesh; they do not flow or "leak" into each other to consolidate themselves in a single substance as they do in the dogmatic conception of *homoousia*. The *barzakh* is, above all, a membrane of division; it guarantees the separation of adjacent terms and refuses their synthesis in the figure of Christ.

The limit is not, however, merely an impassable fault. One must not forget that the imaginal is also the domain in which a link is formed; a zone in which opposing terms—God and man; matter and spirit—coincide. Ibn 'Arabi describes this coincidence of opposites an act of "com-passion." The term is not meant to invoke a moral prescription, but a metaphysics of active relating to what escapes comprehension. *Barzakh* names the site, the condition, of this encounter as one of compassion—which is distinct from actual contact, for there can be no contact with a negative of existence, with what, lacking existence, remains unknown. The "point of contact" is an empty set.

In my citation of Ibn 'Arabi's definition of the *barzakh* above, I inserted an ellipsis in order to reserve the elided passage for a further inspection. Here follows the missing passage: "Though sense perception might be incapable of separating the two things, the rational faculty judges that there is a barrier . . . between them that separates them. The intelligible barrier is the *barzakh*. If it is perceived by the senses, it is one of the two things, not the *barzakh*."[68]

This passage clarifies a number of points. I made a leap earlier from the notion of trans-sensory perception to Aristotle's treatise *On the Soul*, which, I hypothesized, inadvertently handed to Islamic philosophers their own reinvented notion of perception on a plate. The above passage confirms that this is indeed what happened. Aristotle inadvertently exposed the esoteric dimension of perception. Let us run quickly through the argument again to see if we can detect the point at which Aristotle's Arabic translators found their footing.

Aristotle begins axiomatically by stating that all senses sense across a medium or interval and that this interval separates a particular organ from a sensible object. When he examines the case of touch, however, the axiom no longer seems sustainable, for no separating membrane can be detected. The membrane is imperceptible; it "escapes our notice," Aristotle says twice, as if rubbing his eyes in disbelief. Refusing to back down in the face of this lack of evidence, he insists that the membrane that separates organ from object must, in the case of touch, be placed at a lesser distance than in the other senses.[69] The unique closeness of its medium causes Aristotle further to distinguish the sense of touch from the other senses. When we see or hear, he hypothesizes, "we perceive because the medium produces a certain effect on us, whereas in the perception of objects of touch we are affected not by but along with the medium: it is as if a man were struck through his shield, where the shock is not first given to the shield and passed to the man, but the concussion of both is simultaneous."[70] This imagined shield is unlike any one has ever encountered, since it seems to be placed not outside but somehow "seated inside."[71]

Eventually, Aristotle throws in the towel, exclaiming simply, "We are unable clearly to detect" where the medium falls.[72] This is where the Islamic notion of the *barzakh* intervenes and takes over. While it is true that the senses are incapable of locating the medium that is necessary in order for us to perceive, the matter does not end here. For it falls to the rational faculty of judgment to performs this function. Man also thinks with his bodily organs, his objects a. Avicenna's thought experiment "demonstrated" that the first certainty is that "I am." This certainty is not, however, a thought. Thought, which comes later, is necessary to illuminate the certainty of self-awareness, to give form to the "I am," to the *sum*. Were this form rigid, it would cancel out the source whence it came, the sense of the absent presence it is meant to reveal. And so thought thinks not only the form "I am" takes, but also the limit-threshold, the imperceptible *barzakh*. We think because we have access to what comes before the world comes into being, to its opening or threshold.

In his defense of divine images, John of Damascus states that while human nature was once under a curse that enjoined us from touching bodies of the dead, lest we be reckoned unclean, "our nature has [now] been truly glorified and its very elements changed into incorruption."[73] Released from the custody of the law that pronounced the former curse, our bodies have been elevated to a new status of "incorruptibility." Might we not say, then, that our release from the taboo was the result of a new notion of touch, which became available at that historical moment when, as John claims, "divinity [was] united without confusion to our nature"? As we argued earlier, union without confusion, without commingling or synthesis, put paid to the doctrine of incarnation. The *barzakh* is necessary to prevent death, time, and the outside from seeping into the body and exposing it to rot. We touch and that which we touch eats into our bodies, corrupting it. The *barzakh*, however, reconceives time and the outside as internal to the body and the no-longer-tabooed touch renders us incorruptible. This does not mean that the body can escape eventual death (we are not looking for miracles) but that it resists being taken over, infected by the outside. The rot of corruption gives way to the unripeness of potentiality.

As he attempts to explicate what is "essential and original in Freud's thought" concerning the body of the subject, Lacan proceeds by contrasting that thought with an age-old dream lyrically recomposed by Walt Whitman. This is the dream of "total, complete, epidermic contact between one's body and a world that [is] itself open and quivering."[74] What is clear is that this dream relies on the superseded sense of touch as a phenomenon of the periphery, of touch as contact along an epidermic surface. The "electric" body Whitman "sings" expresses a pastoral optimism: that the "perpetual, insinuating presence of the oppressive feeling of some original curse" will finally, somehow, disappear.[75] If Whitman's wistful dream of dispelling the curse is doomed, it is because it is premised on the very idea that elicits the curse in the first place: that the body has a periphery and thus constitutes a whole.

I bring up this old dream for a variety of reasons, the least significant being the fact that some of the work now being written on the subject of touch demonstrates that the dream is still alive. A giddy sense of universal relatedness, of being in touch with the world in its entirety characterized this work, which never thought to question the body's completeness. Our constant refrain has been that every body defined as whole is encased; every frame serves as a coffin. Fully incarnate, it awaits only death. For psychoanalysis, the question was raised by clinical observation. From the first, the bodies that walked through Freud's door arrived in pieces; they seemed to be cut up, to be missing parts. Sometimes the hysterics could not move an arm or leg, or could not control them as they flailed about, because they had no idea of them. It was by trying to figure out why this was so that Freud was led (to cut a long story very short) to his theories of sexuality and the drive. In contrast to Whitman, Freud was led to "emphasize [that the] point[s] of insertion" of the subject into the world were "limit point[s] . . . at the level of what we might call the *Triebe*."

The subject is inserted not along the periphery but at any of an infinite number of limit points, thresholds through which the light of another, suspended, dimension shines. *Triebe*, drive, is like *barzakh*, both a limit and a zone of linkage. And here—as I have been broadly hinting—the analogy does not end.

This is not the place, however, to take this analogy further, and so I will use my final words to turn the discussion back to Kiarostami, who undertakes a reinstatement of the imaginal world—along with its attendant phenomena: the image, touch, the *barzakh*—in a cinema still affected by the taboo against touch, specifically between unrelated men and women. This taboo reposes on the idea that sex is a surface phenomenon that places men at risk of corruption by women. One might speculate that Kiarostami's intention is to lift once again the curse of corruptibility from which Islamic philosophy released us long ago.

2
THE VERTIGO OF ORIGINS

In the beginning was the Cloud. This we know because when he was asked "Where was our Lord before he created his creatures?" the Prophet responded without hesitation, "He was in a Cloud; there was no space either above or below." In this hadith, Cloud is clearly identified as the first locus or precinct, the first thing about which "whereness" is posited. As usual, however, in cases that involve origins, matters are never as simple as they seem. The Arabic word *kan* is in this passage normally translated as was, but the Sufi mystic "Ibn 'Arabi makes clear that 'he came to be'—a meaning equally allowable by the Arabic—is how he understands it."[1] What reason could there have been for this preference if not what is evident on its face: instead of predicating something about God—his whereabouts, in this case—it locates Him in an act of emergence? Yet, the implications of Ibn 'Arabi's translation are not immediately evident.

Further questions arise in response to a more elaborated version of the myth, this one composed by Ibn 'Arabi himself:

> When God created Adam, there remained a surplus of the leaven of the clay from which He created the palm tree, Adam's sister; yet this creation, too, left behind a remainder the size of a sesame seed, from which this tiny fragment God created an immense Earth, the whole of our universe, in which was hidden so many marvels that their number cannot be counted.[2]

The "immense Earth" is here synonymous with the Cloud, insofar as both designate the first locus despite the fact that the second version mentions it last in order of narration. More explicitly than the first, the second version also exposes these oddities: (1) the tiny fragment, which is purported to contain an immensity greater than it would seem capable of containing; and (2) the almost comical nature of the remainder; for despite its apparent diminution—from remainder to the remainder of a remainder—the remainder or surplus (as it is also called) seems, on the contrary, to be refractory to numerical conceptualization. Rather than a dwindling portion of a larger sum, the peculiar character of this remainder resides in its insistent recurrence. Reappearing with each division, the stubborn surplus repeatedly enacts the misalignment of the narrative with its own unfolding. Everything happens as if it were itself responsible for thwarting the linear progress of creation.

Also referred to as the Divine Breath or Imagination, Cloud is one of the intermediary terms—of which there are many in esoteric Islamic philosophy—that designates a zone of separation between opposing terms thus preventing their collapse into one another. In these intermediary zones, relationships are established between terms that do not preexist their relationship, a fact that reinforces the intermediary's status as first. As a concept, Cloud retains several features associated with empirical clouds; vaporous, it names a place of passage and transformation. It is the locus of a subtle movement. The extraordinary conceptual innovation of the Cloud lies in large measure in its avoidance of the standard theological opposition between the Uncreated and His creatures, in which the former is said to bring forth the latter ex nihilo. In the common view, the gulf separating God from His creatures is overcome through the positing of a third substance, a nothing-substance, out of which God unilaterally, and mysteriously, fashions the world.[3] Cloud, on the other hand, is not a separately existing substance between God and the world. Cloud is neither being nor nonbeing but "being in suspense"; it suspends or limits absolute power and maximizes tension.

Allow me to add to this an early warning: the suspending nature of this zone should not be confused with the sort of wavering hesitation that characterizes agnosticism. On the contrary, the concept of Cloud "pierce[s] even the granite of doubt . . . [thus] paralyzing the 'agnostic reflex,' in the sense that it break[s] . . . the isolation of thought and being; [it transforms] phenomenology into an ontology."[4] A Gnostic concept, Cloud contributes to the theorization of a kind of knowing that takes the form of nonknowing, a certainty that forges the pact between the human and the Divine.

All existence is brought forth, esoteric philosophy contends, not out of a nothing (as if it were a material cause), a substance outside God (who would thus function as efficient cause, as a creator in the ordinary sense), but out of Himself, out of the very breath He exhales. As noted earlier, Divine Being is said to be originally in the Cloud, and yet insofar as it is His breath, Cloud seems to be a part of—and thus in—Him. Is God in the Cloud, or is the Cloud in Him? Regarding his creatures, a similar question remains: are they inside or outside Him? From beginning to end, questions of cause and temporality plague this myth of origin even though answers, such as the following, are periodically offered: the Lord is indeed in the Cloud, the Universal Reality, but "the Divine Essence . . . which cannot be conceived as the Lord of anything, is beyond the Cloud."[5] We gather from this that God is not a simple fact or idea. He is both Lord and Divine Essence, in and beyond the Cloud, Revealed and Hidden. But such terminological distinctions are simply unsatisfying without an explanation of how the opposing terms relate to each other. How precisely is the unity of God—*tawhid*—to be thought?

My interest in the Cloud and the questions surrounding it was initiated not by theological concerns but by my admiration for the films of the Iranian filmmaker Abbas Kiarostami, whose commitment to a distinctive form of factual fiction led critics to label his work with the default term *neorealism*. It seemed to me, on the one hand, that these extraordinary films demanded their audience to delve further into the culture that nourished them before burying them under that tired, overused label. On the other hand, I could not quiet my sense that the insights of psychoanalysis were germane to the films.

Details from the films finally conspired with scattered references in Lacan's writings to bring to my attention the work of the French philosopher and Islamicist Henry Corbin. This work became the most inspiring, though not exclusive, source of my knowledge of the Islamic philosophy to which I began to turn for guidance in reading the films. That my decision to follow the path of this *principia domestica* allowed me to hold onto insights derived from psychoanalysis, that Islamic philosophy might open my eyes to Freud and Lacan as often as the other way around, is not something I took for granted but something I found myself fighting for and against, concept by concept.

Why assume that such a project was even feasible to begin with? A quote from Christian Jambet, an Islamic philosopher and former student of Corbin, will serve as my starting point:

> The future of a thought speaks the truth of this thought, whereas the history of its sources fixes its exactitude. The metamorphoses of a philosophy are the effective act[s] of being of this philosophy because philosophy has no history but rather, in the time of systems, expresses schemes whose fecundity or capacity to be transformed through a confrontation with the present, is expressed by its future power. Its "history" is the record of the positions it has taken within the real, which it embodies and engenders.[6]

Relying on a distinction between truth and exactitude, Jambet separates historicity from historicism. He rejects not history as such but the historicist assumption that systems of thought succeed each other in linear fashion and have limited time spans that can be more or less clearly demarcated. Philosophical thought is conceived in this way as systems of time-stamped ideas that go out of fashion as new ones replace them. But if philosophy demands that we contemplate it otherwise, it is because it harbors a kernel of truth. Truth?! I know, what a bloated, outmoded idea this is! What a word to "fling . . . in your faces—a word of almost ill repute!"[7] We moderns no longer officially believe that there is a transcendental perch from which the truth can be spoken. However, the truth at issue for Jambet is not that one, not pompous and whole; it is niggling, carping truth. Normally, we accord to speech and writing a unique direction, an intention to say something about the world that exists beyond it. Truth in the sense used here, however, lacks intention; it is instead *orientated*. I use this term as did Corbin and the Sufi philosophers for whom the Orient was not a geographical territory but a "metaphysical destination." It is not only Sufi mystics who turned our heads in this direction, Levinas also urged us to be aware of it. Language is not merely directed toward the world but turns toward an absolute otherness, absolute in the sense that is not integrated into the world, does not disclose itself there.[8] This orientation disturbs intention and interrupts the forward movement of thought.

Jambet makes his argument in the introduction to his book on Mulla Sadra (1571–1636) to warn readers who might want merely to peruse the Iranian Shi'ite philosophy out of an antiquarian curiosity. Jambet is at pains to point out that Sadra's work has contemporary significance, for it—along with the entire "Avicennian turn" in philosophy of which Sadra's philosophy distinguishes itself as a kind of culmination—reappeared on the world stage during the Islamic Revolution.[9] Khomeini, a self-professed Sadra scholar, attempted to place this philosophy in the service of the revolution by twisting its arguments while laying claiming to them. Prior to this, Jambet points out, Islamic philosophy was thrust into the spotlight at two other moments. The first was the period of German idealism, in which "Oriental" or mystical thought, including that of the Persian mystics, was enthusiastically embraced. The second began in the late 1940s with a dialogue among Christian, Jewish, and Islamic religious scholars and ended at the dawn of the revolution. We will come back to these separate but interconnected moments.

At the risk of losing this important thread, however, I need to pause for a psychoanalytic intermission. The idea that history does not simply move forward but that events at a later moment retain (let us say for now) an underground connection to moments in the past to which they seem to revert is familiar—even overly familiar—to psychoanalytic thinkers. We speak of it often by its German name: *Nachtraglichkeit*. Freud regularly used this term to describe a psychical operation of temporal redirection at odds with a leveled-down chronology, but not always. We now recognize the concept under various names: *après-coup*, retroaction, afterwardness.

But however often these words are used, the concept itself is shrouded in confusion, as Jean Laplanche, to his great credit, has shown. His attempt to resolve this confusion begins by detailing the stark differences between the way Freud and Jung understood this concept. To summarize, while Jung conceived *Nachtraglichkeit* as a movement that reversed the arrow of time by rewriting the past from the position of the present, Freud conceived it primarily as a subterranean operation by which cause takes effect belatedly, in a future at a distance from it. This sharp distinction—which sets up both opponents for failure—is, however, too simple.

That Jung's was a cavalier reduction of *Nachtraglichkeit* to *Zuruckphantasieren*—that is, to retroactive fantasizing or resignification—seems clear enough. In its most cynical form this definition amounts to the assertion that imaginary scenarios are reconstructed "to meet the needs of some present concerns."[10] This psychologization of the operation prevents it from rising to the level of a psychoanalytic concept. Yet, Freud makes a symmetrical error, in Laplanche's view, by conceiving *Nachtraglichkeit* as a delayed form of determinism. In this alternative conception, a first psychic blow is thought to function like a time bomb with a long fuse, producing its effects long after, in a second blow. In this case the "arrow of time" is preserved; a cause, located in a definite past, produces consequences in a determined future. Now, Freud may not have been entirely consistent in the way he expressed his profound disagreement with Jung—and Laplanche's meticulous tracking of Freud's waffling is enlightening—but it is imperative to note that Freud held phantasy in much higher esteem than his colleague did, and this esteem was woven together with a conviction that there was an aspect of the past that could not be eclipsed. Cause and effect are, for this reason, not completely reversible. It is, I believe, this conviction that Laplanche mistakes for determinism.

Freud and Jung are both chastised by Laplanche for neglecting the essential role of the Other in the phenomenon of *après-coup*. "Other" refers, in this case, to another person simultaneously present with the child; it is the speech of this other person that delivers the traumatic blow. Freud's counterargument would be crisp: it is not other persons but the first Other, the unconscious, that is essential for understanding *après-coup*. The point is not only that other persons would fail to appear to us as other were it not for the unconscious, but that it is only as "instance of the unconscious" that *après-coup* reveals to us "a temporal structure of a higher order" and "reopen[s] the debate over cause, a phantom that cannot be banished from thought."[11] We will say more about the concept of *après-coup*—and the thesis imbedded in Lacan's comment—after we have acquired a better understanding of the temporality implied in the concept of the Cloud.

Let us now return to Jambet's proposal regarding the reemergence of interest in Islamic philosophy by examining the second period mentioned, in which Corbin played a major role. Because his work is relatively unknown in the English-speaking world, we begin with some elementary facts, selected for their relevance to this discussion. Corbin met Lacan at Alexandre Kojève's lectures—the two were thus colleagues who exchanged ideas—and Lacan's familiarity with the writings of Ibn 'Arabi and other mystics—especially evident in his *Encore* seminar—is said to have benefited from conversations with Corbin.[12]

While his first studies were devoted to Western philosophy and scholasticism, Corbin was later drawn to the Iranian philosophy of illumination when his teacher, Louis Massignon, gave him a first edition of Sohravardi's (1154–1191) *Philosophy of Illumination* in response to questions Corbin had begun to raise in his own work. Profoundly taken by the ideas of Sohrawardi and other illuminationists, Corbin spent much of the rest of his life traveling back and forth between Paris and Tehran, photographing and translating texts of various Islamic philosophers while maintaining an active intellectual life in Paris. From 1949 (the beginning of the Cold War) until his death in October 1978 (mere months before Khomeini returned from his Paris exile to Tehran to lead the Iranian Revolution), he also spent summers in Switzerland, where he attended the Eranos meetings, which were originally inspired, in 1933, by Carl Jung.[13]

For reasons that will become clear, I will focus on the way this period is represented in *Religion after Religion*—a scholarly, informative book about the Eranos meetings and three of the religious scholars (Corbin, Gershom Scholem, and Mircea Eliade) involved in their proceedings. While Jambet characterizes the dialogue that occurred at the meetings as a critical response to the positivism of Ernest Renan—whose book on the Muslim philosopher, Averroes (1126–1198), put forward the infamous claim that after Averroes's death, Islamic philosophy and science disappeared from the Islamic world, its culture being antithetical to rational thought—*Religion after Religion* makes the (in many respects) antithetical claim that these men, members of a generation in which religion had fallen out of fashion, were guilty, to varying degrees, of secularizing religion by emptying it of its religious core, which was to be found in laws, rituals, and social history.

However, Corbin is selected by the book's author, Steven Wasserstrom, for special and often outrageous ad hominem criticism.[14] The virtual coincidence of the death of Corbin and the triumphant return of Khomeini—"two champions of the soul of Iran"—is dramatized by Wasserstrom as the decisive conclusion of the struggle over the definition of that soul.[15] In his view the Iranian Revolution signaled the start of the "age of the return to religion" and constituted "an implicit repudiation of [Corbin's] idiosyncratic version of Iranian tradition in the name of an authentic indigenous religiosity."[16]

Wasserstrom makes no mention of the battle over Sadra's work staged by the opposed readings of Khomeini and Corbin, let alone try to parse these readings. This aside, not everyone would agree that the battle over the Iranian soul was as decisive as Wasserstrom believes or that any one voice is authorized to define the "authentic indigenous" form of the religion of a culture. I turn to this book not only to parry its criticisms but also because by framing Corbin's powerful reading of Islamic history in world historical terms, Wasserstrom retrieves that philosophy from what might otherwise be regarded a superseded past to accord it a significant role in contemporary political affairs. This is not to imply that it was Wasserstrom's intention to confirm Jambet's thesis regarding the truth of philosophy, a thesis inspired by Corbin himself. In a book of his own translations of texts by Islamic philosophers, for example, Corbin wrote that "our authors suggest that if the past were really what we believe it to be . . . completed and closed, it would not be the grounds of such vehement discussions. They suggest that all our acts of understanding are so many recommencements, reiterations of events still unconcluded."[17] Far from wishing to support this position, Wasserstrom attacks Corbin's polemical antihistoricism as scandalous. The tendency of Corbin to reduce the role played by law in religion, his distaste for what he regards as the overemphasis on the rational elaboration of the doctrines of religious law provoke Wasserstrom's loudest criticisms.

It must be said, however, that despite their bilious tone, his main criticisms of Corbin are not completely out of bounds; similar charges have been lodged by others. That Corbin overemphasized the mythological aspects of Islamic philosophy and idiosyncratically privileged the concept of the imaginal world over the central concept of the unity of God are widely voiced complaints.[18] These charges, which amount to a condemnation of his self-professed esoteric approach, insufficiently acknowledge that Corbin himself always maintained that the esoteric was encountered outside, that "the other world already exists in this world."[19] Our existence in this world is dependent on the fact of symbolization, the theory of which is one of Corbin's major preoccupations. His distaste for the "doctors of law" is often expressed in terms of his understanding of the operation of symbolization. He was of the same belief as Ibn 'Arabi, who held that "if each word of the shari'a has a meaning, the absence of a word has one, too; and man . . . is not to fill in God's silence. [For] the 'holes' in the Law are part of its plenitude."[20] Ibn 'Arabi here affirms a negativity within the law as part and parcel of the latter's very function. Not law as such, but the obloquy of doctors—who mistook their mandate to be the multiplication of strictures, the turning inside out of what is not forbidden into explicit disallowances—is the target of Corbin's contempt. For Corbin, as for Ibn 'Arabi, law does not merely restrict and forbid, but through what it does not say, makes room for the freedom of subjects subjected to it.

It is thus fortuitous that Wasserstrom decides to privilege a rare term, *tautegory*, as the "very watchword" of Corbin's philosophical intervention. As he points out, Corbin borrowed the term "from the Schelling-Cassirer theory of symbolism" and placed it "at the core of his philosophy" in order to abolish the distinction between myth and history.[21] Insofar as it focalizes

Wasserstrom's criticisms of the antihistoricism and antilegalism of Corbin, who indeed once referred to the term as a "privileged imaginal form," tautegory offers an appropriate vehicle by which to reply to those criticisms.

So, what is it? Tautegory is a term coined by Samuel Taylor Coleridge to encapsulate ideas he borrowed from F. W. J. Schelling, who subsequently adopted the term himself. Essentially, it is meant to name a symbolic form distinct from allegory. The *tauto* [a contraction of "to auto": the same] of tautegory is contrasted with the *allos* [the other] of allegory. Allegory establishes a link between two distinct terms to posit a resemblance between them; an allegorical figure is thus understood to represent something other than itself while pretending to be similar to it in some way.[22] A tautegorical symbol, on the other hand, does not represent something other but expresses only itself. Yet, this does not mean that tautegory states an identity or isomorphism. Distinct from tautology, tautegory indicates its own difference from, or unlikeness to, itself.[23] By means of the latter, as Corbin puts it, "the *allo* (the other) of allegory is surpassed, because [tautegory] is the form in which both the one and the other integrally manifest themselves."[24] In short, the tautegorical symbol is not other than the reality it represents; it is the form assumed by this reality or the reality it expresses.

Why does Wasserstrom so stridently object to this form of symbolization? Because it is the "working principle" behind Corbin's claim that "the first and last reason for a religious phenomenon is the existence of those who believe in it."[25] It is indeed true that Corbin rejected the modern tendency to explain religion (away) via psychological, economic, or political terms. By this, we imagine he meant to oppose those explanations of religion that reduced it to an opiate against—or compensation for—intolerable circumstances, otherwise inescapable; or to a strategy for quieting the revolutionary tendencies of the masses. He argued, on the contrary, that if religion had to be dealt with as a fact rather than an illusion, it is because those who believed in religion were caught up in it in an essential way.

This position, as Wasserstrom understands it, summarizes all that is wrong with tautegory: it insists that something can be the cause or the basis of itself, that the simple belief in something makes it so. He, on the other hand, wants to locate religion in the "ethical authority" of laws and customs, in what he calls an "exoteric ethics." He thus regards Corbin's esoteric elevation of the believer's "personal" relation to God as hopelessly secular and modernist in its embrace of individualism.[26] Now, we will argue that far from importing a modern, Western notion of the individual into Islamic philosophy, as his critic implies, Corbin offers from within that philosophy a theory of individuation that repels the notion of an isolated, self-enclosed individual.

The parallels between the antihistoricist and antilegalist stance articulated by Corbin in the name of the philosophers he champions stem from the fact that both reject the idea that they can be grasped from an external position. There can be no history, no religion without the subjects who are caught up in them. It is only the "doctors" of the field who think otherwise. As we will see, it is the fundamental cleavage between the hidden, or apophatic, God and the personal, or revealed God that permits us to think the peculiar curvature by which the subject becomes an essential part of his own beliefs. Were one to surrender tautegory—the privileged term that brings the intermediary precinct to light—this cleavage would fall apart into a simple duality, rather than remain what it is: the as-yet-unpacked unity of God critics of Corbin are right to want to preserve.

This is the proper moment to recall that the second reemergence of Islamic philosophy, by Jambet's count—the period associated with Corbin's monumental reexamination of it—was preceded by an earlier one: the period of German idealism's mythical or esoteric inflection, which is identified in Jambet's account with "the names of Goethe and Hegel" but which we will continue to explore through Schelling's unique contribution.[27] By spotlighting Corbin's use of Schelling's term, *Religion after Religion* may seem to imply that its appearance in this context is further evidence of an illegitimate importation of Western ideas into a system of thought demonstrably alien to it. But such a reading would have to disregard the fact that German idealism's incorporation of esoteric concepts itself opened the door of importation. That Schelling drew inspiration from one of the very thinkers who profoundly influenced Corbin—the seventeenth-century mystic, Jacob Boehme (1575–1624)—and that Hegel went so far as to bestow on Boehme the honorific, "the first German philosopher" are well-known historical facts. Corbin often openly stated that Boehme's ideas could be clearly shown to be convergent with those developed by "Shiite Islam, Ismailis as well as Twelve-Imam Shiites."[28]

Among German idealists, two of Boehme's theoretical contributions were especially influential: (1) the concept of an abyss or groundlessness (*Abgrund* or *Ungrund*, in Schelling's vocabulary); and (2) the reconceptualization of God as the *ens manifestativium sui*, that being whose essence is to reveal itself. The parallels between Boehme's innovations and the hadith that was arguably the most intensely contemplated by Sufi mystics—in which God's desire to reveal Himself is declared—are particularly striking: "I was a hidden Treasure and I yearned to be known. Then I created creatures in order to . . . become in them the object of my knowledge."[29] Boehme's first contribution participated in a larger mystical tendency to define the first principle from which the world emerges as containing nothing of what emerges from it. This is clearly an apophatic principle. Gilles Deleuze takes note—with reference to Schelling, though we can attribute it to the wider apophatic tendency—that the nothing at issue in his work is *me on*, which is to say a relative nonbeing or a not yet being, and not *ouk on*, not absolute nonbeing or nothing at all.[30] The Arabic word, *ma 'dum*, used by the Sufi mystics, had the same meaning: "nonexistent [but] not a mere nothing."[31]

We are now prepared to return to the initial questions raised by the Cloud that stands center stage in the myth of creation. In the reference just cited, Deleuze is distinguishing Schelling's position from that of the Neoplatonists, whose concept of emanation defined the process by which God's creatures proceeded from Him. Corbin often refers to the alternative process conceived by Islamic philosophers as a "divine dramaturgy" and forcefully distinguishes it from that of emanation.[32] In doing so he borrows another of Schelling's derogatory term, *unilateral monotheism*, to describe the latter.[33] The Sufi mystics and Schelling, after them, lodge the same complaint against the Neoplatonic conception of emanation: it proceeds in a single direction. A one-way path leads from a prior substance, the One, to the multiplicity that emanates from it. This supposes a necessary relation between the One and the multiple; not only is it necessary that God create, but the relation between Him and his creation is a necessary one. Emanation thinks the One as preeminent, as a sort of model for the expressions—individual the beings—that proceed from it and maintain toward it an allegorical relation, or relation of resemblance. In this way, the One serves as a binding, totalizing force; it coagulates what emanates from it.

Because the God of the mystics is inextricable from His apophatic status, a unilateral procession from Him, which would attest to—or define—His divinity, was summarily ruled out. Moreover, in order to remain faithful to the Qur'anic verse that rejects the Christian dogma of incarnation, Sufi philosophers denied the proposal that God had a son and refrained from according Him the role of progenitor. Conceived thus, not as a sovereign Lord from whom His creatures issued and on whom they were completely dependent, He was regarded more as a suzerain. The bond between Him and His creatures was maintained not by analogies and laws but by com-passion, initiated by the Lord's passionate longing not to reproduce or define Himself in his like, but to manifest Himself. This is by no means a simple idea, for the question immediately arises: to whom? There seems to be no way around it: the idea of manifestation, presupposes, in Corbin's words, "*eo ipso* the second term: the one to whom it manifests itself."[34] The "second term" refers here to God: He manifests Himself not to human subjects, to whom He remains opaque, but to Himself. We must make clear that God, as the second term, is not "presupposed" in the sense that that the manifestation merely reveals what was always already there. Each manifestation is accorded an original, unique status. That which comes forth from the in-between world of the imaginary is first, without precedent. God is ceaselessly created.

This point is evident in the terms used to designate these manifestations: *theophanies, epiphanies*. It is not that God was in the Cloud—where the past tense of the verb *to be* functions merely as a logical copula that situates God in a place: no, He came to be there in an act of being: boom! Just like that! Theophany and epiphany both imply an unpredictable appearance, untraceable back to a preexisting object. This is what makes them homologous to tautegories, which do not represent a given, some preexisting reality but are themselves what they represent.[35] Corbin attempts to explain this by reverting to Martin Luther's flash of understanding (his own small epiphany) regarding the proclamation contained in the psalm verse, "Through your justice you liberate me." The young theologian suddenly realized that this meant that the attributes we attribute to the divine are those we experience in ourselves. They are original with us; as Corbin puts it, we "'create' the God in whom [we] believe and whom we worship."[36]

Upon offering this explanation, Corbin immediately issues a warning, knowing full well that it is likely to become "a source of malicious glee to the rationalist critic and a stumbling block to the orthodox theologian."[37] Do not make the mistake of dismissing this idea as an example of psychologism or sociologism—or, we would add, of retroactive fantasizing—for it only appears to assert that God is nothing more that "a projection of consciousness." This is indeed the way Wasserstrom understands Corbin's arguments regarding the "personal God" of revelation—as a carryover from the Western obsession with individual psychology. But Corbin is quick to set his future critic straight: we are dealing here, he says, "not with an a posteriori fabrication but with an a priori fact of experience, posited along with the fact of our being."[38] We do not retroactively fantasize a God of our choosing. The personal or revealed God cannot be properly understood psychologically, but has to be approached as an ontological matter. While it is true that the personal God of each individual emerges from an act of being, the individual is not its simple agent. For she is brought forth from it, comes to be in the act itself. The act is ungraspable through a chronology, for it is the issue of a "pre-eternal pact."[39]

Nor does the fact that God's creatures are not the simple agents of the act mean that they are not free. Recall that the divine dramaturgy whose logic we are attempting to understand offers a radical rejection of unilateral monotheism, in which individuals come forth out of a One that is their precondition. Then recall the famous Qur'anic verse that states, "No compulsion in religion."[40] This statement is trivialized if is taken to refer *only* to "the faithful," for we could not be free were God not also. Ismaili thought distanced itself from the Neoplatonic schema by introducing—in relation to the act of being—the concept of an imperative: Be![41] Were it be regarded as the compelling of an act, this imperative would violate the Qur'anic injunction against compulsion. The only way to read it, then, is as a "forced choice." As Lacan explains it, a choice is forced insofar as only one of the choices is viable since the alternative cancels the possibility of choice. Had God not opted for being, neither He nor we would ever have been. His choice, made in pre-eternity, was nevertheless a choice, a free act through which God freed or absolved himself from the absoluteness of his nonbeing. By this act, God's yearning to be known is defined as something other than evidence of a lack; it is defined, instead, as a positing, as a choice of "pure alterity," that is, a choice of being.[42] The act brings the revealed God and beings into being at the same time; they emerge as correlated terms.

Let us pause here to consider what this divine dramaturgy or mythical account of creation makes of the created world of being. It conceives being as contingent inasmuch as it is not grounded in any substance or by any necessity. It exposes itself as a world that might not have been. This is a surprisingly modern conception of the world. Is it too modern? I have in mind a comment Slavoj Žižek made about Schelling: "The paradox . . . is that it *was his very 'regression'* . . . *to* [a] premodern theosophical problematic which enabled him to overtake modernity itself."[43] I raise these antihistoricist musings in the context of my interest in Kiarostami and my desire to account for the precise nature of the realism we encounter in his films. Is there a way in which this seeming regression to premodern, Sufi creation myths makes sense of the surpassing modernity of his realist vision? Other chapters pursue aspects of this question further. I raise it here to underscore my general thesis that his modern cinema reinvokes the mythical spaces of the imaginal world—the Cloud—places where being is *suspended*; grounded not in a prior substance, but in the derivation of activity out of passivity.

Let us return to the myth of creation where we left off, only now to confess that I passed over earlier, without comment, Corbin's claim that the act of being is posited along with "an a priori fact of experience." I take Jambet to be making this very point when he notes that "the effect of the . . . act [of being] . . . is indeed to consecrate the ontological priority of the One."[44] This point seems to strike a discordant note, for the argument we have been following denies any such priority. It implies that there never was a time when God, entirely alone, created the world. For were He precedent to His manifestations, being would forfeit its status as original, as revelations or epiphanies. The latter would become thinkable in advance of their actual appearance. But since God has to appear to someone (to beings), somewhere (in a symbolic order, endowed with the capacity to manifest him), they must be present at the origin. To reject, for all these reasons, the unilateralist concept of cause is, however, not to forswear an alternative concept. To do so would be to sacrifice the very idea of epiphanies, of being as contingent, and open the door to miracles.

Consider a recent instance of the latter: at the end of his boldly argued defense of contingency, *After Finitude: An Essay on the Necessity of Contingency*, Quentin Meillassoux surprises us by entertaining the possibility of what amounts to miracles on the grounds that contingency means that anything can happen; nothing is ruled out. This is a vivid illustration of how a modern idea—unassisted by the sort of "regression" offered by Schelling and Islamic theosophists but also psychoanalysis—goes wrong. Here is Lacan, defending Freud's career-long insistence on this point: "Freud shows clearly that . . . there can be no such thing as a miracle. It must, he says, have a relation with causality."[45] "It" refers here to the subject, specifically in the context of Freud's well-known dictum, which Lacan is attempting to unpack: *Wo es war, soll Ich werden* (Where it was, there must the subject come to be). Is this not strangely reminiscent of the mystical dictum: the essence (the imperative) of relative nonbeing (*me on*) is to manifest itself (to come into being)? The subject emerges in being through an act. Epiphany or miracle? What is the difference if not that the modern, idealist conception of antifoundationalism is regarded simply as lack; it has no further consequences, plays no further role, in being. This is how miracles are produced: without constraint, ex nihilo. In mystical thought, however, nonbeing is implicated in being. This is how we have understood Jambet's claim that the original choice is for pure alterity: not simply for being over nonbeing but for being that is somehow irreparably perturbed by its very lack of ground, constrained.

The alternative concept of cause—which the phrase "ontological priority of the One" compels us to contemplate—originates in being or in the symbolic itself. It originates, Jambet says, "belatedly [*après-coup*]."[46] Now, if the causal logic of *Nachtraglichkeit* occurs between two times, the logic of creation seems to conform neither to the determinist (supposedly Freudian) nor the idealist (Jungian) options Laplanche spells out. For the logic of creation, meant to free religion—both God and the faithful—from compulsion, does not begin at the origin but instead at the point that originates the origin. It is nondeterminist. And yet, the concept of the origination of the origin is ungraspable as mere fabrication. It resists the idealist notion of retroactive fantasizing. We consecrate, or attest to, the ontological priority of the One, acknowledge its antecedence as irrefutable, beyond doubt. Precisely because it is ungrounded, being can only affirm itself through repetition—not a repetition of an existing thing, for this would reduce being to a secondary status. Being repeats itself, but in doing so, it produces a surplus with which it fails to coincide. This surplus is not a retroactive meaning but a by-product of our efforts.

We witnessed this very occurrence, in fact, in Ibn 'Arabi's version of the creation myth, in which a surplus or insistent remainder, kept reappearing at each iteration. This remainder, which we can never get in front of, insists on an irreversibility of the arrow of time more implacable than the one to which Laplanche attends, which travels from a determinate point in the past to another in the future, however delayed. This "indivisible remainder," to use Schelling's name for it, harkens back to an absolute past or cause, absolute in its radical undisclosedness. "Anticonceptual," "indefinite," and "unborn" are the words Lacan chooses to describe it; an "inconceivable and unverifiable real, 'beyond' naming," says Jambet.[47]

The ineluctable negativity of this One earned it the name the Hidden God, but the temporality of the origin proves once again that what is hidden is never but what is missing from its place. If he is beyond every disclosure, it is because he never assumed the place of origin, never existed before being. If he comes to be post factum, it is as "the origin that never was . . . not a time that passed away . . . [it] only is in and through the Present as the presence of a haunting absence, that which we have just missed."[48] In short, and as remarked earlier, quoting from Lacan, he is "a phantom that cannot be banished from thought."

This idea of cause cedes none of the previous arguments regarding the priority of being. What, then, does this lost, phantom cause do? It introduces thought. It allows being to appear to reason, to become subject to questions. Again, that being is contingent does not mean no laws apply, that anything is possible. Although mythology is often thought to be fundamentally opposed to rational thought, the Sufi myth of origins shows how the former secures a place for the latter.

3

FROM THE CLOUD TO THE RESISTANCE

It is the third phase of Henry Corbin's career—the period between 1946 and his death in October 1978, during which the French philosopher traveled back and forth between Paris and Tehran—that particularly interests Steven Wasserstrom, author of *Religion after Religion: Gershom Scholem, Mircea Eliade, and Henry Corbin.*[1] And while it is all three scholars named in the title, it is particularly Corbin whom Wasserstrom accuses of offering a woefully insufficient response to the disenchantment of the world, a curse supposedly wrought by modernization's rationalization of our lifeworld.

The problem plaguing these scholars' critical proposals struck Wasserstrom as elementary: they remained uninterested in offering a "workable socioreligious program" and instead chose to present a mere "aesthetic critique" drafted from "an imaginal god's-eye view" of the world. Rather than starting out "from the concrete given of the modern city or the modern body," their arguments took off "from [a] heavenly city and the transfigured body."[2] The fact that Corbin died in Paris mere weeks before Ayatollah Khomeini left this city of his exile to return to Tehran in order to take the reins of his country in the final days of the revolution is a terrible irony. The polemic of *Religion without Religion*, however, views the historical events as proof that the authentic religious thought of Khomeini prevailed in reality over the other-worldly mysticism of Corbin and his colleagues. The "battle over the soul of the Iranian people," as he refers to it, was in the end decided in reality.

I wish to challenge Wasserstrom's view of this history and will do so via a reading of a film by Abbas Kiarostami, *First Case, Second Case*. This film was begun in spring 1979, during the revolutionary moment Wasserstrom evokes as validation of his negative assessment of Corbin's views on religion and his own confidence in Khomeini's victory. I do not pretend that the terms of my argument would please or persuade Wasserstrom since they are drawn from the very theoretical arsenal he condemns. My attention to Kiarostami's film should thus be counted as one more effort to persuade since, as I will argue, the film offers viewers a glimpse of Corbin's theoretical propositions as they were played out in concrete reality, in the homes and on the streets of the modern city of Tehran.³

Before examining the film, I will offer some background. One of Wasserstrom's general criticisms is that the very concept of a "history of religions"—the very attempt to think religion in the plural—betrays the questionable status of the joint enterprise in which these scholars were engaged.⁴ In the world of everyday reality, people belong to *a* religion, in the singular, to a concrete practice and a codified set of beliefs. In other words, religion relies on objective legal systems, official hierarchies, and orthodoxies. Thus, the notion that there might be a "secret history" of religions that linked them strikes Wasserstrom as a dubious construct woven out of a yearning for a transcendence and a totality whose disappearance from our atomized, rationalized world these scholars deplored. This speculation opens the door for his presentation of their work as a misguided effort to reenchant the dreary postwar reality they bemoaned by dredging up esoteric ideas long ago junked for what they are: unscientific phantasmagoria.

Alongside the three scholars who are his focus—scholars of the three monotheisms or religions of the Book—Wasserstrom periodically references some of their fellow travelers, Walter Benjamin being one of them, who participated in the same retrograde desire for re-enchantment as did they. It is thus not possible not to think—nor to think that Wasserstrom might not be thinking, dismissively—of Benjamin here. For in "On Language as Such and on the Language of Man" as well as in "The Task of the Translator," the German philosopher laid out a theory of language in which one language's translation into another is conceived not merely as more or less susceptible to being carried out, depending on the abilities of the translator, but as language's essential aspect. That is, Benjamin's theory of language takes the "impartability" or translatability of language—rather than its propositional content—as its central fact.

By its very nature, language is that *in* which—not *through* which—we communicate. Language cannot be thought in the ablative, reduced to a tool box of names we paste on things. By assigning impartability to language as such, Benjamin conceives it as something more and other than this, as a promise (*Versprechen*). In the terms of the mystical tradition of Islamic philosophy with which Corbin is concerned, language is thought, similarly, as belonging to the "prophetic essence of man." Put briefly, this means that man is he who speaks the truth, where truth is not measured by the adequation of language to an external reality. It implies, on the contrary, an "inadequation of man as prophet to the language of the divine speaker, the absolute subject supposed to speak." More, while this inadequation is constantly struggled against, it is "never vanquished in the infinite exegesis of the letter."⁵

Stated thus, this conception of truth can only seem opaque. The terms permitting its articulation still need to be presented and examined. I intend to do this, but if I offer this conception of truth, prematurely, it is to enlist Benjamin as another ally against Wasserstrom's criticisms, which are rooted in the highly debatable position known as nominalism. The pillars of this position are (1) language is a tool we use to name preexisting things; and (2) in reality, there are no universals that gather up or collectivize individual things. Nominalism abhors the One, which it dismisses as a mere abstraction that serves to efface the concrete existence of things. At stake in the warring positions between Wasserstrom and Corbin is thus the very concept of the One, more specifically the concept of the "unity of God"—*tawhid* in Arabic—a concept central to Islamic philosophy and religion.

I will focus for the remainder not on the group of Eranos scholars but on Corbin specifically and on the unique conception of the Oneness of God he brings to light through translations and detailed readings of numerous Islamic philosophers. My intention, however, is to offer a critique of the reenchantment thesis with which Wasserstrom tars the entire Eranos project. In an attempt to hold together the various strains of my argument, I will focus primarily on one of Corbin's essays, "Apophatic Theology as Antidote to Nihilism." There are two reasons for this choice. First, the essay was delivered as a paper in Tehran in October 1977 at an international colloquium devoted to the question of whether or not Western thought permitted dialogue with other civilizations.[6] At this moment, the tensions that would explode in a revolution months later had already begun to broil. Second, after alluding to current questions concerning technology, Corbin suggests in this essay that these questions should be held in check until the commonplace proposition that "socio-political systems spread out from the contemporary West across the whole planet are the secularizations of earlier theological systems" had not been sufficiently interrogated.[7] That proposition might be summarily stated as follows: Secularization is an operation that "leaves intact the forces it deals with by simply moving them from one place to another. Thus, the political secularization of theoretical concepts does nothing more than displace the heavenly monarchy onto an earthly monarchy."[8] We see from this that Wasserstrom is correct to accuse Corbin of openly challenging the secularization thesis, but—as I will argue—this was not because he wanted to reenchant the world by reinstalling God in his allegedly former position.

A sigh of impatience is detectible at this point in Corbin's rebuttal of the secularization thesis. Yet, the contestation Corbin lodges against this supposed hierarchy confronts a seemingly insurmountable hurdle, given that the religion of Islam is well known to prize submission (*taslim*) as the proper posture of religious subjects to their Lord. It is therefore necessary to point out that in Islam, the religious subject is not obliged to submit herself to any external entity or exoteric authority. The religious posture does not require subjects to submit themselves to the *religio* (the bondage) of norms.⁹ Quite the contrary, "the hypothesis of a delegation, of a representation of the divine authority in human authority [was until fairly recently] impossible a priori [in Islamic thought].... Nothing that resembles a minister or pope, even less the secularization of religious authority under the leader of a sacralization of the political body" can be found in the Qur'an or in any proposal made by religious philosophers.¹⁰

The proposal that secularization results from the placement of a new term in the superior position of an older hierarchy would make no sense to Islamic philosophers, who conceived the religious relation between God and man to be forged laterally, not hierarchically. From the perspective of Islamic theosophy, it would be more correct to say that the hierarchy secularization sought to take over from religion was one of secularization's *own invention*. For this reason, Corbin views secularization as a much more destructive operation than is ordinarily acknowledged. It does more than plant its own flag on the hill of Divine Being; it attempts to efface every trace of God. In brief, it orchestrates a complete obnubilation of the dimension of the divine. And it cloudes over, occludes, the middle term known in Islamic philosophy as the Cloud.¹¹

Corbin makes only slant connections between technology's ascendent place in the modern world and secularization, but his remarks are provocative. What he observes, and vigorously condemns, is the nihilism that dominated the discourse on technology. He regrets its characterization of technology as a weapon of the West, one that the West believed, throwing up its hands, inevitably rendered dialogue between modern and traditional cultures impossible. If these cultures could no longer speak to one another, it was not only because technology had ruined any chance of their finding a common language but worse: technology had, by this point, pushed traditional cultures to the verge of extinction. One needs to remember that the "Apophatic Theology" paper was delivered at a moment when the "clash of civilizations" rhetoric that pitted the West against cultures soon to be laid to rest—was in this moment ramping up. The anticipated annihilation of entire cultures is evoked by Corbin's use of the term *nihilism*. The latter names a virulent form of agnosticism, an indifference, or unwillingness, to acknowledge others sufficiently to engage them in dialogue. Simply said, nihilism is a wanting-not-to-know anything about any dimension other than that of the finite, empirical world.

In the face of this seemingly invincible negativity, Corbin refuses to surrender to the inevitability of its triumph. He goes on to argue that the unrelenting blindness of sociopolitical systems is incapable in and of itself of destroying what it refuses to see. Qualifying it as a "plenary" concept, he suggests that if secularization has an air of viability about it, it is because it claims to be part and parcel of a phenomenon that is itself indisputable: the geographical spread of Western thought across the face of the planet. "Secularization" is, in many respects, a blander term for the disease Iranians called "Westoxification," or "Occidentosis."[12] While there is no disputing the fact that this disease had colonized the world by the time it was identified, its success did not automatically insure its victory.

In fact, the term itself highlights its own limits. For the aspiration of Western thought was simple: it sought to spread itself over and thereby to conquer the whole world. This ambition is limited precisely because it aims to take over merely the finite world, which is to say that world which lays claim to wholeness. Here, then, is the problem: by refusing to acknowledge another dimension, the infinity of otherness, secular or exoteric thinkers blinded themselves to the fact that this otherness flees from them. That of which they wanted to know nothing was not some inert territory or substance but an active element whose potential use to them lay in their permanent inability to grasp it. What fled, escaped, withdrew from them was precisely what they were hell-bent on covering up. That which was impossible to grasp was simply denied. This is the key point behind Corbin's bleak description of nihilism as a "desperation or cynicism" that had lost consciousness of the fact that the gates that [it itself] shut [were] closed."[13]

Fortunately for us, a cinematic version of this argument was produced to give us a concrete sense of the still winnable battle between the exoteric forces of nihilism and the esoteric hold outs against it. The film, *The Wind Will Carry Us* (1999), was directed by Kiarostami. In it, a television documentary film crew from the modern, global city of Tehran travels to a "primitive" village in Northern Iran to film the traditional mourning ceremony that is slated to follow the demise of a one-hundred-year-old woman currently at death's door. Despite the fact that the village is visibly undergoing an extensive technological upgrading, and the ritual ceremony is revealed to have been "secularized"—it now serves as a means of climbing the ladder of financial and social power—there is evidence throughout the film—primarily in the unbent postures assumed by the villagers before the clueless camera crew—that a sacred dimension remains intact.

To quote Corbin, "We understand here by 'sacralization' the announcement, recognized by intimate sentiments, of a sacrosanct transcendental world . . . within the phenomena and appearances of this world."[14] The young boy from the village who acts as a guide for the film crew seems to speak for Corbin when he reprimands the crew's director for suggesting that the village has "hidden" itself from the wider world. It is the director, the boy points out, who has blinded himself to the existence of the village. It is clear in this film that the sacred realm occupies a place not above mundane reality but in its interior, which remains unseen only by the distracted televisual crew.

To the negativity of nihilism and agnosticism, Corbin offers as antidote a radically different form of negativity: apophatic theology. Iranian-Islamic philosophy is centered around a dark God: not a God with evil or vengeful attributes, a God who wishes us harm, but one devoid of any attributes by which He can be known or recognized. Devoid of features, apophatic, this God does not perform the functions of a father. He is no progenitor, nor do His creatures bear His likeness.[15] Common to nihilism and the conception of an apophatic God is the idea that the other is unknowable. But here the similarity ends. The former refers to an inability or refusal to know, while the latter breeds knowledge of a dimension of finite reality that flees knowledge but is nevertheless known. To avoid the convulsive syntax necessary to describe this form of knowledge, one modern Gnostic scholar proposed that the term *gnosis*—literally, a knowing—might faithfully be translated "acquaintance."[16] The Lacanian term *encounter* offers, I suggest, a similar but more effective solution inasmuch as it is understood as shorthand for a "failed encounter." The encounter with God (the Other) is always missed, for He is, by definition, that which flees or retreats from us. What is encountered—according to the Gnostic tradition as well as psychoanalysis—is a limit beyond which it is impossible to pass. Psychoanalysis has a word for this limit: *unconscious*. Those who take psychoanalysis, and thus the unconscious, seriously are inheritors of this sturdy Gnostic tradition.[17]

A significant part of his unfortunate misreading of Corbin's contributions to Islamic philosophy owes to the confusion of Wasserstrom regarding the nature of Gnosticism. To give his audience a sense of the pessimism from which Corbin's desire for re-enchantment supposedly took off, Wasserstrom directs us to read *Avicenna and the Visionary Recital*, in which Corbin stands accused of manifesting a gloominess rivaling Heidegger's tenebrous vision of a darkened world abandoned by the gods, where man has been transformed into a mass and suspicion and hatred run riot.[18] Now, while Gnosticism is accurately associated with a belief in an absolute knowledge that is tragically out of reach of fallen beings who remained chained to their mortal, earthbound bodies, Corbin is at pains to show how thoroughly—and with what consequences—the position of the Ismaili Gnostics on which his own work focuses "modifies the radical pessimism of the early Gnostics."[19] Among these Ismaili philosophers, knowledge was regarded not as unattainable but as inexhaustible. While they, too, maintained that absolute knowledge was out of reach, it was for an entirely different reason: absolute knowledge does not exist. One cannot know all because there is no all. The real world is forever in a state of incompletion. Moreover, the "new" Gnostics, as Corbin sometimes refers to them, conceived thought's relation to the body not as an unfortunate tethering to a finite substance that dooms us to perpetual ignorance (as earlier Gnostics would have it) but as a productive and indissoluble bond.

This bond led Ismaili Gnostics to contemplate a third, intermediary term between bodies and thought. It would be a mistake, however, to reduce this term—which Corbin referred to as the *imaginal world*—to a simple positivity. While the imaginal functions as a link, it is defined is negative terms as a limit. Which is it, a limit or link? This question is misleading, improperly formed. It implies that something is squeezed in between God and man or between thought and bodies or form and matter, terms radically opposed to each other by older forms of Gnosticism. Corbin averts this misperception by recommending that we approach the imaginal world as a "speculative" concept, by which he means a device, something like a mirror—that permits something that is absent to appear in its absence. The imaginal world is filled only with nonbeing.

Avicenna and his esoteric followers stood in stark contrast to the rationalist tradition that aligned itself with Averroes. The latter tradition adamantly rejected the imaginal realm, but this was not because this realm was thought to be inhabited by angels—surprisingly, rationalists had no quarrel with angels—but because the imaginal placed a wedge between God as first principle and the mortal intelligences who were said to emanate from Him. The rationalists objected to what was to them the inconceivable proposition that the imaginal interrupted and thus dismantled the chain of causal necessity. Were the imaginal truly operative in the world, this would mean that Divine Being, the necessary first principle, had "withdrawn from participation in the act of being" and had somehow "originated its own limit."[20] To the rationalist, this idea was heretical; for esoteric philosophers, it was essential.

The rationalists had every reason to object to the new Gnostics who threatened their most cherished claims. But one must be specific about what rationalists stood to lose. It was not the *necessity* of God that was for these Gnostics in dispute. Even as He was said to withdraw, to flee or distance Himself from the mundane world, God retained His status as a necessity or, stronger, became a hyper-necessity. In the beginning, what we find is not a first or efficient cause but a self-impeding gesture that prevents God from becoming one with Himself and thus from becoming a primordial figure or first principle from which His creatures would logically flow. The new Gnosticism radically recast the relation between necessity and possibility. Rather than contraries, they conceived the terms as operating in concert. An imperative "must" would emerge to open rather than restrict the possible.

FILMING THE REVOLUTION

My objective thus far has been to demonstrate that Wasserstrom is less than a reliable reader of Corbin. He misconstrues the philosopher's project as an effort to reenchant the world rather than—as I am arguing—an attempt to restore to everyday reality what the rationalists "covered over" or removed from reality by elevating laws and other exoteric apparatuses of power above it, in a position of decisive control. I can only concur, however, with Wasserstrom's conviction that the ultimate battle between Corbin and Khomeini, both practiced readers of Islamic philosophy, must be and was decided by actual events. Let us thus return to these through a reading of Kiarostami's film *First Case, Second Case*, which was in production at the time of Khomeini's return to Tehran.

I credit Khomeini as the inspiration for my approach to this debate, for it was he who drew attention back to the question of technology with which Corbin opened his "Apophatic Theology" address at a colloquium titled "The Impact of Western Thought," held in Tehran several months earlier. Khomeini delivered his first public address after landing on Iranian soil on February 2, 1979, at Bihishti-i-Zahra, the cemetery where many of the martyrs of the revolution were buried. Justly castigating the Pahlavi monarchy for a list of crimes, the newly arrived leader soon came to the one that served as the revolution's flash point: the Shah's cinema, which he vehemently condemned: "Why was it necessary to make the cinema a center of vice? We are not opposed to cinema, to radio, or to television; what we oppose is . . . the use of media to keep our young people in a state of backwardness and dissipate their energies."[21]

In this address as well as in his *Last Will and Testament*, published posthumously, Khomeini decried what he regarded as the greatest threat facing the nation of Iran: its debilitating reduction to a "state of self-estrangement from its own perceptions." He attributed this estrangement to a reconfiguration of the Iranian sensorium, whose "fundamental attachment to film technologies—the eyes to the camera, the ears to sound technologies"—had reprogrammed it and placed it under the remote control of the West.[22] Khomeini refrained, however, from placing blame on technology as such. Rather than dismissing cinema as a Western contaminant, he issued a call for a new use of technology and later provided state funding for a cinema that would devote itself to the reeducation of the Iranian people in the values and ways of Islam. The new counter-cinema, as he envisioned it, would cure the Iranian people of the Westoxification that had polluted their senses. It would restore the Iranian sensorium by washing out the eyes and unstopping the ears of Iranian citizens.

What is beyond question is the fact that Iranian cinema emerged after the revolution fully purged of its reliance on cinematic precedents, East and West. What is questionable is Khomeini's exoteric agenda. While his revolutionary fervor and selective phrasing borrow from his long study of Mulla Sadra—particularly the latter's conception of an "existential revolution"—Khomeini adopted a course that ran counter to the views of the revered philosopher whose poached rhetoric he turned on its head. What Khomeini advocated for was a conversion of the philosopher's intentions into "the old clerical project of the collective representation of the hidden imam . . . [a project that would rewrite] gnosis into law and Islamic politics."²³

The sensorium cleansing the Supreme Leader had in mind was radically at odds with the position of the Ismaili Gnostics. For what he aimed to do is cleanse—that is, sanitize and strip clean—the sensoria of individual Iranians from them. His goal was to replace their sensoria with a sensorium, an overlay of orthodoxy, of laws that were not subject to contestation and a techno-theocratic regime that would exert control over every aspect of the lives of the Iranian people. What was censored by the rigid modesty system he later installed—not only to oversee and control cinematic production but everyday life as well—was the intimate relation each subject must have to herself for any "existential revolution" to be possible. In short, Khomeini sought to bury the esoteric dimension of Iranian lives under a stockpile of laws and an invasive gutting of interiority via the "system of hijab."

I am less interested at this point in detailing the crimes of the post-revolution regime than in allowing Iranian cinema to reply to Khomeini and by extension his advocate, Wasserstrom. As is known, the unprecedented nature of this cinema was partially obscured by its initial characterization as "neo-realist." Hamid Dabashi, an insightful authority on Iranian cinema, attempted to counter this confounding claim by identifying the "nominalism of the image" as a unique feature of these films.²⁴ I am sympathetic to Dabashi's strategy, which draws attention to the way the image itself, and not just the slight narratives of everyday incidents, offers viewers a reality stripped of excess ideological or metaphysical trappings. A world cleansed of generalities, restored to itself. Yet "nominalism" is the wrong term to deploy in this context.

I would argue that much of Iranian cinema, and Kiarostami's work most notably, is decidedly antinominalist. And I would challenge Lacan, who while denying that he was himself a nominalist—"my starting point is not that [a word] is something like a nameplate which attaches itself, just like that, onto the real"—goes on to reject the alternative position, which was known in the early debates as the "realist" position. Of the latter, Lacan has this to say: "The point is not to be a realist in the sense in which one was a realist in medieval times, in the sense of the realism of universals."²⁵ Something is wrong here. The position of Lacan is, in fact, very similar to that of the "realists," if you count among them—as you must—Avicenna, whose intervention in this debate was incisive and eventually by the esoteric Islamic philosophers who came after him. The paradoxical One conceived by these philosophers owes its paradoxical nature precisely to their conception of the real—*al-haqq* in Arabic. I will return to this point and will go so far as to propose that Iranian cinema should be regarded neither as nominalist nor neo-realist but as neo-Gnostic. Nowhere is this more apparent than in the cinema of Kiarostami.

The filming of *First Case, Second Case* began in early January 1979, at the tail end of the revolutionary struggle, and was broken off when the Shah unexpectedly fled the country on January 16. Khomeini arrived in Tehran on February 1, delivered his cemetery address the very next day, and nine days later declared the existence of the new Islamic Republic. This seemingly simple act of nomination signaled the hijacking of the Iranian Revolution from the Iranian people and its delivery to a new state that would be put in place almost overnight. But Khomeini's return had another, more local, effect: it rendered useless much of the footage Kiarostami had already shot, specifically a series of interviews conducted with experts from the Shah's regime. Several of these experts were immediately replaced by Khomeini's appointees, while others who remained in place feared being caught on tape uttering opinions that would not be tolerated in the new state order. This situation would likely have spelled the end of the project for most directors, but not for Kiarostami. After a six-month hiatus, he resumed filming.

The film opens with a teacher at a blackboard, his back to the class, as he draws a large ear with elaborate folds to the accompaniment of the clattering sound of his chalk hitting the board. This sound is interrupted by another emanating, it seems, from behind his back. In an attempt to discover its source, the teacher turns around to locate the guilty party. The reverse shot reveals a row of innocent-looking boys, none of whom betrays the least bit of guilt. There is something disturbing about this reverse—or answering—shot insofar as it fails to answer to the one preceding it. But the audience is not given any time to ponder the import of the disquieting effect, for the teacher immediately takes the initiative of responding to what troubles him: his inability to determine from their faces the guilty party. He then issues an ultimatum designed to extract from the students a confession. He orders those in the back rows to stand in the corridor until one of them admits to making the noise or is betrayed by his classmates; if neither outcome results, all the students will be expelled. This is followed by the series of interviews with experts and family members of the boys who have been disciplined by the teacher.

Upon returning to filming, Kiarostami made two significant revisions. He added a second case that was neither filmed nor envisioned before the hiatus. While in the first case, the boys remained united, refusing to identify the culprit, in the second, one boy snitches, thus saving himself and the others from expulsion. The second revision consists of the removal of some experts from the old regime and the addition of others newly installed. All respond to the questions put to them regarding the wisdom of the teacher's ultimatum and what a proper response to it might be.

The interviews elicit a range of observations about the bonds that unite individuals to classmates, families, professional, political and other groups and the responsibilities these bonds entail. What one takes away from them is less the differences (present but relatively minor) among the interviewees than a certain unanimity. The responses offer collective confirmation of the overwhelming popularity of the revolution. This fact struck many, including—famously—Foucault, who took a special interest in the Iranian revolution.[26] In "The Constitution of the Subject and Spiritual Practice," Jambet examines the impact the revolt had on Foucault's theoretical project. This is not the place to go into Jambet's argument. Suffice it to say that it draws attention to the fact that the revolt occurred in a "messianic" moment to which historicists remain blind.[27] As the interviews in *First Case, Second Case* make plain, the struggle that defined the revolt of the nation was less between parties, classes, or socially defined genders than an esoteric battle in which speakers were overpowered—that is to say, impassioned—by their own speech.

THE SUPREME SCIENCE OF THE REAL

In debates regarding individuation, the process through which individual beings emerge from the One, esoteric philosophers maintained a realist position. Again, the contrary, nominalist position rejected abstract entities, whose primary role was to aggregate or collectivize actual individuals. No less opposed to the idea of aggregation, the realists were at the same time unwilling to deny the existence of relations among individuals. These had to be forged by the individuals, not directly by the One. There had to be, in other words, a paradoxical One, a One that was superior to unity.

The royal road to this paradoxical conception of God runs through an understanding of the relation between His radical apophasis and His manifestations or "theophanies." Devoid of attributes, Divine Being would seem incapable of inspiring anything other than agnosticism. Yet, as we learn from the hadith, "I was a hidden Treasure and I yearned to be known. Then I created creatures in order to be known by them," God is in fact made known. By whom? Ibn Arabi's faithful translation adds to the translation above, the following phrase: "in order to become in them the object of my knowledge."[28]

In this crucial hadith, the paradox of the One is dramatized by a scenario in which God assumes specific attributes—that is, He is *individuated*, or absolved of His indeterminations—but without forsaking His negative, indeterminate status. The reasons behind this drama have been rehearsed: the God of Islam is not a first principle and cannot precede His creatures. Rather, He comes to be through them. The imaginal world separates God from the multiplicity of individuals; it and disrupts any causal relation No chronological account is given of the dependency of individuals on His priority. In lieu of logical chains of entailment, esoteric philosophy invented not a narrative, but what Corbin refers to as an "intra-divine drama" in which God and man come into existence at the same time. This drama consists less than a single scene than a mere movement in which God, the Absolute, "step[s] out of His absoluteness" to become manifest in the world.²⁹ God emerges for the first alongside His creation but also, as we will see, as a shadow or stranger.

Ae note of caution will forestall misunderstanding: that He reveals Himself in the world does not imply that He submerges or incarnates Himself in it. Ibn 'Arabi's strategic translation, quoted above, prohibits the pernicious suggestion that God is reducible to what we know of Him through His manifestations. It is to prevent this misunderstanding that Ibn 'Arabi repositions God not simply in His manifestations but also as their perceiver. The Sufi mystic places Him in the position of a mirror on whose surface theophanies become visible, while He Himself remains veiled, *unseen*, behind His manifestations. In other words, He goes forward as a shadow, masked. In brief, the theophanic forms do not nullify His apophatic status, which remains intact. Apophasis and theophanic forms operate together as an irreducible antagonism. The manifestations fend off agnosticism and operate on behalf of knowledge, while His retreat from the world prevents His imprisonment in, or absorption into, intelligible forms.

Presumably, the latter is understood as a means of preserving His greatness even if it strikes us initially as a self-defeating contradiction. Let us take the time to address a further question, "In what does this greatness consist?" If God is "greater" than anything we can conceive, greater than any intelligibility theophanies permit, does this greatness necessarily entail His existence?³⁰ The answer of the mystics is "No." God does not exist, but do not be so hasty as to conclude that He is dead. It means that God *is* nothing. To the question "Which is greater existence or nothing?" the mystics answered, "Nothing." This is, as I understand it, part of the point Corbin makes when he opposes affirmative exoteric theology—the very notion of religion Wasserstrom stiffly defends—to negative apophatic theology. The negativity at stake in the latter, Corbin goes on to say, is not one that "needs to be absorbed, but, contrarily, a positivity to be conquered."³¹ Nothing is not a deficit for which we need to compensate; it is a plenitude of which we must make use.

It is difficult to know where to begin when there is no beginning, so let us remind ourselves of our goal: to determine why seemingly contradictory terms—God's apophatism and His theophanies—do not cancel each other out, and why nothing is not less but greater than existence. Intimately entangled, these issues can be pursued simultaneously. While His escape from His revealed forms appears to exhibit a bad infinity in which God continually slips through their grasp, as though they were inadequate to the task of fully capturing Him, the logic at work here is wholly different. The point is not that these manifestations—or epiphanies—are weak or dim; it is, rather, their effectivity and capacity that stand out. Without the epiphanies neither we nor God Himself would know anything about Him. The neo-Gnostics inspired by Ibn 'Arabi agreed on this point: "there is nothing more luminous than knowledge to throw light" on God.³² The illumination knowledge provides does not merely delineate the bounds of Divine Being, but embraces all bounds. This means that, manifestations also attest to the positive fact of God's inexistence and, in this way open our eyes to an actual infinity.

Much of this has been said earlier in other contexts: neo-Gnosticism prizes knowledge not simply for making the world intelligible but also for acquainting us with the unknowable; the unknowable is unknown because it does not exist. Inexistence is. Thus far, we have been fed a pretty strict diet; how is it that it has brought us to this banquet of actual infinity? We must hold in mind the fundamental proposition: there would be no God were it not for the individuals, the persons, in whom God discloses Himself. There is no God but for the creatures in whom He is individuated. On the other side, far from reminding them of their limitations as finite creatures unable to scale the heights of the Divine, the retreat of God lifts them from their finitude by ceaselessly producing a remainder: His hiddenness. While the manifestations represent a "conquest . . . of the original indetermination" through their very existence, God's flight—which is not from finite being but within it—creates in individual creatures, a hidden interior.[33]

At the close of "Apophatic Theology," Corbin castigates nihilistic sociopsychologies for "den[y]ing to human individuality . . . something unborn. [As a result of this denial] everything that it is, it will have to receive from its environment, from the omnipotent pedagogy that takes charge of it."[34] Elsewhere, Corbin offers synonyms for the "unborn," referring to the "uncreated" or "un-engendered." If God is greater than that to which His manifestations attest, it is not because He exists on a higher plane, but because He is thus "of the order of the nonrealized" or "is manifested to us as something that holds itself in suspense in the area . . . of the unborn."[35]

The last two terms—the "nonrealized" and the "unborn"—are taken not from Corbin, but from Lacan, who deploys them in an attempt to rethink the notion of cause in relation to the unconscious. The philosopher and the psychoanalyst do not just happen to use nearly identical phrases; they offer the same answer to the same question: how to think a negativity—a God who retreats, an unconscious—that is not simply negative, that does not simply subtract but also adds to reality? Ibn 'Arabi offers a clear statement of this: "The Manifest has a stronger—that is to say, more inclusive—property than the Non-manifest, since the Manifest [is] both creation and the Real, while the Nonmanifest [is] the Real without creation."[36]

Before it emerged as a major concept of Lacan's return to Freud, the real (al-haqq) was central to Iranian philosophy. Now, while "the word haqq is a noun and an adjective signifying truth, correctness, rightness, appropriateness, real, sound, valid and so on," in its specific ontological sense "it is rendered as 'real' or 'truly real.'"[37] As such, the real designates, as it does for Lacan, an intransigence that exceeds any reality and is associated with Truth rather what are commonly or conventionally regarded as truths. This does not suggest that the real is the Being of beings, being's superlative. The real has, on the contrary, the status of a limit at which we encounter the unborn, the infinity of all that is un-engendered. If there is a dehiscence of the One, it is for two reasons: none of its manifestation can exhaust this infinity, and the One does not unify its manifestations. The One in retreat binds His theophanies anonymously, not in the manner of a cult figure, whose attributes command the devotion of those who owe obedience to Him, but precisely as an occulted figure.[38] God flees the role of common denominator or essence. It is in this sense that He is "superior" to unity.

Let us return to the mandates guiding our argument: (1) situate Kiarostami's film in relation to the revolution it films, and (2) return to earlier points requiring further elaboration when it was possible to do so. At the beginning, we defined Truth, quoting Jambet, as "not the adequation of the representation to the thing but the inadequation of man as prophet to the language of the divine speaker, the absolute subject supposed to speak." It is now obvious that Truth does not start out from anything that is already given. It should also be clear that this "inadequation" of man cannot be understood as a failure to reach an ineffable God whom we approach with no hope of knowing. If there is, beyond everything that exists, as the Islamic mystics held, an infinity of unborn objects, knowledge is that which responds to the longing for the unborn. For this reason, knowledge is regarded as an insatiable thirst for more knowledge, rather than something constitutionally doomed to failure.

One phrase in Jambet's definition of truth, "the absolute subject supposed to speak," resists immediate comprehension even if we do now have the means to comprehend it. We grasp what is meant by the phrase "absolute subject supposed to speak"; we need to distinguish the suprapersonal God from the personal God who sustains the ego. Nominalists, as we noted more than once, regard language as the means we deploy to designate things. It must finally occur to us as we proceed in this argument that manifestations, theophanies, operate as elements of a radically different conception of language and signification than the one to which nominalists reduced it. It is suddenly easy to see that the "speaker" does not stand outside a language she wields as an instrument, but discovers herself through language, which she only "half speaks." Kiarostami often made this very claim when he noted in various interviews that his films were "half-made." One cannot, after all, know oneself apart from language; rather, we find ourselves through it. If there is Truth, it would be untrue to say that we speak it; Truth speaks through us. The Qur'an has this to say about it: "You did not throw that when you threw, God threw" (viii:12). If there is no first principle that we might name "God," it makes no sense to turn around and name it "man" instead. There is no such principle to name. There is only a Mobius-shaped structure in which a person bears witness to an elsewhere within herself, with which she neither unites nor breaks from. This elsewhere is an inexistent priority, which we are describing here as a "wanting to speak" or a "yearning to be known."

LISTEN!

Thus far, I have been characterizing Kiarostami's realism as "neo-Gnostic," in an attempt to distance it from alternative characterizations, as "neo-realist" or "nominalist." The problem with the latter, which sought to save the concrete individual from its dissolution in some abstract ocean, was its inability to imagine an open form of collectivity. Kiarostami's characters keep gesturing toward others even if the real that interrupts his reality principle often defeats these attempts. The documented interviews that comprise much of *First Case, Second Case* attest to these attempts and their difficulties, as well as the urgency that impels them. In *The Project for a Scientific Psychology*, Freud introduced a concept, *die Not des Lebens*, which implies something stronger than "vital needs," something that *wishes* and acts as an "urgency . . . a state of emergency." Die Not des Lebens alerts "consciousness that it has to deal with the outside world." When Kiarostami claims to "use documentary to get at lies," he evokes this same state of urgency. There is an impasse at which point a wish, in this special sense, demands a lie—which is, here, tantamount to "Truth," insofar as both lack foundation in any existing cause and offer no attempt to adjust themselves to existing reality. Both are fictions in an effective sense. We will return to this point shortly.

Thus far we have dealt with the issue of individuation as it is manifested in the documented interviews that comprise much of *First Case, Second Case* and have neglected the fiction—those scenes involving an exoteric teacher with a kind of mad-scientist demeanor, who attempts to draw an anatomically correct ear—with "outer," "middle," and "inner" written in chalk above each part—and the students whom he wants to punish for interrupting his lesson. On the human sensorium? Perhaps. One of the most extraordinary facts about the film is that it creates the documented interviews from the fiction. The real interviewees are called upon to answer the pressing questions posed by the fiction that precedes it.

Beyond the theoretical question of individuation they bring to our attention, the interviews also constitute a record of a highly charged historical moment. Many of the people interviewed would have been known to the Iranian audience at the time: for example, Ezatollah Entazami, one of the most highly regarded actors in Iranian cinema, famous for his role in the much-loved film, *The Cow* (Dariush Mehrjui, 1969), and Masoud Kimiai, the famous *Filmfarsi* director. The two women interviewed—Jaleh Sarshar and Ehteram Broumand—appear unveiled, shockingly so, given the fact that in a few short weeks such immodesty would be severely punished. Sadegh Ghotbzadeh, a close consultant of Khomeini and the director of radio and television of the Islamic Republic of Iran at the time he was interviewed, would be executed in 1982 for allegedly plotting against Khomeini.

Because the first set of interviews was filmed just before the revolution ended, and the second during its still-very-much-undecided aftermath, they do not simply straddle the event by recording actual people and opinions but also, and most importantly, manage to illuminate the fact that the present veils the not yet, the undecided, the unborn that lurks behind it. The impossibility of the real, the radical impasse at which knowledge encounters is own limit, becomes palpable in this way. At this moment, all is on hold, in suspense. It is at this moment that a need arises and signals to consciousness that it has to deal with a world beyond itself.

Many of the interviewees associate the teacher and his authoritarian tactics with the Shah's brutal police force, the SAVAK. "Big ears," as they say, were assumed to be everywhere, hyperalert to any infraction of the law, part of the everyday espionage of a hated regime whose only chance of survival was to pit its citizens against each other. It thus seems legitimate to associate the ear drawn on the blackboard—in its supine position, as if it were an "ear to the ground"—with the recently ousted regime. A question then arises: what is the relation between this ear and the sound that interrupts the teacher's tedious lesson?

To answer this question, I will return to my earlier observation that the "answering shot" that confronts the teacher who has turned around to see what is going on behind his back—the shot of a row of students—is perplexing. In the few, brief analyses the film has so far received, the sound's source, if it is mentioned at all, is attributed to an unidentified student's banging a pen on his desk. This explanation is plausible if one focuses merely on the nature of the sound. And yet, it is downright baffling that any such speculation is ventured. For what must strike us as a bit "off" is not just that the boys are completely poker-faced, their placid image at odds with the banging, but that no image of its source is offered to the film's viewers. None! We are instead presented with an acousmatic sound, a sound that is deliberately unanchored in the image. Like pain, sound radiates, unless it is tied to a place, that is, to a source in the visual field. It is even impossible at times to determine whether an unanchored sound originates outside or inside the ear. In sum, the sound whose source the teacher is intent on ferreting out evades the outer or esoteric ear he designs to detect it. Acousmatic, the sound refuses to allow itself to be assimilated into the space of the classroom. Hailing not merely from behind the teacher's back but from beyond the diegetic space itself, it draws attention to a dimension that flees from framing.

It is also notable that the rhythmic tapping distinguishes itself from the irritating clattering of the teacher's chalk. To my ears, at least, the former recalls the rhythmic beating against the walls of a leper colony by one of the lepers as he recites the days of the week in Forough Farrokzad's film *The House Is Black* (1962).[39] In this film, the beats break up the unending darkness and the uninterrupted passage of time that seal the isolated colony off from an elsewhere, from a world beyond it. The sound of the slaps and the chanting of the days create a minimum of sociality, that is to say, a kind of protolanguage addressed to another. And they create this space of otherness within the confines of their colony—not, as we see at the end of the film, by simply exiting through the massive doors that normally imprison them.

Hamid Dabashi is perfectly correct to contest humanist readings of Forough's film, which look past the lepers to invoke our "common humanity" and to insist, instead, that the film demands that we look at the lepers in their singularity.[40] While this is an essential observation about the film, it also underscores the nature of the esoteric philosophy that informs it; for the latter is a philosophy not of abstraction but of illumination, in which individuals are not subsumed under an abstract universal that defines a human essence they supposedly share. Individuals are each accorded what can be described as a pristine status; each illuminates Divine Being uniquely.

In my reading, Kiarostami's acousmatization of the rhythmic tapping in *First Case, Second Case* formally radicalizes the scene from *The House Is Black*. But to what end? What does this off-screen sound contribute to our understanding of the film and to the philosophy of illumination? I have been arguing that the purely negative definition of the God of the Gnostics—as unassimilable, un-engendered, neither being nor nonbeing—is not evidence, as Wasserstrom at one point suggests, of a gloomy vision of the world, which Corbin and his Eranos colleagues attempted to reenchant. On the contrary, the Gnostic philosophers illuminated a power that is occluded by abstract philosophies. It is not yet entirely clear, however, what the God of the Islamic mystics contributes to this process of illumination, or what this God-in-retreat adds to the world that forms around Him. Corbin responds to these questions with a simple—and unexpected—answer: "He is not, but causes to be."[41] What can "cause" possibly mean here given what has already been made clear: God is not a creator, not a father. He does not enter into the act of creation but comes to be only through His creatures. Corbin continues: "Even beyond the One, He is the "Unifier Who 'monadises' all the monads. . . . Thus the *tawhid* takes on the aspect of a monadology . . . it separates this 'Unifier' from all the Ones He unifies, it also affirms Him."[42] God is not a numerical One, a one in a series, but remains outside it.

We have thus returned to the paradoxical One, a One superior to unity, via a different route. From this perspective we are able to give a name to the acousmatic sound in *First Case, Second Case*: it is an echo! This is at least the word Leibniz chose—before he adopted the term *substantial vinculum*—a bond or tie—to name that which linked the monads without collectivizing them.[43] Like the Islamic Gnostics, Leibniz set out to challenge the nominalist contention that groups were only ever abstract entities that effaced the individuality of their members. Nominalists regarded individuals, or monads, as worlds unto themselves, independent of relations to others. By characterizing it as an original echo, Leibniz sought to conceive a bond that was untraceable back to a source. What linked the individual monads had to be estranged from any first principle that determined their nature. For this reason, the link had to remain purely acoustical, as unlocatable as every *acousmetre* is. The echo could only issue, then, from beyond being, from beyond anything that already existed. Leibniz argued that while the echo had a massive effect on all the monads—while it "monadise[d] all the monads" by holding them together—it did not dictate the forms they assumed. Far from effacing their individuality, the echo demanded it. And that was all it did.

Holding onto Leibniz's felicitous term, we can now return to Kiarostami's film and to the Gnostic philosophers to address from their side Corbin's claim that God is not, but causes, the monads to be. Up to this point, the apophatic God might seem to have been burdened by a kind of impotence, an inability to "father." However, as Jambet warns, "we must be wary of believing" that the negating of His attributes "entails dispossessing God of His" ipseity.[44] Not a mere nothing, the apophatic God of the Gnostics retains a generative power. Although He does not enter into the act of creation, but remains ever in retreat, refusing assimilation into being, there issues from Him—that is, from God knows where—an imperative: "Be!" God does not "cause" His creatures to come into being in the sense that term has when one speaks of a chain of cause and effects. At the point where the chain breaks down, He demands that they come into existence.

To make sense of this, let us return the matter of the uncreated, or unborn, which I casually described as infinitely greater than what is. It is necessary to proceed cautiously here so as not to confuse the unborn with a simple latency, something preformed and awaiting actualization. Nor should we make the error of reducing the infinity of the uncreated to a numerical sum, to an infinite number of finite things. What is paramount is the negative prefix: the unborn, the uncreated. At the limit the Gnostics termed *the real*, thought encounters something that is withheld, something to which it comes infinitely close without being able to grasp. If this moment is not marked by failure, it is because the unborn is not an endlessly deferred destination outside of thought. The unborn emerges within thought. The uncreated presents itself in the face of a superabundant, originary demand—call it echo or imperative, their functions remain the same. They signal the dispossession of reality's finitude and call upon us to create what has never been created, to give birth to the unborn. The term *originary demand* is meant to imply that the imperative is a fact of thought; that is, it must be assumed to account for the effectivity of thought. In a different, but closely related context, Corbin insists—citing approvingly the work of his contemporary, Etienne Souriau—"it is not in our power to prove the existence of God.... The only proof accessible to man is then to accomplish His presence."[45] This implies, as we have come to understand, that man "accomplishes God's presence" by coming into existence in his own, unique way. The imperative does not itself originate anything; it does not instruct thought what to think or how we are to be.

Nor does it suggest that the imperative lends itself to arbitrary thinking, for the imperative, crucially, demands obedience. It calls upon thought to submit itself to and obey it. Here we return to the Arabic term *taslim* (submission, obedience). It should now be clearer how thoroughly the Divine imperative overturns the demand for blind obedience to religious legislation and prescriptions. It is also possible to see why the differences proposed by Wasserstrom between religion, as defined by laws and customs and religion as defined by poets and mystics, is not as absolute as he would have us believe. The imperative demands that thought submit itself to it, that is, to something within it that is too close to be an object of thought. The echo, or demand, is—again—nonpredicative; it demands only that thought abandon itself to the rigors of thinking. Those who oppose the neo-Gnostics miss precisely this point; thought is obliged to rethink itself again and again. Corbin underscores this point by repeatedly warning against confusing the imaginal with whimsy. It is incorrect to say that the imaginal brings things into existence ex nihilo, for this implies a chronology with nothing as its first term and thus makes no sense. The imaginal operates medially; it sews or binds body and soul, nature and culture.

While Islamic philosophers identified this inexistent place of mediation from which the imperative resounds by names we have already cited—*imaginal world*, *Cloud*, among others—Freud chose to call it "drive." He openly acknowledged that the term named his "mythology" and appeared to him "as a concept on the frontier between the mental and the somatic, as the psychical representative of the stimuli originating from within the organism and reaching the mind, as a measure of the demand made upon the mind for work in consequence of its connection to the body."[46] Given the centrality of this concept for psychoanalysis overall, it is not surprising that Lacan embraced Freud's term and definition.

But it is also unsurprising that he chose to alter Freud's wording slightly, as he does in *The Sinthome: Book XXIII*, where he defines drive as "the echo in the body of a fact of saying." Lacan justifies his emphasis on hearing and his choice of the organ that detects it based on the fact that the ear "can't be sealed, shut, or closed off."[47] He thus appears to acknowledge in Freud a distinctive Leibnizian resonance—while windowless monads may fail to see, they cannot shut their ears to a surplus otherness that comes from speech itself. For Leibniz, as well as for Freud and Lacan, the resonating echo is housed within what Islamic philosophers referred to as a "subtle body," a body dispossessed of its finitude. This is so not only because it is through their bodies that the monads are linked to other monads but also because the body escapes thought and is thus that which thought suffers. Rather than develop this point here, we return again and finally to our main concern.

First Case, Second Case was made in a moment when everything was up in the air. While a mighty cacophony broke out on the streets of Tehran, Kiarostami asked his film's audience to refocus their attention by lending their ears to the imperative that was calling thought to order. It would soon become apparent that events would move in a different direction—one that sought to render Iranian ears deaf to the internal echo that sounded in each of them. The Supreme Leader preferred an agenda of indoctrination that would swoop all Iranians up in a nominalist nightmare of a docile whole. Kiarostami would go on from here to make a series of films to oppose this agenda. Finally, in Homework (1989), he turns off the sound rather than listen to small children mouthing violent sentiments they learned by rote but did not understand.

4

BATTLE FATIGUE: BODIES AND RESURRECTION

Taste of Cherry, winner of the 1997 Cannes film prize, is the bleakest film in Abbas Kiarostami's oeuvre. By 1988, Iran's devastating eight-year war with Iraq, which erupted on the heels of the bloody 1978–1979 revolution, had finally ended, but battle fatigue and disillusionment are still palpable throughout the film. Explicit references to these conflicts and the lingering presence of militia, together with the desperate conditions of day laborers, who hang around looking to pick up whatever work they can, serve as reminders that capitalism had been operating behind the scenes all along, manipulating and prolonging the conflicts for sheer financial gain. The lush vistas of many of the director's other films are sadly absent, here replaced by a flinty, peri-urban landscape. Bulldozers emit harsh sounds as they claw the ground as if to rip out—root and branch—the lone tree on a hill, a signature, sheltering presence in many of Kiarostami's films, here appears forlorn. That this is a world made up almost entirely of men is an indication not of the director's indifference to the plight of women, as some feminists complained, but of the arid conditions that everywhere quash desire and foster despair.

Sometime before the film began, Mr. Badii apparently made a decision to commit suicide, for he spends most of his screen time trying to accomplish what turns out to be this not-so-simple task. The film focuses on his preparations for accomplishing his resolve. Regarding Badii's nihilistic decision, Kiarostami had this to say in an interview: "The choice of death is the only prerogative left to a human being with respect to God and social norms. Because everything in our life has been imposed on us from birth, our date and place of birth, our parents, our home, our nationality, our build, the color of our skin, our culture."[1] If Kiarostami felt compelled to offer an explanation, it is because the narrative does not.

Badii, an urban, educated, middle-class man who minds his health and drives a Land Rover, seems to have been favored by God and social norms, unlike the out-of-work laborers from Iran's ethnic underclass, who struggle to eke out a living. There is no hint of anything lacking in his life, no particular circumstance that might have produced the sense of unfreedom and despair he exhibits. This does not, however, retract the suggestion that Badii's despondency is related to the grim political and economic conditions on view in every frame. By making its protagonist a cipher, the film compels us to question the site of traumatic inscription. Rather than a psychosocial narrative about the debilitating effects on the psyche of this new form of poverty, Kiarostami gives us something different. In place of psychological depth, he focuses on psychic interiority.

To understand this difference, I will supplement Kiarostami's explanation with a passage in which Emmanuel Levinas describes a situation very much like the one in which Badii finds himself:

> There exists a weariness which is a weariness of everything and everyone, and above all a weariness of oneself. What wearies then is not a particular form of our life—our surroundings, because they are dull and ordinary, our circle of friends, because they are vulgar and cruel; the weariness concerns existence itself . . . in weariness existence is something like the reminder of a commitment to exist . . . [and] the impossible refusal of this ultimate obligation. In weariness we want to escape existence itself, and not only one of its landscapes. An evasion without an itinerary or end, it is not trying to come ashore anywhere.[2]

Kiarostami's film, I will argue, is legible through the concept of fatigue elaborated by Levinas in *Existence and Existents*. This concept helps highlight the odd arduousness of the film's trajectory and allows us to examine both the contemporary issues at the film's center—issues of war, capitalism, and their relation to fatigue—and the philosophical background informing Kiarostami's image-making practice.

While the antipathy of Kiarostami to narrative and character psychology is acknowledged, little has been written about the source of this attitude in what is regarded as a heretical strain of Islamic thought. Henry Corbin, one of the most important Islamicists of the twentieth century, is known not only for enlarging our understanding of this philosophical tradition but also for introducing Heidegger into French circles. In fact, Corbin claimed that he found in Heidegger a critical key to understanding Islamic philosophy. This claim is, however, a bit of an exaggeration, for as he continued to take direct inspiration from philosophers such as Sohravardi and Mulla Sadra, he was obliged to part ways with his German mentor on several substantial matters. Heidegger was also a preliminary and abiding inspiration for Levinas, and yet in *Existence and Existents* the French philosopher expressed a "profound need to leave the climate of his mentor's philosophy."[3] I will suggest that if Corbin and Levinas strayed from the confines of Heideggerian thought, it was to meet up in a similar place: a place that happens to be known in Islamic philosophy as the Eighth Climate. The latter is another name for the "imaginal world," a meta-geographical or hiero-historical realm in which "empirical experience displayed to the senses [is absolved and] real apparition restored."[4] This is a speculative realm, ontologically real, despite having no existence in reality.

CORPOREAL CADUCITY

In 1943, Lieutenant General George S. Patton was disciplined for two infamous slapping incidents in which he struck soldiers across the face upon learning that they had been placed in evacuation hospitals not due to wounds sustained by enemy fire but because they were suffering from "battle fatigue." This term seemed, at the time, to have replaced "shell shock," the term used by Freud to describe war neuroses: traumatic effects of battle that appeared to have no direct physical cause. Patton's anger was undoubtedly ignited by the suspicion that these soldiers were mere malingerers—"cowards," as Patton called them—who had trumped up a fake illness to get out of the work of war. Yet the double slaps just as surely had another cause: Patton's frustration with corporeal caducity, the ultimate unfitness of the human body for the job at hand. War has a way of piling up worn out, wounded, and dead bodies and thus throwing the fragility of our corporeal condition in the face of even the most arrogant and bellicose among us.

What interests me about the ascendency of "battle fatigue" over alternative terms is precisely the tenacity with which it refuses to surrender the body to the merely mental, its resistance to allowing the physical domain to fall prey to thought. Fatigue clings to the body. While it is possible, for example, to speak of a laxity of attention as a fatigue of concentration, "fatigue," even in this case—and for solid historical and philosophical reasons—does not let go of its relation to the body.

From the waning days of the nineteenth century onward, fatigue emerged as a problem whose very insurmountability spawned utopian dreams not only of its eradication but of the body's eventual obsolescence. Why? Because war and capitalism—and who in the last century would think of separating them?—have little patience for the down time that human bodies require. An account of this obsession with fatigue is given in Anson Rabinbach's *The Human Motor: Energy, Fatigue and the Origins of Modernity*, which centers on the German concept of *Kraft*, a universal energy or force that became the fetishized focus of much late nineteenth-century science.[5] Many of the names that crop up in the study—including those of Hermann von Helmholtz, the German pioneer of the theory of thermodynamics, of the laws of energy's maintenance and loss, and Gustav Fechner, who introduced theories of energy conservation into psychology—are familiar to readers of Freud and Marx. These readers will be able to glean in the crucial notion of Kraft the tentative beginnings not only of the notion of Arbeitkraft but also libido.

Devoted, however, to the Taylorist regime of the late nineteenth and early twentieth century, and a worn out vocabulary, Rabinbach's book calls for an updating. Jonathan Crary's 24/7: Late Capitalism and the Ends of Sleep responded to this call by dwelling on a new form of unmitigated capitalism, which—devoid of the utopian impulses that once characterized early modern industry and buttressed by a capacity, thanks to advances in science, to remain unblinkingly awake—regards fatigue with an unprecedented enmity.[6]

The aim of 24/7 is to expose the latest phase of what we can think of as capitalism's war on bodies and to imagine ways of resisting it. To this end, the book looks kindly on dreams and sleep as precious reserves to be defended against the incursions of capitalism (even as it rejects entirely not just Freud's work on dreams but also the whole of psychoanalysis) and evokes as an ally the work of Levinas (without giving any real account of the latter's argument or its specific conception of fatigue). The price Crary pays for this double neglect is a failure to get beyond the notion of a physiological need for sleep, even as he rails against the capitalist reduction of human existence to its bodily needs. What he legitimately seeks from Levinas is philosophical support for his desire to reimagine a being-in-common with others that would spring us from the trap of self-isolation in which capitalism seeks to place us. The refusal to attend seriously to Levinas's argument and its outright dismissal of Freud diminishes the books argument.

Now, had Crary not simply dismissed The Interpretation of Dreams, he would have discovered there the extraordinary thesis that certain dreams testify to what Freud calls a "wish to sleep," a wish Lacan later described as "the greatest enigma" of Freud's new science.[7] Not a response to a physiological deficit, this depsychologized wish involves something more profound: an ontological declivity. In German, this wish is manifest in the term, Wiederholen, in repetition; etymologically, a "hauling" by which the subject "drags [himself] into a certain path that he cannot get out of."[8] In the Freudian context, Lacan says that it retains all "its connotation of something tiring, exhausting."[9] If "nothing is more enigmatic" nor central to the structure of psychoanalysis than Weiderholen, the idea itself precedes psychoanalysis and is present in Islamic philosophy's conception of ta'wil, a tenacious exegetical return to and repetition of obscure origins ends up in the nonplace of the imaginal world, the Eighth Climate. The key to ta'wil Corbin claims to have found in Heidegger was precisely the latter's conception, at the beginning of Being and Time, of hermeneutics as just such a "hauling back."

Levinas began writing Existence and Existents in 1940 while he was retained in a forced labor camp. Although he had by this point already become disaffected with Heidegger's philosophy, the rift could only have been aggravated as the official motto of National Socialism (and unofficial motto of capitalism), *Arbeit Macht Frei*, was being mounted on the gates of various concentration camps. Heidegger's thesis—that *Dasein* was consigned in its Being, that it had to assume as a task what was given—must have begun to seem even more unpalatable. During his imprisonment, Levinas composed his reflections on fatigue, which he conceived not as something that befalls a worn-out subject but as contributory to the event of the subject, its coming into existence. Stated simply, fatigue is defined as a turn away from the world and a return to anonymous existence, or to what Levinas refers to as the *il y a* (the "there is"), a term he substitutes for Heidegger's term *es gibt*. The substitution removes *Dasein*'s "preunderstanding" of, and concern for, Being to introduce a note of indifference, even an inhospitability, into the field of Being.

The concept of "being-toward-death" is the primary target of both Corbin's and Levinas's critique of Heidegger. For now, however, we will follow the argument of Levinas, which—viewed from its widest angle—proceeds from the general observation that the "development of biological science in the 19th century . . . had an incalculable influence on the whole of contemporary philosophy."[10] "Including Heidegger's" is implied. From this point, Levinas sketches an argument that resonates in the one Foucault sets out in amplified form decades later regarding biopower's roots in this same science. While previously the living and living things were assumed to have been given life, which thus belonged to them, in some "quasi-perceptible fashion," the nineteenth-century life sciences transformed life into the object of a struggle to preserve itself. From here on out, it became possible to define life as having a purpose or final cause, namely life itself.

Foucault famously characterized the shift to biopower as an abandonment of "the ancient right to take life or let live" in favor of the adoption of a new conception of power as that which "foster(s) life or disallows(s) it to the point of death."[11] Yet, while biopower retreats from the business of death, which is no longer a territory it commands, the ultimate threat of death is what gives the concern for life its urgency. It is to save Heidegger from association with this "bio-problematic" that Derrida warns us against confusing Heidegger's being-toward-death with a privileging of the end of living, or perishing, or "kicking of the bucket."[12]

Being-toward-death's goal must not be confused with biological death, for what is at stake in Heidegger is, rather, death in its "proper" sense, death as one's "*ownmost* possibility," as uniquely mine. By anticipating my death, I do not experience my own expiry, for the sovereignty of death ensures that it never discloses itself to me in actuality. In being-toward-death, I instead confront the "closest closeness one might have," which is for Heidegger the possibility of the impossibility that is death.[13] That is, I confront not the absolute Nothing that annihilates all possibilities but the "nothing actual," which is to say, possibility itself. Through our anticipatory stance toward death, we discover our capacity to transcend not death (which remains ineluctable, certain) but the limitations placed on us by our having been thrown into the world. That is, we cease to be limited by the ontic dispositions thrust on us before we had a chance to choose them—"our parents, our home, our nationality, our build, the color of our skin, our culture" (to borrow—why not?—Kiarostami's list)—and become capable of all the possibilities available to me on this side of death. The anticipation of death throws open being in its totality, in all its possibilities, and discloses our primordial power to transcend our ontic limits.

This is not the place to adjudicate Derrida's claim that Levinas confuses Heidegger's "proper" death with perishing; rather, we will focus on Levinas's stated objection, which is that being-toward-death appeals to an ontological finality. This critique focuses on *Dasein*'s concern for Being, its care for existing. Levinas's complaint (which is similar to Corbin's) is that Heidegger constrains us within the horizon of Being. The following assertion clearly articulates this complaint: "There is, according to Heidegger, a circuit that leads each moment of our existence to the task of existing; thus in turning the handle of our door we open the totality of existence, for beyond the action[,] we have already traversed the intermediaries separating this action from our concern for being itself." [14] The threat of nothingness, of being's imminent annihilation, demands that every act serve as a means to a specific end: the endurance and conservation of being. Just as Aristotle's finalism of the Good sacrificed, or dismissed, excess pleasure as accidental, as mere aberration, so the finalism of Being sacrifices desire, along with all the intermediary instances through which the teleological circuit passes.

Levinas theorizes a "voluptuous" about which the finalism of Being has neither knowledge nor interest. Critics have expressed disappointment with a saccharine note in *Taste of Cherry*, which they read in the film's title and in the episode in which Bagheri, a taxidermist who attempts to dissuade Badii from his goal by recounting his own battle with suicidal thoughts. The simple pleasure of eating a few mulberries was sufficient to persuade him to go on living. Let us put it this way: Badii is not Bagheri, cherries are not mulberries, and the film is much too dark to be lightened by such humble pleasures. Nor, for that matter, for anything like "the depersonalization of slumber, [which would allow us to] inhabit a world in common, a shared enactment of withdrawal from the calamitous nullity and waste of 24/7 praxis," the remedy offered by Crary as relief from this praxis, to ameliorate the situation. We must take care not to confuse Levinas's notion of voluptuousness or Freud's notion of desire with "acquisitiveness." [15]

Desire seeks neither assuagement nor the nullification of singularity; it is exorbitant, an opening onto an unsettling alterity. Before we learn that his approaches to random men are part of the search by which Badii hopes to find someone willing to assist in his suicide, the film lends credence to the suspicion that he is soliciting sex from them. Along with the men he approaches, we in the audience initially misread Badii's goal. The question, however, is this: Why did Kiarostami plant this suspicion in the first place? We know he is not above such a thing, for in interviews he has confessed to filming a can rolling down a hill because he "needed" an emptiness. In that case what he needed was a pause, a break in time; what he needs in *Taste of Cherry* is to associate Badii's death drive, from the beginning, with sex. We will return to this later, but at this point we want to insist that the film presents the goal of Badii's journey not in finite terms, as a mere surcease of his burdens and sorrows, but in terms that are exorbitant. Desire, as we noted, devotes itself not to a comforting pleasure but to a scandalous otherness. Not unlike Levinas, Kiarostami indicts the metaphysical calamity that grounds capitalism's refusal to affirm the exorbitant nature of desire, which—far from sustaining the care for being—actively relaxes it. That desire must be regarded as unsacrificable should be evident, *a contrario*, in the fact that under capitalism, so many, like the work-deprived workers in Kiarostami's film, are forced "to eat, drink and warm [themselves] in order not to die, [for them] nourishment becomes fuel, as in certain kinds of hard labor."[16] To those to whom this is not evident, *Existence and Existents* attempts to open their eyes to "the lies of capitalist idealism."[17]

Rudolph Hoss, whose decision it was to display the infamous Nazi motto at the entry of Auschwitz, is said to have regarded that motto as a "mystical declaration that self-sacrifice in the form of endless labor brings a kind of spiritual freedom."[18] Levinas's argument is a stiff rebuttal of that declaration; it opposes itself to "every labor mystique, which [appeals] to themes of joy and freedom."[19] Ultimately, the mystique of freedom-promising labor relies on the supposition of a lack or deficit, which the subject seeks to overcome through the willing sacrifice of her labor in return for some greater, perpetually deferred gain. This calculation reposes on a duality: on the one side, constraint and the despair arising from it, the matter of the body, dense with the weight of its frailties and its inert resistance to will; on the other, the effortless effort of freedom and will, able to overcome frailties and resistance as long as it keeps its eye on the rewards that await us in the future. A naive notion of matter as inert substance is met with an equally naive notion of action as propelled by a freedom "simply present and ready" to do whatever it wants, a freedom as "free as the wind" (as Levinas sarcastically put it) or as a "flowing river" (as the mother in Kiarostami's film, *10*, too credulously declares to her properly incredulous son).[20]

THE TWO DEATHS

This notion of freedom as simply there from the start, a potential we originally possess and can make use of at will, discounts the intermediaries of "satisfaction and avowal" and reduces the body to its physiological caducity, and fatigue to spent energy, to mere waste.[21] To overturn this capitalist idea of freedom, Levinas theorizes fatigue not as an entropic dwindling of energy but as a deeply enigmatic movement of return that "describes a closed circle" that effaces "every ulterior finality."[22] Fatigue—which is fatigued with the future—recoils from the latter and from existence itself, not to escape but to coil back toward existence from a slight distance. Fatigue installs a lag or interval within existence, a present that interrupts the link tying the moment before to the moment after.

It is by virtue of this interruption that fatigue can be said to form a *closed* circle; otherwise, the phrase is misleading insofar as this circle represents a kind of opening rather than a closing. It would be more accurate to describe it as Lacan does, as a "short circuit." As opposed to that circuit which is magnetized by the future, or "which leads every moment of our existence to the task of existing," fatigue is magnetized by existence as a never experienced past, a lost rather than final cause. It forms a circuit in which "I am obliged to pick up again the discourse . . . bequeathed to me . . . because one can't stop the chain . . . and it is precisely my duty to transmit it in its aberrant form to someone else."[23]

This short circuit is homologous to the realm I invoked earlier, that of the Eighth Climate or imaginal world, in which heterogeneous terms emerge not as entirely separate but as implicated in one another. Steeply schooled in protestant theology, Corbin describes what occurs in this realm by borrowing from Martin Luther's explanation of *significatio passiva*, or passive meaning. Puzzled at first, the young Luther, in a flash of insight, suddenly understood what the psalm verse in *Justitia tua libera me* [liberate me in your justice] meant: in attributing to God the justice that makes us just or the holiness that hallows us, we do not confer these qualities "upon divine Essence as such . . . [but] discover [these qualities] only insofar as they occur and are made within us, [that is] according to what they make of us, insofar as they are our passion."[24] With respect to the Eighth Climate, this means that what we encounter in this region is not the divine Essence but rather the fault in being instituted by His primordial withdrawal from us. Thus, the qualities we experience are not His but those excited in us through our passive relation or exposure to the fault created by His retreat. We emerge as modes of being, as subjects, through our relation to our own alterity or our capacity to be affected by His withdrawal. The heterogeneous terms brought together in this imaginal space—as in Levinas's notion of the present—thus constitute a primitive duality, composed (again) not of two separate terms but of the disjunct term of a subject stretched between an active and a passive pole, between a past that never was and a future that is not yet.

This explains perhaps a peculiarity in Kiarostami's manner of filming *Taste of Cherry*. Although the film consists mainly of a series of dialogues between

Badii and the passengers he picks up along the way, there are not only no two-shots of the interlocuters but in addition, when one or the other partner of the dialogue is being filmed, there is no character off screen in the other seat. The other seat is always empty. While the film appears to promote the importance of camaraderie, the fond memories of which Badii retains from his experience in the military, Kiarostami's focus is on the sense of an inner otherness, which is the condition of the possibility of the subject's appreciation of the otherness of other persons, and on the treacherous nature of our relation to a lost past, which is both horrifying and a source of joy.

Let us break off here to return to the notion of entropy in its historical association with fatigue and the development of psychoanalysis. It is known that Freud was seduced by Fechner's contention that the psyche sought to maintain libidinal excitation in a state of equilibrium, despite copious evidence of the inefficacy of this principle of constancy. That there was at work in the psyche "a circuit at the limit of sense and nonsense" that ran counter to the arc of self-preservation, progress, and mastery seemed irrefutable, and thus again and again Freud acknowledged the existence of a "daemonic force" at odds with the tendency toward progress and well-being.[25] Yet, because his "Fechnerism" continued to get the better of him, even at times in his remarkably bold *Beyond the Pleasure Principle*, he attempted to remain within the conceptual framework of principles of thermodynamics by embracing its second principle and suggesting that this daemonic counterforce behaved "somewhat like entropy."[26] With this, drive's recursive movement became confused with a winding down to the state of inanimation, of a total vastation of energy.

This account runs counter to the notion of drive Freud develops elsewhere, in which drive entails a maximum perturbation rather than a winding down. Consider, for example, his concept of *Hilflosigkeit*, or radical helplessness. Faced with Otto Rank's proposal that the trauma of birth results from the loss of the mother, which arouses the child's anxiety, Freud objects that this thesis, while promising, "floats in the air" without an argument to sustain it.[27] His counter-argument amounts to the proposal that the child suffers not from the simple absence of his mother but from a lethal, suffocating jouissance that marks her presence. The special fault of *Hilflosigkeit* is "introduced, perpetuated in man in relation to [a dimension of externality or otherness] infinitely more fatal for him than [is the external world] for any other animal."[28]

In other words, we misconstrue the infant's wild cries of helplessness by treating them as inarticulate pleas for the mother's presence; what provokes them, rather, is an overwhelming imminence that announces to the child that he will be taken back up into the mother. If, as Freud says, the "initial helplessness of human beings" makes us dependent on the "extraneous help of an experienced person" and establishes helplessness as "the primordial source of all moral motives," we would be wrong to conflate this lesson with the humanist assumption that man's helplessness is founded in lack, in inadequacies, which the society of others makes whole.[29] The child finds himself not so much abandoned as alone with an "essentially alien [existence that] strikes against" him.[30] The society of others is salutary only insofar as it distances us from the threat of the latter.

This notion of *Hilflosigkeit* helps us to read the distinction Levinas draws between existence and existents. That he separates existence from existents has often be said, including by Derrida, who admonishes Levinas for not understanding that in Heidegger's thought, "nothing is more clear" than the fact the "Being is nothing outside the existent . . . and does not exist outside [the existent] as a foreign power, or as a hostile and neutral impersonal element. . . . Being is not an *archia* which would permit Levinas to insert the face of a faceless tyrant under the name of Being."[31] This criticism—that Levinas is smuggling in ontic content under ontological clothing—misses the mark. Levinas does not dispute the fact that existence is nothing outside the existent; what he disputes is the characterization of this nothing as a simple nullity.

Far from separating existence from existents, Levinas insists that existence is irremissible, that we are riveted to it in a way that sometimes suffocates us. Overturning Heidegger's thesis that the "closest closeness one might have" is to the possibility of impossibility, Levinas associates this closeness with impossibility, as a blockage of breath and a comprehension that leaves the existent utterly helpless. This negativity or fault concerns not a "contingent fact—the frailties of [the human] organism" but a radical impasse or fault in being itself, and, "far from being an 'insult' to freedom, [this fault, which exposes us, fatally, to a dimension of otherness] is freedom's faithful companion."[32] Two points must be stressed: first, this "special fault" is strictly homologous to the one we encountered in our discussion of the withdrawal of divine Essence, where its positive valance was highlighted; here, its threatening aspect is brought to the fore. This variation defines the treacherous nature of our relation to this fault. Second, it is with the neglect of this impasse in Being that Levinas charges Heidegger.

While *Dasein* is threatened by the definiteness of death, which remains unimaginable, Levinas's existent is threatened by an indefinite limitless.[33] The unimaginable nothingness on which Heidegger's notion of being-toward-death reposes comes under assault by Levinas, who adamantly opposes the idea that nothing lies outside being and like "an ocean . . . beats up against it on all sides."[34] Appealing first for support to Bergson's argument that negation no longer makes any sense when applied to the whole of being, Levinas nevertheless declines to endorse Bergson's counterproposal that there is something that escapes negation. This demurral indicates a willingness to accept the idea that there is a residual entity, a vital force, that is immune to negation. Rejecting both positions, Levinas asserts there is something that negation cannot cancel. It is not a thing, does not exist, and falls not outside being but within it; there is an internal, ineliminable fault within being itself. He describes this indefectible nothing as the murmuring "presence of an absence," a dense atmosphere of nothingness, lying in the very heart of being.[35]

Something is primordially lost, withdrawn from us, leaving us not only unsupported but helplessly exposed to the atmosphere of a potentially lethal alterity. It is from this helplessness that Mr. Badii suffers. For him, "everything-has-already-been-imposed-at-birth" is not the ontic affliction Heidegger describes, a condition of immanence to be transcended by anticipating and assuming his ownmost death. "Already imposed at birth" is an ontological condition that stifles him, prevents him from coming into being. And yet, while there is no "faceless face of a tyrant" hidden "under" existence, as Derrida's criticism would have it, no content, no "something" hidden in the impersonal "there is," it is also true that this atmosphere of presence can, as Levinas plainly states, "appear later as content" as the face of tyranny.[36] Whenever the always already lost past is recast as a once actual past of which a people have been robbed or which they themselves have squandered, the figure of tyranny presents itself in the engineering of efforts to recover the loss. It is precisely the fact that the radical impasse of being has emerged as content in the combined forces of war, capitalism, and theocratic-legalism, to which *Taste of Cherry* testifies.

As previously indicated, the remarkable premise of the film is that Badii feels obliged to solicit the help of another person to accomplish his suicide. He thus attempts through long conversations to convince three strangers he happens to meet—a Kurdish soldier, an Afghani seminarian, and a Turkish taxidermist—to assist him. Curiously, he does not ask his potential accomplices to help him perform the deed itself—he will take this on himself—but to come along afterward to see to his burial. It would be a mistake, however, to regard Badii as a sort of Polynices, searching for his Antigone. He is not looking for a symbolic sprinkling of dust, a ceremonial gesture to spare him the ignominy of dying in the open like a dog. No, Badii's request is more puzzling and oddly excessive: he requests that his companion call out his name twice, toss a few pebbles at him, and then throw twenty shovelfuls of dirt on his grave. It appears that he requires an accomplice not to perform the obsequies that would mark his demise but to make sure that he is well and truly dead.[37]

This suggests that Badii is plagued not by the anxiety that accompanies being-toward-death but by the impossibility of dying. That is, it appears that he has lost faith in the possibility of dying.[38] It is undeadness—or to use Levinas's phrase, "the indefectibility of existence itself"—that fills Badii with horror. It presses against him, stifles him; it is what he wants to put an end to through suicide. But if the "there is" of anonymous existence insists beyond every negation, how can suicide succeed as a strategy? How can Badii be assured that he will die given that it is the very indefectibility of existence that drove him to contemplate suicide in the first place?

Taste of Cherry is not the only Kiarostami film to focus on death. The Wind Will Carry Us, which features a graveyard as one of its primary locations, tells of a documentary news team that has descended on a small village to film the funeral of a one-hundred-year-old woman, who does not oblige the filmmakers by dying until well after the plug has been pulled on their project. Life and Nothing More tells of another documentary filmmaker who visits a small village after an earthquake claims the lives of many of its inhabitants; it is up to the living to figure out how to go on. It seems that it is the death of others that is Kiarostami's theme, and this is true, I argue, of Taste of Cherry as well. For while in this film it is the protagonist's impending death with which the film is concerned, it is still the death of others (unknown ancestors) that motivate his quest. It is their death that imposes on him the burden of existence, binding him irremissibly to a radically lost, because never experienced, past.

In Difference and Repetition Deleuze produces a reading of Beyond the Pleasure Principle that continues to challenge the "Fechnerism," that periodically reemerges in Freud's argument, sending it off course. Against Freud, Deleuze insists that "death does not appear in the objective model of an indifferent inanimate matter to which the living would return."[39] This idea acknowledges only one aspect of death, one that

> signifies the personal disappearance of the person, the annihilation of this difference of the person, the annihilation of this difference represented by the I or the ego. . . . This is a difference which existed only in order to die, and the disappearance of which can be objectively represented by a return to inanimate matter, as though calculated by a kind of entropy. Despite appearances, this death always comes from without, even at the moment when it constitutes the most personal possibility.[40]

Deleuze is here chiding Freud for allowing the personal aspect of death to prevent him from paying more attention to death's strangely impersonal aspect, which Maurice Blanchot succinctly described as

> that which is without any relation to me . . . [it is] the unreality of the indefinite. . . . It is not the irreversible step beyond which there would be no return, [but] that which is not accomplished. . . . It is inevitable but inaccessible death . . . it is that toward which I cannot go forth, for in it, I do not die, I have fallen from the power to die. In it they die; they do not cease, and they do not finish dying . . . [it is] not the term, but the interminable, not proper but featureless death.[41]

The "they" in question, unlike the inhabitants of the world into which *Dasein* is thrown, cannot be outdistanced through an ecstatic flight of transcendence, nor do they have anything to do with the ontic limitations of everyday banality. Instead, they figure a ceaseless limitlessness. In an argument that seems designed to discredit Heidegger's concept of being-toward-death as well as localized misfires in Freud's conception of the death drive, Deleuze claims that "death cannot be reduced to negation . . . neither the limitation imposed by matter upon mortal life, nor the opposition between matter and immortal life."[42] This is not to deny the scientific fact that at death the body acquires the inertness of matter but to grasp the manner in which death occurs to the subject.

It is never as our own but as something that happens to others that death occurs. Freud proposed that even though the subject can accept the abstract idea of death, his own death is completely unacceptable to him. All men are mortal, and while I may count myself among them, I—in my singularity—escape the universal condition. Blanchot's phrase "one dies," on the other hand, should not be read as an abstraction, a generality added by the intellect but as a *reality in the subject* that renders her indefinite. It is precisely because we are not protected by the umbrella of the universal that we are subjected to the torrent of interminable, featureless death. That is, "one dies" is not the equivalent of "all men are mortal" but the result of the fact that man is marked, in the absence of a ground, with an uncertain purpose. It is not just that he lacks the specificity of a predetermined nature but more: this lack inhabits him as a presence. Similarly, when Levinas ascribes to the "there is" the impersonality of "it rains," he posits a term homologous to Freud's impersonal term id. In both cases a preindividual reality is supposed to operate in the subject, a loss not preceded by a having, a "wound [that] existed before me."[43]

Deleuze ends his discussion with a statement that reflects on Badii's precise dilemma: "in confronting these two aspects of death," the impersonal and ceaseless and the personal and definitive, "it is apparent that even suicide does not make them coincide."[44] The death of an individual is incapable of bringing to an end the unending "one dies." This is, I have been arguing, what perturbs Badii throughout the film: his inability to die. But does he discover the lesson of suicide's futility?[45] Does he come to realize that suicide will not resolve the issue of "everything imposed at birth," will not stop the murmuring of the dead?

ONE MORE EFFORT TO THINK EFFORT

I will attempt less to answer this question than to develop further the terms in which the question should be addressed. While capitalism regards the frailty of the body, its susceptibility to a fatigue brought on by labor, as a kind of insensitivity to the motivations of will—a will that navigates a world filled with dangers to be avoided and opportunities to be seized—Levinas offers a radically different theory of fatigue and its relation to the body. While he begins by characterizing fatigue as a numbness, he defines it not as a paralysis of will but as a numbing caused by an overexposure to the remorseless murmuring of the *il y a*. The reduction of sensation is defined as an obscure sort of activity within the inactivity of suffering.

Freud characterizes pain in *The Project* in a similar way. He suggests that in his "theory [that quantities of excitations produce facilitations] pain . . . leaves permanent facilitations behind . . . which possibly do away with the resistance of a contact-barrier entirely."[46] In short, a radical passivity or overexposure to otherness requires a membrane of separation from the impersonal, overwhelming *il y a* in order for a subject to emerge. The numbing effect of fatigue enables effort to install the separation necessary to allow an intimate relation to this otherwise corrosive otherness.

Levinas is quick to add that the existent—the subject—gains through fatigue a foothold in existence, not in the world. This cautionary distinction marks its distance from the rationalism of Aristotle, to which—Levinas argues—Heidegger remained heir. The mistake common to both is their supposition that beings enter into a preexisting world even if the harmony they establish there, according to Aristotle, is denied by Heidegger's insistence that *Dasein* is not "at home" in the world. Levinas sets his philosophy upstream from the accounts of these predecessors, at a point where no division exists between inside and outside and the concept of the uncanny marks not *Dasein*'s position in the world but the existent's relation to itself. Levinas thus rejoins and updates a tradition that began with the challenge mounted against Aristotle by Avicenna, who vigorously maintained that the subject's relation to itself was a primitive phenomenon and not—as Aristotle believed—derivative of the subject's relation to external objects. This is the capital point of Avicenna's "flying man" experiment. The individual is not first situated in a place in the world; it *is* place, the primordial event of localization.[47]

The distinctive lexicon of *Existence and Existents*—fatigue, indolence, sleep, rest, and so on—is polemically selected to unknot the work-freedom link and interrupt the capitalist argument subtending it. Levinas thus makes claims such as the following: "The possibility of sleeping is already seated in the very exercise of thought . . . It is qua thought, here, already sheltered from eternity and universality. . . . [Sleep] is not a new life which is enacted beneath life; it is a participation by nonparticipation, by the elementary act of resting."[48] This is to say, we can refuse to accept the world as it is; we can close our eyes and dream—that is, bring about—another world.[49] The 24/7 rhythm of capitalism is here replaced not by a simple dream but by the rhythm of repetition, which allows us to imagine the inexistent.

"Repetition is essentially inscribed in *need*, since need rests upon an *instance* which essentially involves *repetition*," says Deleuze.⁵⁰ I have emphasized three terms in this statement to foreground their co-occurrence, for they together disambiguate each other: "need" cannot be conflated here with "vital needs" but means "something that wishes," in Freud's strong sense. "Instance" also suggests an urgency or pressing demand as well as a decisive process, and "repetition" in this context returns not to the same but to the place where something escapes it, to the place where a fugitive elsewhere is glimpsed from behind, in the moment it withdraws from us.⁵¹ To say that fatigue, like the death drive, insists beyond reason, beyond the needs of survival or the preservation of being, is not to say that it has the force of inertia that inevitably ends in a state of inanimation.

It is necessary to distinguish, in short, between insistence and inertia.⁵² Inertia continues on the same path unless, or until, it is met by another force—such as death—sufficient to stop it in its tracks. Fatigue—and the death drive—insist, and this insistence insists not on a specific trajectory or goal but on its own repetition. The insistent form of repetition is met with its own form or resistance, but this time it is internal rather than external. Repetition gives rise to its own resistance, or its own failure, for it continuously produces a difference it merely circles but does not contain. It is in this moment that the death drive is eroticized, when a surplus jouissance arises to mark this heterogeneity, the foreignness of the subject's body to itself. This is also the way in which despair—precipitated by a failure of belief and a consequent retreat from any goals or care for being—fails: by meeting unexpectedly an element it cannot consume, a heterogeneity that paralyzes doubt by providing proof of a true alterity.

In Levinas's terms, the existent's heterogeneity is produced through fatigue's recoil from the excessive presence of anonymous existence. As a result of this recoil, destiny ceases to weigh on us—as it does on Badii—"like heredity," as if we were "born without having chosen [our] birth."⁵³ Still, it weighs down on us. For while destiny is no longer experienced as an external constraint against which we must struggle, constraint remains evident in the very effort of fatigue, which slackens the grip of the il y a without entirely slipping from the latter's hold. And while he insists on tying the existent to a "here" rather than a far-off, ecstatic "there," Levinas insists on retracting the future by refracting it back into the present. The distant destination of the future—in which the hoped-for recompence of one's labor will arrive— belongs to the economic order of capitalism, which uses it to discredit the importance of the present. The point is not just that the promise of future remuneration will justify a sacrificed present is a scam but also, and fundamentally, that the devaluation of the present relies on a false notion of time.

For the present, as Levinas conceives it, is the moment in which an incision is made in eternity. The present is that moment at which the link to the moment before is cut and time is from there (re)started. The present is the time that effort and fatigue take to interrupt destiny's implacable march forward.

To debunk the mystique of labor, Levinas restores the present—that devalued, waste-time on capital's ledgers—to its proper value; it becomes, in his account, the time needed for time to exist. He also advances a further argument to prevent another false sense of freedom from entering through the back door. While it is through effort, exerted in the present, that the subject emerges as something that holds together as an entity, despite its division, this effort extracts from the present a price: it will be incapable of extending itself. The present cannot last, cannot leave a legacy, but remains evanescent. This is to say that the present can never be the *place* of the subject, the span of its sovereignty. There seems, at first, nothing extraordinary about this argument, which appears only to reproduce the commonplace notion of the fleetingness of the present. But rather than regarding this fleetingness as something to be mourned, Levinas revalues it as the condition of the subject's freedom from any predetermined destiny. The "ransom," as he calls it, that must be paid for our freedom from the past is that we can never own our freedom. It is improper to suggest that we free ourselves, for we owe this freedom to our passivity to the otherness that attaches itself to us, to a doubling up of ourselves that occurs in the present.

It is well-known that Derrida regarded the present as an enemy of otherness, an illusory moment of the subject's self-presence. Levinas's position is plainly contrary in that it defines the present as the moment in which the subject encounters itself as an ungraspable excess. It is in the present that the movement of fatigue—which consists not only in the recoil from anonymous existence but also a turning back to it—takes place. The infrangible nature of the subject's bond with its self, its sense of its own "inwardness," is thus forged there.[54] Levinas does not invent this notion whole cloth but joins a long philosophical tradition that stretches from Avicenna to Maine de Biran and beyond, where it is through its relation to its *body*, specifically, that the subject acquires its inner sense.[55] This relation of intimacy with our bodies lacks the assurance of that illusory self-presence of which Derrida was rightfully suspicious. As Levinas points out, we cannot "merge with [our bodies] with the innocence of Narcissus espousing his own image."[56] Rather than reflecting a comforting image of ourselves, the body presents itself to us in the guise of a shadow, or blind spot in our nonetheless indubitable consciousness of self. Our own bodies, the felt region of self, remain—despite their inalienability—alien, improper.

A body is not something we are but—as even common parlance acknowledges—something we have. Subjects have bodies, though not, of course, in the way we have umbrellas, which are notoriously easy to lose even when we try or just happen to forget them. Our relation to our bodies is more intimate than the one we maintain to objects and more like the one we have to our past. Indeed, *Existence and Existents* seems implicitly to argue that it is through our relationship to our bodies that we can have a past other than the one imposed on us at birth by biology or culture. Since Levinas is not explicit on this matter, however, we will need to supplement what he does say to establish the relationship. Admitting that that he is not the first to resist the reduction of the body to a substance, he distinguishes his position from that of others who convert the body into a kind of corporealized soul that expresses some inner truth of the subject. For Levinas, the body is not something that dwells within us but is instead the condition of inwardness.[57]

At another point, he acknowledges his debts to earlier philosophers on this score, citing prominently Maine de Biran, who famously theorized the subject's relation to its body in terms of effort's encounter with an internal resistance. Levinas's criticisms of Biran are mainly these: (1) he conceived effort based on the subject's will, and (2) he cast his argument as a theory of the way in which the subject discovered its body.[58] The underlying problem, as Levinas sees it, is that will and discovery both presuppose an already existing subject. Biran thus fails to consider the way in which embodiment is constitutive of subjectivity.

To push further the relation between temporality and the body, we might return to a Deleuze's examination of Freud's conception of the death drive. After making brief references to fatigue, Deleuze makes the following claim: "A scar is not the sign of a wound, but of 'the present fact of having been wounded' . . . [the scar] contracts all the instants which separate us from [the wound] into a living present."[59] It is in "Remembering, Repeating, and Working Through" that Freud formulated this very proposition. After ruminating on the odd compulsion of patients to repeat past traumas during analysis and wondering aloud what in fact repetition repeated, he offered this conclusion: "We have made it clear . . . that we must treat [the patient's] illness not as an event of the past, but as a present-day force."[60] Can we not define the body, based on this insight, as the present-day force of the past? As the present-day force of an intimate past?

Freud attempted in "Remembering, Repeating, and Working Through" to distinguish the psychological notion of remembering—in which an already constituted subject loses a memory and dredges it up again by reestablishing its links to other memories and perceptions—from repeating. The latter is no longer a psychological notion, first because the past that is repeated in analysis was never experienced by the subject and was thus never linked to other memories or perceptions. While remembering stitches up a hole in memory, repetition makes a hole in the psychic fabric; something breaks into the analytic scene to disturb its coherency. The abrupt emergence of the past is an "event" in the same way Levinas uses the term when he says that "the body is itself [an] event that realizes the condition for any inwardness."[61] There is no subject to be found in the pure slide of signification or in the chain of associations that string themselves out in the analytic situation. It is only with the apparition of this scar that a subject emerges.

Now, it is widely known that the peripatetics regarded the body as matter molded by a beautiful form. The harmony between the opposing terms was guaranteed by a belief in a final cause. Once the latter lost its credibility, an impersonal illimitable force—that had until then been obscured and held in check—was unleashed. Freud's metapsychological writings on repression and the unconscious linger on the notion of a primarily repressed jouissance, or impersonal id, an archaic and alien force, which resembles, in many respects, Levinas's concept of the il y a. It is in relation to this impersonal instance that the subject is, for Levinas and Freud, thought.

In his commentary on Freud's essay on "Negation," Jean Hyppolite argues that the emergence, of the subject relies on "making possible something like the use of the unconscious, all the while maintaining the repression," or, it is a matter of finding a way of "having the unconscious at one's disposal even as one refuses it."[62] The anonymous force of the id (and, we might add, of the il y a), ceaseless and indestructible as it is, compulsively repeats itself, remaining indifferent even to death. This fact is ultimately what the claim that repression cannot be lifted suggests. While what is primarily repressed cannot be appropriated or transmuted into something recognizable, Freud contends that "recognition of the unconscious on the part of the ego" can and does occur "in a negative formula."[63] I am suggesting that our sense of embodiment presents itself in a negative formula, as being attached to something with which we cannot coincide.

BODIES AND RESURRECTION

As I noted, Avicenna was a key figure in a long line of philosophers who located the body in an opacity within conscious thought. Prescinding the claims of reality, he argued that an obstacle, a negativity that could not be reduced by thought, constituted a primitive awareness of an immanent otherness. Our sense of embodiment, along with the sense that we persist in time, is dependent not on the ego and its illusions of will, control, or self-identity but on the fact that we are riveted to something that escapes will and intention, and disturbs our sense of identity. I recall Avicenna's pivotal role in this long legacy to help reset the stage for a return to our specific concern: *The Taste of Cherry*, whose central character is overwhelmed by a vague despondency from which he can imagine no exit other than suicide. All his resources seem to have been exhausted. Capitalism regards constraint as external to the efforts of labor. Constraint overcomes effort by force, causing fatigue—an inability to keep up the effort required to accomplish the task at hand or, in extreme cases, to go on living. A different diagnosis of Badii's condition can be derived from Levinas's argument that fatigue and despair cling to constraint—that is, to irremissible existence, to an oppressive "atmosphere," he calls the *il y a*. By clinging to the *il y a* while allowing its hold to slacken, fatigue creates a space from which effort lurches forth.

Throughout the film, Badii has driven around in a desolate landscape, his attention rigorously focused on his goal. The penultimate sequence takes place in a different location, at his home as he awaits the taxi that will take him to his gravesite. A noticeable retreat from intentionality characterizes the sequence. Shot from outside his apartment, the scene is enclosed in the vast darkness of night. Badii, smoking a cigarette, regards the impersonal night with a sleepless intensity as he moves restlessly from room to room, making, we imagine, his final preparations. We cannot be sure of this, however. For the fact that he is seen from outside suggests that it is he who is being watched by the ceaseless, indifferent darkness. It is possible that it is he who is exposed to an anonymous gaze.

"The vigilance of insomnia which keeps our eyes open has no subject," Levinas writes, almost as if commenting on Badii's situation.[64] While attention, "which presupposes the freedom of the ego that directs it," navigates a world filled with dangers to be avoided and opportunities to be seized, the vigilance that defines insomnia turns away from the outside world. It remains helplessly awake to the anonymous rustling that lives on, refusing to disappear from the world of objects that normally holds it in abeyance and implies the impossibility of sleep or any sort of respite from wakefulness. And yet, Levinas concedes, if I am aware of being an object of anonymous vigilance, I must be so in such a way that my "I is already detached from my anonymity."[65] My very awareness implies that I have allowed a minimal distance to slip between myself and that vigilance in which my subjectivity is eclipsed. Levinas's theoretical description of vigilance is poised on an edge of discernibility as fine as the one on which Kiarostami films the penultimate sequence.

The sequence is followed by an equally subtle shot: a close-up of the face of Badii tightly framed by the edges of the grave he has dug for himself. A cinematic close-up is not reducible to the function of showing a detail from a larger scene; rather, its true function, Levinas explains, is "to stop the action in which a particular is bound up with a whole, and let it exist apart."[66] The close-up has been theorized as a shot in which the cinematic conceit that the screen offers viewers a window on the world is abandoned. The close-up exposes the screen as a surface—not a mere surface but one that suggests something is happening behind it.

In Kiarostami's *Shirin* (2008), for example, 114 spectators (111 of whom are well-known actresses) stare out from the screen the audience watches at a film screen in front of them, which we in the audience do not see. If we are unable to reduce these actresses to mere objects of our look but regard them, rather, as actively engaged in looking, it is because they are not situated in a world they must navigate—in events going on around them or on the unseen screen. Their active looks are inward-turning, ignited by their affective encounter with what is transpiring within themselves. While the action on the unseen screen may occasion this affective encounter, it is not the cause of what they actively see. In short, the actresses are deliberately not situated in a world, so as to allow us to see their look as situative, engaged in redefining their relation to an emerging world.

Now, if Badii's close-up suggests that he, too, has come to his senses, that Badii has been awakened to his embodiment, there is reason to believe that he may abandon his suicidal goal. In the theoretical treatises of Islamic Gnostics, the body ceased to be thought as the earthly anchor that doomed subjects to their finitude. Bodies became thinkable as a source of resurrection—not into another world but in this world. One can become other than one is. The film's coda, I would suggest, is a this-worldly scene of resurrection. It is set no longer in the autumn of the nominal narrative but in spring. The actors—no longer in character—appear alongside Kiarostami and the film crew, as if engaged in a postproduction sound check, while moving about freely amid soldiers on maneuvers. This appears to be a new world, technologically transformed by the abandonment of cinematography in favor of video, a very grainy video. The coda catches its audience by surprise and offers itself with all the ungainliness of a newborn, or of a dynamic present, still in the process of forming.

II

PILLOW SHOTS

5

MAY '68, THE EMOTIONAL MONTH

Emotions ran high in Paris in May '68, particularly among students in the universities. Sensing the peril of ignoring the groundswell of emotion, faculty responded immediately but variously. Some conservative old fossils attempted to quash the rebellion, while more liberal-minded, avuncular types "took to the barricades," casting their lot with the student radicals. Both camps allowed themselves a little more passion than usual, precisely because "usual" seemed to have evaporated in the hurly-burly of dissent. In the upheaval, everything seemed to have been turned upside down and inside out, including reason, which—suddenly agitated—became clouded with roily sediment. Less cool-headed and clear, reason became crimson-faced.

The response of Jacques Lacan did not fit, however, into either camp. Aligning himself neither against nor on the side of the student radicals, he simply accused them of not being radical enough, of behaving like unwitting flunkies of the university against which they imagined themselves to be in revolt. Detecting in their cries a plea for a new Master, he warned that they were on the verge of getting one. The monitory finger he held in their faces assumed the form of a year-long seminar, *Séminaire XVII: L'envers de la psychanalyse (The Other Side of Psychoanalysis)*.[1] In this seminar Lacan maintained that although the students wanted to believe they were abandoning the university for the streets, the university was not so easily abandoned. Rather than let them go, it had already begun to take over them—as well as the streets. In other words, certain elements of their revolt reflected academic business as usual.

The reversals or flip sides referred to in the seminar's title produce discourses other than psychonalysis, those of the Master, the Hysteric, and the University. That is, the specific operation of "reversal" referred to in the title is that of the "quarter-turns" or rotations that produce the differences between psychoanalysis and these three discourses.[2] Yet the title also refers to a reversal within psychoanalysis itself, operated by Lacan who turns classical Freudian theory upside down and inside out to produce a more revolutionary version of it, and thus to redefine the "analytic discourse" as a new social bond.

At the end of the seminar, this social tie is rendered in a distilled formula that exposes the ultimate ambition of the analyst—who, in her impossible role as analyst, operates on the analysand—as rather unseemly. The final aim of psychoanalysis, it turns out, is the production of shame. That which Lacan himself describes as unmentionable, even improper to speech as such, is mentioned (and mentioned only) on the threshold of the seminar's close. The seamy underside of psychoanalysis, the backside toward which all the twists and turns have led, is finally shame: that affect whose very mention brings a blush to the face.[3] Why is shame given such a place of honor, if we may put it that way, in the seminar? And what should the analyst's position be with respect to it? Should she try to reduce it, get rid of it, lower her eyes before it? No, Lacan proposes that the analyst must make herself the agent of it; her task is to provoke it. Looking out into the audience gathered in large numbers around him, he accounts for their presence in his final, closing remarks thus: if you have come here to listen to what I have to say, it is because I have positioned myself with respect to you as analyst, that is, as object-cause of your desire. And in this way, I have helped you to feel ashamed. End of seminar.

I want to allow what Lacan is saying to sink in. In response to May '68, a very emotional month, he ends his seminar, his long warning against the rampant and misguided emotionalism of the university students, with an impassioned plea for a display of shame. Curb your impudence, your shamelessness, he exhorts, cautioning: you should be ashamed! What effrontery! What a provocation is this seminar! But then, what are we to make of it? Because the reference to shame appears so abruptly and only in the final session, without elaboration, this is not an easy question to answer. One hears echoes of the transferential words of Alcibiades, who has this to say in *The Symposium* about Socrates: "And with this man alone I have an experience which no one would believe was possible for me—the sense of shame."[4] But to detect the vibrations of this precedent is a far cry from understanding what to make of it.

To sort matters out, one looks for hints that might be seen in retrospect to have been dropped along the way and might now steer us in the proper direction. Shame did emerge as a topic of interest in earlier seminars. In *Seminar VII: The Ethics of Psychoanalysis*, for example, Lacan compared shame to beauty, noting that the two functioned similarly to mark a limit. And in *Seminar XI: The Four Fundamental Concepts of Psychoanalysis*, in his discussion of Sartre's scenario of the voyeur at the keyhole, he dwells for a bit on the phenomenon of shame as if to justify Sartre's contention that it marks the "birth of the social." In *L'envers*, Lacan does not develop this argument, but his suggestion that analysis ought to induce shame vaguely confirms it. One of the most fruitful paths to follow, however, is the one laid down by Lacan's remarks on affect, since shame would seem to be an affect, although this is not so easily said.

That the return to Freud via Saussurean linguistics was guilty of a disastrous neglect of affect was, by May '68, not a new charge. Lacan had dealt with it before, particularly in *Seminar X*, the seminar on anxiety. But it is not difficult to understand why the charge was resurrected by the students who confronted him, during the course of this very seminar, on the steps of the Pantheon. The perceived hyperrationality of the formulas drawn on blackboards by their structuralist professors seemed arid and far-removed from the turmoil that surrounded them, from the newness of extraordinary events, the violence of police beatings, and from their own inchoate feelings of solidarity with the workers. A grumbling sense that something had been left out, that something inevitably escaped these desiccated and timeless structures, was expressed in the renewed demand that Lacan begin redressing the university's failures by recognizing the importance of affect. They had had it up to their eyeballs with signifiers and all the talk about them, which only left a whole area of their experience unacknowledged: precisely the fact of their being agitated, moved by what was happening in the here and now.

Lacan responded, how? By drawing more formulas on the backboard. But let us at least credit him with this: he bent over backward to point out that he was not simply talking the talk, he was . . . well, he was fitting his structures with feet. Indeed, he mentions this over and over: my structures have legs. They *do* march; they *do* move, my four-legged creatures. If he keeps repeating this joking reference to his four-footed structures, it is not because he is delighted with his little metaphor but because it is not a metaphor. The movement in these signifying structures is real, which is how we know they do not ignore affect, as many had charged.

Affect is included in the formulas of the four discourses. But where? A negative answer first: one misses the point if one tries to locate affect—or jouissance, in Lacan's preferred vocabulary—in any of the individual symbols that compose the structure. Affect (again, affect) is not to be treated as a local element that can be simply added to the chain of signifiers like that. This is in fact what Lacan himself did in his earlier work when he theorized jouissance as outside discourse. Defining the relation between the signifier and jouissance as antinomic, he localized the latter in a beyond. A positive answer begins by noting that what is new in *Seminar SXVII* is the emphasis Lacan gives to Freud's critical assertion that only ideas are ever repressed; affect, on the other hand, is subject to displacement. The latter phrase can mean two things: (1) that an affect can attach itself to a substitute signifier or object, rather than the one proper to it; or (2) affect can be displaced from itself. The first option is easily grasped; one can, for example, become enamored of some person or place because it reminds one of someone one once loved. This does seem to rise to a psychoanalytic insight, however, as it deals with "feelings," rather than affect. The intriguing option is the second, mostly because we do not yet know how to distinguish feelings from affect. It is the latter which poses the questions with which psychoanalysis is concerned.

I will begin from a distance, hoping to catch a certain emergence of affect in ongoing French debates around the heady period of May '68. Consider this passage from an essay published by Gilles Deleuze in 1967, that is, between the years of Lacan's *Seminar XI* and *Seminar XVII*:

> The first effect of Others is that around each object that I perceive or each idea that I think there is the organization of a marginal world, a mantle or background, where other objects and other ideas may come forth.... I regard an object, then I divert my attention, letting it fall into the background. At the same time, there comes forth from the background a new object of my attention. If this new object does not injure me, if it does not collide with me with the violence of a projectile (as when one bumps against something unseen), it is because the first object had already at its disposal a complete margin where I had already felt the preexistence of objects yet to come, and of an entire field of virtualities and potentialities which I already knew were capable of being actualized.[5]

In this description, perceptions, or representations, are conceived less as limited than as wrapped in a mantle of indetermination; they emerge as if from a peripheral vision. A surplus of perception, an indeterminate "more," creates a kind of buffer zone that ensures perceptions do not simply follow from antecedent perceptions but emerge smoothly from their penumbra. The source of this mantle or surplus is what Deleuze calls here "the Other"; it is an Other who "assures the margins and transitions of the world" and "fills the world with a benevolent murmuring." In his later work, Deleuze rebaptizes this benevolent Other with another term, "affect," and he defines affect (specifically in the books on cinema) as the participation of the actual in the virtual and the virtual in the actual, as seen from the side of the actual thing. In this later work, he will argue that an actual, individual perception participates simultaneously in a preindividual or impersonal field, just as in the 1967 Tournier essay where he claims that it participates in the field of the Other.

But something changes in the later work when the Other comes to be referred to as affect. At this point Deleuze's account becomes less Merleau-Ponty-esque. Affect is not quite as "benevolent" as the Other. For affect does not confirm the existence of a stable world—to guarantee, for example, that the back of a house meets up with its front in some consistent way, as Merleau-Ponty would say—nor does it protect the subject from "assaults from behind," as Deleuze puts it in the earlier essay. In that essay Merleau-Ponty's account of the relation between the gaze and the visible is invoked as a critique of the analysis given by Sartre in Being and Nothingness—it is as if Deleuze had attempted to take Merleau-Ponty's side, rather than Sartre's, as Lacan did (up to a point) in Seminar XI. However, the later Deleuze assumed a more "Sartrean" stance, insofar as he conceives affect as more disruptive, more antagonistic than "murmuring"; less a mantle surrounding perception than perception's inner division, its dislocation from itself.

So, Deleuze began at this point to associate affect, as did Lacan, with dislocation, but this does not yet settle the precise question we posed about this dislocation. According to the first alternative, which I described as non-psychoanalytic, the displacement refers to the way perception is distorted by a quantum of affect that wanders inappropriately into an otherwise objective field and burdens or blocks it with a subjective excess of feeling. In order to dismiss this option Brian Massumi offers a Deleuzian-inspired analysis of an experiment in which subjects were instructed to match a color swatch with some cherished object about which they were invited to reminisce. As Massumi notes, the subjects in the experiment frequently mismatched the fondly remembered object with a "too-blue" swatch. In the common misinterpretation, the excess of color would be viewed as a sure sign of the *affected* character of the choice. The choice of the excessive hue would indicate an excessive quantity of feeling, a surplus of personal feeling that would not have been elicited had the subject maintained a purely objective relation to the object. Affect is here misunderstood as a quantitative surplus, a value-added personal touch, "To me his eyes seem very blue." On this much at least Deleuze and Lacan agree, the excess of affect is qualitative rather than quantitative; it opens another order; for Deleuze, it is the virtual, for Lacan, the real. In psychoanalysis, affect does not familiarize, domesticate, or subjectivize—on the contrary, it estranges. It causes us to lose what Lacan once called "that belong-to-me-aspect so reminiscent of property." Objects, persons, even the self become alien to the subject. Rather than immediacy, affect bestows a distancing effect, not a homeliness but an unhomeliness.

Freud and Lacan both associate affect with movement, albeit in different ways. Massumi, following Deleuze, states that "affect inhabits passage," adding this metaphor: in the same way, "an excess of activity over each successive step" constitutes the "momentum of walking."[6] Just as walking would grind to a halt if there were no excess of movement over and above the simple addition of one step to another, so, too, would signification and thinking stop dead in its tracks if thought did not exceed the simple succession of signifiers or logical steps. Each step, signifier, or thought must not merely follow its antecedent but emerge from within it.

That Freud tried to theorize thought as movement is often lost on his readers, in part because he chose to describe this movement as a "discharge." To forestall this casualty, Lacan attempted to rescue Freud's misleading term from the biochemical context in which it was sunk, insisting boldly, "what affect discharges is not adrenalin but thought."[7] Affect is discharged, its oppressive threat diffused, by thought, which slips from the grasp of, or distances itself from, the affect that otherwise holds it back. If readers of Freud, were blinded by the word "discharge," readers of Lacan were blinded by the term "signifier." They were misled into believing he had neglected affect altogether. Counting only signifiers among the elements of his system, they saw no room for affect, never noticing that one of these, the one Freud called *Vorstellungrepräsentanz*, was unlike the rest. It does not fit in the signifying chain, for it turns backward toward upon itself.

ANXIETY: SISTER OF SHAME

As we know too well, thought does not always plunge ahead. It grinds to a halt, becomes inhibited, and ceases to move forward. In these moments, movement is reduced to a state of agitation, a kind of inexpedient running in place, held in the grip of affect, or what we commonly refer to as anxiety. To those who accused him of neglecting affect, Lacan always answered in the same way. He pointed to the fact that he devoted an entire seminar to anxiety, and this should have been enough to dispel the fears of his detractors regarding his lack of interest in the matter. It did not. For, Lacan argued, anxiety is the *only* affect. Guffaws from his audience, which began counting up a list of others on their fingers. What if Lacan is right? What if other affects are not so much distinct from anxiety as they are transformations of it? This would mean that if we wanted to come to some understanding of the nature of shame, we would be well advised to start by trying to understand anxiety.

Earlier I noted that psychoanalysis does not conceive affect as offering subjects immediate, personally experienced knowledge. The commonplace assertion, "I know what I feel," does not hold up under psychoanalytic scrutiny. Given this psychoanalytic skepticism on the matter, some might be taken aback by Lacan's insistence that anxiety carries with it a sense of certainty. It is not something with which we can truck. There is simply no give at this point; we are brought up short. Anxiety is a sign, pointing directly at . . . at what?

In *Anxiety: Seminar X*, Lacan adopts Freud's argument (borrowed from Schelling) according to which anxiety (expressed in the phenomenon of the uncanny) occurs when that which was repressed and should have remained hidden becomes visible. What should have remained hidden is not something, but the absence of a ground. It is thus not something, not an immovable, resistant object that thwarts the subject's endeavors, but an absence that occasions anxiety. In order to register this point, Lacan invents for it a name, "object a," to distinguish it from any and all empirical objects.

While it first appears in *Seminar X* to clarify the concept of anxiety, the object a, which Lacan touted as his major invention, is developed further in later seminars. In *Seminar XI*, for example, Lacan goes so far as to invent a modern myth, the myth of the lamella, to showcase it. There it appears as a kind of anarchic, runaway object let loose from any empirically conceived biological body that might have been thought to contain it. In *Seminar XVII* this mythical lamella, undergoes some biotechnological tinkering. The little organ is made over into a small gadget or gismo. The neologism employed to designate this genetically engineered device, this little nothing, is "lathouse." In Lacan's new ultra-modern myth, there is no heavenly sphere, naturally, for it has long ago been set to rest. All that remains of the world beyond the subject is the "alethosphere," which is a kind of high-tech heaven, a laicized or "disenchanted" space filled nonetheless with every technoscientific marvel imaginable: space probes and orbiters, telecommunications and telebanking systems, and so on. The subject is now a "terminal" subject, plugged into various circuitries, suited with wearable computers, and fitted with artificial, remotely monitored and controlled organs, implants.[8]

The myth is probably inspired by the section of *Civilization and Its Discontents*, where Freud speaks of modern man's capacity to remake himself as "a kind of prosthetic God," to replace every lost appendage or damaged organ with another, superior one endowed with fantastic powers.[9] In this alethosphere (*alethosphere* because this space and everything in it is built on the demonstrable truths, rigorous and mathematical, of modern science), the prosthetically enhanced, plugged-in subject does not need to flee reality to indulge his pleasure principle, for he can now remold reality in accordance with it. In other words, in the ultra-modern, advanced capitalist world, the pleasure principle and the reality principle are no longer in competition but have merged to form a kind of corporation. The image Freud paints is of a friendly takeover of the pleasure principle (or of jouissance, as Lacan would put it), for reality presents jouissance with a set of blueprints for the global cyber city of its dreams. Lacan stresses the underside of this merger. As the twentieth century wore on and the utopian view of science gave way to dystopian visions, while capitalism grew more muscular, it became more difficult to hold onto the idea that pleasure had the power to program reality. The reality (of the market) principle was clearly calling the shots, telling the pleasure principle in what to invest and what pleasures ought to be sacrificed to get the best returns on those investments.

One of the best depictions of the takeover of pleasure by reality is still to be found in Walter Benjamin's notion of aura. Benjamin writes as though aura was destroyed when we began by means of capitalist production to bring things closer to us, and yet he taught us enough to know that the aura did not exist before capitalism, that aura appeared for the first time with the emergence of capitalism, specifically as that which had been lost. This loss, however, had a rather odd effect since the eradication of the intervening existence between us and things created "the unique phenomenon of a distance" and a now more rigid, indestructible aura. How are we to understand this logic if not in the terms Freud gave us: an original loss, the difference between satisfaction anticipated and satisfaction obtained, which is recuperated by being embodied or imaginarized in objects with a certain sheen that we no longer simply want, but want more of? Prosthetic gods, we do not simply bring our fantasies closer to reality, more within reach; we experience their remodeling by the market into *mise-en-scènes* of the postponement of desire. The gleaming, globalized city erected in the alethosphere turns out to be ruled by, as in Fritz Lang's *Metropolis*, an occult, maimed wizard named Rot[z]wang. This figure represents the S_1, or master signifier, placed in the bottom-left corner of Lacan's university discourse, the master who is castrated and reduced to the level of superegoic urgings to "keep on yearning."

In the alethosphere, the merger of the principles of reality and pleasure is coextensive with a merger of subject and Other. Patched into a surface network of social circuitry, the subject "interfaces" with the Other. This interface is not to be confused, however, with what is in Lacanian terms referred to as "extimacy." The notion of interface (which pretends to antiquate the psychoanalytic conception of the subject) is only the most recent retooling of that phenomenological assumption against which Lacan repeatedly railed; namely that the whole of the subject's corporeal presence is engaged or chiasmically intertwined with the Other,[10] "directed in what is called [its] total intentionality."[11]

At a certain historical moment, that moment when the social configuration Lacan calls the "University Discourse" was first set in place, reality—including man—began to be conceived as fully manipulable. Man came to be viewed as a being without foundation, without roots, or as so intertwined with the Other as to be infinitely moldable. This is the heart of the conception of the cosmopolitical subject, nomadic, homeless man of the world. Capitalism drives and profits from this conception of the malleability of man, but we have not yet said enough to know how it does so, how it gets us to surrender ourselves to it or what it is we surrender. The first point that needs to be made is this: if the subject becomes conceivable as completely intertwined with the Other, this is because modern science comes to be conceived as universal, as having triumphed over and supplanted every other realm and every other form of truth. Man is totally taken up, then, without exception, into the Other of the scientific world.

Without exception? This is, of course, the critical issue and one Lacan will persistently mine. According to a long tradition that includes Freud himself, anxiety is distinguished from fear on the grounds that unlike fear, it has no object. We noted this earlier and promised to return to it. Here we are, approaching it from a slightly different angle. Anxiety is intransitive, as opposed to fear, which is transitive. Lacan does not go against this tradition, so much as give it its teeth. Anxiety, he asserts with full conviction, is "not without object." Why? What does he gain by this? The standard criterion "with or without object" offers a simple choice between two contradictory or mutually exclusive terms that pretend to exhaust the field of possibilities. Being or nothingness.

Freud seems to have understood that this boundary did not merely divide fear and anxiety; it also had the potential to divide the scientific and reason from the unscientific and irrational. And Freud did not want this. He did not want his science, psychoanalysis, to be construed as a study of irrational phenomena; the workings of the psyche, no matter how troubled, or at odds with reality, did not fall outside the pale of science. This may be why he kept trying to model anxiety on some form of actual threat, even at one point proposing a "realistic anxiety" after which signal anxiety might be patterned. The sentiment of anxiety is one of hard certainty, and he felt no impulse to question this, to characterize that feeling as a delusion: that is, to dismiss this certainty as unfounded, as having no basis in reason.

Lacan's formula, "not without object," is fashioned out of the same concern as Freud's. The first thing to observe is that the formula has a definable rhetorical structure, namely that of litotes or understatement. Through the rhetorical figure of litotes, one is able to affirm something by negating its contrary. I recount an actual example. A graduate student, having finished his exams, sits nervously on the steps outside the exam waiting for one of his professors to inform him of the results. Several pass by without saying a word to him. Finally, one professor takes pity on him and stops to tell him the truth: "I would be lying to you if I told you that you passed." Here is a more upbeat example: "I am not unhappy with the way things worked out." These examples affirm that the student has failed his exam and that I am happy about the way things worked out, even though they have not literally been said. Litotes demonstrates that there is a surfeit of signification over what is said. Not stated, but—once again—understated, in and by a negation.[12] Lacan, cleaving to Freud's own theory of anxiety and his wish to accord psychoanalysis the status pf a science grounded in the actual world, finds through this rhetorical ploy a way of saying that while anxiety does not, like fear, have an object in the actual world, neither is it something that is only "in one's head," divorced from reality. The point is, rather, that reality itself has what we might call a "backside" or an "esoteric" dimension, which is not actual, but its fount. I noted earlier that the historical proposition that everything, including man, is malleable implies that he is without foundation, without roots. This is at any rate the view of the scientific/capitalist world. Yet we have had occasion to observe that man is "not without foundation," "not without roots."[13] Something insists on disrupting the progress of deterritorialization, time and time again.

Now, to say that one is "not without roots" is different from saying that one has roots in some racial, ethnic, or national tradition, as those who engineered the turn to "identity politics" are wont to say. But by way of exploring this critical difference, I want to return to Lacan's myth of the lathouses, the non-objectified objects that appear from time to time in the alethosphere. Man, the prosthetic God of this alethosphere, is uprooted from every foundation, ungrounded, thus malleable, but from time to time, and without warning, he encounters one of these lathouses, which provokes his anxiety. The chiasmic intertwining of man and big Other, the absorption of the former in the latter, falters. Man is pulled away, disengaged from his foundationless existence in the Other; he grows deaf or indifferent to the lure of progress. This disruption is not followed, however, by a retreat from the publicity of "pleasure-reality incorporated" into privacy, simply. For what we encounter in this moment is not the privacy of a self without others but the esoteric dimension which Lacan named "extimacy."

Within the seemingly well-oiled, smooth-functioning alethosphere, the mythical object a assumes the character of a malfunctioning, toy-like, mechanical thing that interrupts our linear path forward. An example of such an object is found in Charlie Chaplin's *City Lights*. In this film the little tramp—who merely wants to blend seamlessly into modern city life, to give himself over to it—is thwarted by the importunate sound of a whistle he previously swallowed and which keeps calling him back to himself. In an early text, *On Escape*, Emmanuel Levinas draws our attention to this scene, proposing that the inadvertently ingested whistle "triggers the scandal of the brutal presence of [Charlie's] being; it works like a recording device, which betrays the discrete manifestations of a presence that Charlie's legendary tramp costume barely dissimulates."[14] This whistle is the equivalent of Lacan's object a in the technological field of modernity. If Charlie cannot be totally absorbed into the world of his surroundings, this is because he is, in Levinas's phrase, "riveted to his being" and thereby uprooted from the uprootedness of modern life.

As Levinas puts it, in the capitalist world, where man feels himself "liable to be mobilized—in every sense of the term," there insists nevertheless a palpable counterweight, a disturbance that lends our "temporal existence . . . the inexpressible flavor of the absolute . . . [and gives rise to] an acute feeling of being held fast" or being unable to desert or escape being.[15] In other words, Levinas associates the feeling of being riveted, of the inescapabilty of being, to life under capitalism, as though the counterweight preventing us from becoming totally absorbed within the universal world of capitalism also acted in some paradoxical way as the driving force of our full participation in the latter. I will examine this proposition in a moment, after saying a bit more about the central concept of this text.

The phrase "riveted to being" is revealing. Rather than simply and immediately being our being, coinciding with it, we are ineluctably fastened, stuck to it—or it to us. (Levinas describes this being as "adhering to" us; just as in his own myth of the lamella, Lacan describes the object as "sticking to us.") The sentiment of being riveted to being is one of being in the forced company of our own being, whose "brutality" consists in the fact that it is impossible either to assume it as our own or to disown it. It is what we are in our most intimate core, that which singularizes us, that which cannot be vulgarized and yet also that which we cannot recognize. We do not comprehend or choose it, but neither can we get rid of it; since it is not of the order of objects—but rather of the "not without object"—it cannot be objectified, placed before us and confronted.

The sentiment of being doubled by an inhuman, impersonal partner, who is at the same time me and disquietingly alien, is, of course, the psychoanalytic equivalent of Levinas's sentiment of being riveted. In each case we feel ourselves "enclosed in a tight circle that smothers";[16] in each case everything transpires as if we bore engraved on our backs or scalps a defining mark we could not read nor even see.

RIVETED TO JOUISSANCE: LEVINAS WITH SARTRE AND LACAN

In his commentary on Sartre's voyeur, Lacan makes the strong point that the gaze that "assaults [the voyeur] from behind" (to recall Deleuze's dismissal of this idea, as mentioned above), or that looks at him from a place he cannot see, is the voyeur's own, not another's. This brings Lacan's reading close to that of Levinas: the gaze that looks at me is that of my own being to which I am riveted. But Lacan goes further in his revision of Sartre, and this revision has no precedent in Levinas. Sartre is adamant that the gaze must always be "manifested in connection with . . . a sensible form."[17] If he insists that the accidental sound of rustling, or some other sensible disturbance, is necessary to evoke the gaze, it is because he—like Freud before him—does not want anxiety to be confused with an imaginary phenomenon. Lacan would concur that a sensible experience is required for the feeling of anxiety to arise but is reluctant to attribute this experience to accident in the same way. Is it an accident, he asks, that the gaze manifests itself at the very moment the voyeur peers through the keyhole?

Lacan's suspicion has a traceable provenance. For an almost identical suspicion is voiced by Freud in one of his case studies. When a young woman patient of his makes the delusional accusation that her lover has planted a hidden witness somewhere to photograph their lovemaking and thus disgrace her and force her to resign her position, he questions her closely and discovers that the onset of the delusion coincided with a specific accident. Lying half-dressed beside her lover, the woman suddenly "heard a noise like a click or a beat." It was this click that the woman later interpreted as that of the camera photographing her and her lover. From the beginning, Freud does not doubt that there was a click or beat, but he protests that he cannot believe that had the "unlucky noise" (which the woman's lover identifies as coming from a clock on the far side of the room) not occurred, the delusion would not have formed. That is, he remains suspicious of the sound's purported origin. After further speculation, however, he draws up the courage to go "further in the analysis of this ostensibly real 'accident.'" He now risks the following hypothesis: "I do not believe that the clock ever ticked or that there was a noise to be heard at all. The woman's situation [that is, her lying half-naked on the sofa] justified a sensation of a knock or beat in her clitoris. And it was this that she subsequently projected as a perception of an external object."[18]

Lacan follows Freud in rejecting an explanation that would link the onset of the delusion of being photographed—in the one case, or the feeling of being gazed at, in the other—to an accidental external sound. Yet, like Sartre, Freud and Lacan both insist on locating a sensible cause for the uncanny sense of being observed by another. The sensible disturbance for Freud and Lacan, however, is the subject's own surplus jouissance, the libidinal knock or beat of the signifier on some part of the body. We summarize the difference that Lacan introduces this way: while Sartre likens our sudden awareness of the presence of the gaze to the opening of a kind of drain hole in our world,[19] James Joyce, in "The Portrait of an Artist," identifies this drain hole with the obscene sound it makes: "Suck!" Joyce thus approaches more closely Lacan's view. And in relation to Levinas's argument, we can now make the point that the being to which we are riveted or stuck is, specifically, jouissance. It is our own jouissance that cannot be escaped, gotten get rid of, even though we never manage to claim it as our own. It is jouissance that not only singularizes us but also doubles and suffocates us. If in the crawl space of our solitude we bump up against an otherness that refuses to leave us alone with ourselves, it is because of jouissance we can say—as Sartre says of the Other's gaze—that it "delivers me to myself as unrevealed."[20] Jouissance makes me who I am while preventing me from knowing who I am.

Here is what we have thus far: Freud's half-clothed patient reclined in an erotic attitude beside her lover, Chaplin's little tramp in his legendary costume, and a voyeur peering through a keyhole. All three, concentrated in some activity, are caught off guard by a disturbance (audible in all three cases) that thwarts their willed concentration, seems to come from outside, from some other place, but actually comes from the very core of their being. In each case the disturbance functions as a counterweight, an unexpected resistance that causes a swerve in the main flow of activity. Freud speaks in his essay

"On Narcissism" of an easy exchange between object libido and narcissistic libido, as though one could be converted into the other without loss. But at a certain point, he insists that there is a residue of nonconvertible narcissistic libido that does not enter into the exchange, the back-and-forth flow. At the point of disturbance, the moment of anxiety, it is this nonconvertible narcissistic libido—this jouissance that cannot be vulgarized or distributed—that we encounter.

Outside the experience of anxiety, this inalienable remainder of narcissistic libido is never directly experienced but remains hidden behind its object-libido "emanations," or behind our absorption in the activities and objects on which we are concentrated. One might have imagined that the direct experience of this surplus, this abrupt uprooting from our uprooted absorption in everyday life, might have brought with it a sense of mastery rather than this sense of inescapable anxiety. But instead of breathing freely, we begin to asphyxiate in the air of an overly proximate otherness. This sense of being overburdened and doubled by jouissance, of an embarrassed enchainment to a body too much, or (once again) of being "enclosed in a tight circle that smothers," is the automatic result of the encounter with our own jouissance. But this is not the end of it.

ANXIETY IS NOT SIMPLE

Up until now, I have simplified matters somewhat, pretended it was anxiety simply that was in question all this while. In fact, anxiety has almost imperceptibly shaded over into moral anxiety and shame anxiety, or guilt and shame, in the various discussions we have been following. Let us take the last first. In truth, Sartre did not define the encounter with the gaze as an experience only of "pure monition" or anxiety but also as one of shame. And Levinas did not define the experience of being riveted to being only as nausea or anxiety—"this fact of being riveted constitutes all the anxiety or nausea"[21]— but also as shame: "what appears in shame is thus precisely the fact of being riveted to oneself."[22] The conflation of anxiety and shame is almost total, as when Levinas says, for example, "the phenomenon of shame, of a self confronted with itself . . . is the same as nausea."[23]

The only gap Levinas opens between nausea and shame is a brief moment of hope in which we imagine we might be able through pleasure to escape. Shame simply underscores the disappointment of this hope; shame is, in his view, the affective recognition that escape is impossible, that we remain tethered, without any hope of escape, to something we cannot assume as our own. It is precisely at this point that Lacan parts ways with Levinas, although we must note that in his later work Levinas does find a kind of escape from the chokehold of the il y a that is not unlike the one we find in the final session of *Seminar XVII*, where Lacan advocates what he calls his *hontology*. There he attempts to disable anxiety's "precomprehension" of the subject in order to define shame as the subject's ethical relation toward being, his own and the other's.

Lacan described anxiety as an "edge" phenomenon in the seminar he devoted to the concept, while Levinas called it a "limit situation."[24] At this edge or limit the subject is bound to an Other, whose terrifying grip retards the subject's entry into the world. Anxiety restrains the hand of the writer, preventing her from composing her thoughts; it stays the sword of Hamlet, preventing him from avenging his father. It stuns and immobilizes the protagonists of that postwar cinema that Deleuze designates the "cinema of the voyeur," converting the would-be action heroes into passive witnesses of an incomprehensible event. The anxiety of the hysterics was evident in their paralyses. Freud diagnosed their cause as reminiscences, not memories of some event that happened to them in the past, but some unlived past.

Levinas reminds us that in that anxious moment when we encounter our being, we encounter ourselves, in Heidegger's language, as *gewesend*—that is to say, as being the one who thus has been. In this account of anxiety we are doubled by an alien and yet intimate other. The "origin of [our] own person," where who I am in the present converges with who I was in the past. The unassimilability of the experience is due to the fact that this past is not a modality of the present, of actual or realized events that once happened, but rather of "that portion of the powers of the past that has been thrust aside at each crossroads where [actual events] made [their] choices."[25] In other words, the edge on which anxiety touches is that of the unrealized, the "thrust aside," powers of the past that might have caused my personal history or history *tout court* to be otherwise. This past is a burden that can never be laid to rest, even though the subject who must support the weight is at risk of annihilation. It is this burden that makes anxiety "the supreme instant from which we can only depart."[26]

The experience of anxiety is, in Levinas's account, one of being "riveted" to an "immemorial past," which was never experienced. It insists that we are born into an identity that we never chose, but which chooses us. In the first annotation to *On Escape*, Jacques Rolland notes a striking similarity between the language of this book and "The Religious Inspiration of the Alliance," an essay Levinas wrote in the same year, 1935. In the essay, Levinas wrote: "Hitlerism is the greatest trial . . . through which Judaism has had to pass. . . . The pathetic destiny of being Jewish becomes a fatality. One can no longer flee it. The Jew is ineluctably riveted to his Judaism." He also wrote that a youth "definitely attached to the sufferings and joys of the nations to which it belongs . . . discovers in the reality of Hitlerism all the gravity of being Jewish"; "In the barbarous and primitive symbol of race . . . Hitler recalled that one does not desert Judaism."[27]

The phrasing of the sentences is indeed similar to *On Escape*'s description of the manner in which, as Rolland translates it, "the existent is compelled to its existence," or in the manner in which one is riveted to one's being. This hints at a problem in the argument Levinas offers in *On Escape*, which does not fully succeed in theorizing an escape. Had it succeeded, Rolland might not have been able to collapse a racist, anti-Semitic view of the situation of Jews with that of the views of the Jews themselves. In the experience of anxiety, one has a sense not only of being chained to a jouissance that precedes and overwhelms us, but is also opaque. The opacity of this enjoyment makes it inassimilable. In the eye of the anti-Semite, the situation is different: the Jew is viewed simply as riveted to his jouissance; if that jouissance is opaque, it is only to non-Jews. The anti-Semite reduces the Jew to a single pole of the oscillation between the certainty and the indecisiveness that constitutes anxiety, the painful, irresolvable tension occasioned by the certainty that one is called and the impossibility of knowing what one is called to. In the anti-Semite view, being a Jew is an uncomplicated compulsion; a Jew knows what it is to be a Jew and cannot be otherwise. He lives his life serving the irremissible fate that has chosen him. In brief, a Jew is a Jew, not only irremediably but immediately. This according to the anti-Semite.

MORAL ANXIETY

In *Seminar XVII*, Lacan claims that anxiety is the "central affect" around which every social arrangement is organized; every social link is approachable as a response to, or transformation of, anxiety, the affect that, as we noted, functions as counterweight to existing relations. The intolerable inhibition, the debilitating helplessness induced by the encounter with one's own jouissance, must admit of some escape for society to be possible. Opposing the "analytic to the university discourse," Lacan opposes the response or exit strategy of the latter in terms that bear ominously on questions of race, ethnicity, and national identity, at which Levinas's text hinted. The What kind of response does the university discourse, the discourse Lacan linked to the rise of capitalism, offer? A scene from psychoanalytic literature gives us some insight. The curious behavior manifested in this well-known scene by Freud's patient, the Rat Man, occurs at a time when he "was working for an examination and toying with his favourite phantasy that his father was still alive and might at any moment reappear. [The Rat Man] used to arrange that his working hours should be as late as possible in the night. Between twelve and one o'clock at night he would interrupt his work, and open the front door of the flat as though his father were standing outside it; then, coming into the hall, he would take out his penis and look at it in the looking-glass."[28]

What was the Rat Man trying to glimpse in the mirror? That bit of surplus or narcissistic jouissance-being to which he felt himself, in his bouts of anxiety, riveted. If he could now assure himself that this jouissance-being were here now in front of him, reflected in this mirror, then it would no longer be behind, an unreadable hieroglyph occupying his blind spot. He would be able to grasp it, possess it; it would cease to possess him. That is, he would no longer have to regard it as an inappropriable, foreign thing. Between the Rat Man and his anxiety, Freud explained, a principle of renunciation was interposed. It took shape around the patient's father and was experienced as the internal voice of conscience. This voice uttered prohibitions in the form of demands for implementable cost-benefit assessments: "What sacrifice am I prepared to make in order to . . . ?"[29] The impossibility of escaping jouissance was transformed into a prohibition that sounded more like an investment strategy, while what Freud frequently referred to as "moral anxiety" substituted itself for originary anxiety. The danger from which the Rat Man sought to flee was no longer his inappropriable enjoyment, which had produced his originary anxiety, but a hostile and obscene superego. One flees, or attempts to flee anxiety, by obeying the superegoic demand to enjoy in a productive way, or by banking one's "jouissance credits" in anticipation of some "cash out" to come in a new, improved high-tech future. You see what happened: the rat of a foreign, surplus jouissance was exchanged for the florins of a countable, accumulative surplus-value; a question of being converted into a problem of having or, more precisely, of having more.

In the Rat Man's mirror, jouissance becomes a spectacle, something to be seen not only by the Rat Many but by others as well, a kind of merit badge that displayed his value. One cannot help being reminded of "The Impromptu at Vincennes," which took place during the period *Seminar XVII* was being delivered, where Lacan warned a group of students that they were playing the role of helots, serfs of the state, by parading their zealous enjoyment for all—especially the state—to see and enjoy.[30] There is compulsion in this display of enjoyment-as-identity but not the same one experienced in the state of originary anxiety. I noted earlier that in his book, *On Escape*, Levinas suggested that an intimate connection exists between the sentiment of being riveted and capitalism. We can now see more clearly why this connection is made and how, finally, it misses the mark. The problem is that Levinas fails to properly distinguish moral anxiety, anxiety, and guilt. For capitalism is founded on a *transformation* of anxiety—the originary feeling of being riveted—into guilt. This transformation is undertaken in an attempt to escape the unbearable condition of anxiety, but in doing so, it indentures the subject to a cruel, insatiable superego and to a past that is no longer immemorial but, on the contrary, compulsively memorialized.

We were pursuing hints in Levinas's text that the sentiment of being riveted was connected to the question of race and all those forms of identity that are ours by virtue of birth rather than by choice. This connection is suggested in relation to a specific characterization of anxiety or being riveted as the feeling of being burdened by a "nonremittable obligation." From this sentiment to that of being weighed down by an inexpiable debt is a short step, but to take it without being aware of the distance traversed leads to the inappropriate conflation of originary and moral anxiety. That Levinas makes the error of too quickly conflating the experience of being riveted with those of culpability and debt proves nothing so much as the effectiveness of the superego, of guilt, in the modern world. Why should our admittedly infrangible attachment to that which precedes us and drenches our enjoyment in its indelible colors be characterized as a guilty one? There is no good reason for it, but if the equation of the past with guilt and debt is endemic to modern thought, it is because the superegoic evasion or recoil from anxiety retains so much influence over thought, up to and including Freud's. Critiquing the familiar Freudian myth of the murder of the primordial father by sons who try to atone for their crime by reinstating him in an idealized form (as all-loving and loved by all), Lacan disentangles guilt from originary anxiety and prepares the way for an alternative escape from the latter.

What is the point of Lacan's critique? This myth of the father underwrites the reign of the superego. The superego is nothing other than that jouissance—which grabs the subject by the throat and incites anxiety—in altered form. This transformation might be describes as the conversion of a force (jouissance as object-cause of desire) into a power (the superego).

What is the difference? Steven Connor puts it this way: "For something we want to call a power, there is a notion of an agent that precedes and deploys the power, a who looming through the what. A force, by contrast, exerts itself, and exerts itself on itself." The difference between force and power lies, in other words, primarily in this distinction between an exertion, which does not imply a coercion of one thing by another, and exercise that does. "A power is exercised as one exercises a right, or one's right arm, a prerogative or property, something apart from ourselves," Connor goes on to say.[31] Power seizes possession of that on which it is exercised; it realizes itself in its objects by appropriating them, stamping them with its identifying mark. Creation, on the other hand, is a force, not—properly speaking—a power.

The painful tension experienced in anxiety gives way in moral anxiety, or guilt, to a different sort of split, one more easily imagined by *dramatis personae* engaged in a power struggle. In fact, the second topology of Freud, in which he thinks of the psyche as a struggle among agents—ego, id, superego—is to a large extent the result of his increasing fascination with the superego. The feeling of guilt is the sentiment that a power—the superego—internal to the subject and acting on him or her is exercised by an external agent. Freud thought of this external agent as parental interdictions that had been internalized by the subject; in *Seminar XVII*, Lacan instead attributes the role of agent to accumulated knowledge. This improves on Freud by locating the authority of parental interdictions in a wider social source.

The Lacanian reidentification of the agent of power also permits us to see more clearly what happens in the transformation of anxiety into guilt. Freud described the superego's power as that of prohibition, specifically the prohibition of jouissance. But Lacan sees this power not as a prohibition of jouissance as such but rather as a prohibition—or better, a dissolution or blockage—of the disturbing enigma, the enigma of being, which jouissance poses. The unmistakable and baffling certainty that forms the ground of anxiety vanishes in guilt in favor of a pursuit of knowledge. Let me reiterate this point: certainty is transformed into not only knowledge but also the relentless pursuit of ever more knowledge. The "inexpressible flavor of the absolute" that Levinas discerned as a feature of temporal existence under capitalism finds its explanation here. For the "acute feeling of being held fast" no longer comes—as Levinas indicates in his confusion—from being riveted to a jouissance we cannot assume because it remains opaque to us but rather from being riveted to the pursuit of ideals and goals we cannot obtain because they withdraw from us.

To continue translating into the terms of the present discussion: guilt takes flight from the enigma of our jouissance-being, not from jouissance as such. The guilt-laden, anxiety-relieved subject still experiences jouissance, but this jouissance is characterized by Lacan in *Seminar XVII* as a "sham," as "counterfeit."[32] The fraudulent nature of this jouissance has everything to do with the fact that it gives one a false sense that the core of one's being is something knowable, possessable as an identity, a property, a surplus-value attaching to one's person. Sham jouissance intoxicates one with the sense that all our inherited, unchosen identities—racial, national, ethnic—root us in an actual past that may be lost but is not [for all] that inaccessible insofar as we can have knowledge about it and about how to restore it in an ideal future. What anxiety exposes as ungraspable or unclaimable jouissance is that which the guilty shamelessly grasp for in the obsequious respect they pay to a past sacralized as their future. The feverish pursuit of this future—conceived both as their due and as a repayment of their (unpayable) debt to the past—is a poor substitute the guilty accept in the place of real jouissance.

Let us allow ourselves a little surprise, however, at finding that the universalizing tendency of the university discourse does not end up forsaking these inherited identities or differences but welcoming them with open arms, those of the idealized father. At the moment the university students stepped forward on the political stage as presumptive actors, Lacan responded by agreeing with them that the university had, indeed, ill-prepared them for their role. It had seduced them into settling for the inglorious role of serfs of the superego, compelled to add mortar to the thickening barricade against anxiety, against the enigma it poses. With reference to their feeling of fraternity with the workers, he warned that we are always alone together and that the students ought to mind the gathering storm clouds of segregation already visible in the alethosphere.

The mounting threat of segregation was a major concern of Lacan during this period. In 1967 he wrote, "Our future as common markets will find its equilibrium in a harsher extension of the processes of segregation." And in 1968, he repeated the warning, "We think that universalism . . . homogenizes the relations among men. On the contrary, I believe that what characterizes our time . . . is a ramified and reinforced segregation that produces intersections at all levels and that only multiplies barriers."[33] He reiterated his concern about the rise of racism in his television interview, which aired in 1973. Lacan's point was not that segregation would reemerge in the form of a return of the repressed but that it was being positively fomented by the universalism of the university and the occult power of the superego. Since 1970, segregationism has indeed returned in the form Lacan predicted, curiously partnered, rather than at odds with universalism and with the universities that became home to "identity politics." One of the most remarkable instantiations of this association in recent years has been, as Jacques Rancière was the first to point out, the extension of humanitarian aid to the very ethnic enemies with whom we are simultaneously at war.[34]

Here the logic of the psychic transformation we have tried to describe plays itself out on the big screen of world events. We shore up our increasingly fractious identities, exercise our rights in the name of identities we believe we possess, while locating our underlying "humanity" in our basic impotence in need of aid, our own lack of force.

SHAME ANXIETY

It is only against this background that Lacan's call to shame makes any sense. His recommendation does not call for a renewed prudishness but, on the contrary, for a relinquishing of our sham jouissance in favor of the real thing. The real thing—jouissance—cannot be "dutified," controlled, regimented; rather, it catches us by surprise, like a sudden, uncontrollable blush on the cheek. It is not possible here, in this brief conclusion, to do justice to the concept of shame (though I will do so in a later chapter). I do not want, however, to end quite so abruptly as Lacan ends his seminar and so will say a few more words—only.

Alain Badiou has identified one of the dominant traits of the last century as its "passion for the real," its frenzied desire to remove every barrier that frustrates our contact with the real. If this has a familiar ring, it is because a similar diagnosis was proffered by Nietzsche, who complained that our age was one in which we sought to "see through everything." Nietzsche further characterized this passion as a lack of reverence or discretion, a tactless desire "to touch, lick, and finger everything."[35] The passion for the real treats every surface as an exterior to be penetrated, a barrier to be transgressed, or a veil to be removed. The violence of this passion insists in each penetration, in each transgression, and in removal, and is exacerbated by the fact that each arrives on the other side only to find that the real has fled behind another barrier.

It is hard not to recognize in this passion the logic subtending the university discourse as Lacan presents it in *Seminar XVII*. Nor is it difficult to see, in this context, that the antidote of shame proposed by Lacan follows on points made by Nietzsche and Freud. Shame is, as Freud put it, a "mental dam" against the "aggressive instinct" or the destructive passion for the real.[36] Lacan's neologism, his *hontology*, its suturing of shame and being, acknowledges not a flight from being, but a flight into a being that shelters us from the ravages of anxiety.

6

THE CENSORSHIP OF INTERIORITY

Iranian films are an exotic experience for audiences accustomed to Hollywood dominated cinema. Not just for obvious reasons but because what is obvious—the foreign locations, customs, and people, everything we actually see on screen—is produced by a different distribution of the visible and the invisible and an alien logic of the look.

One of the most spectacular heralds of Iran's 1978–1979 Islamic Revolution was the torching of spectacle. Movie theaters—in one horrific case, with the audience still in it—were set on fire and incinerated, presumably by fundamentalists. Fittingly, in this respect, Khomeini spoke, in his first public appearance as Iran's new leader, not only of his intent to restore the authority of the mullahs and to purge the country of all foreign influences, Eastern as well as Western; he also broached the question of cinema directly. As might be expected, he vehemently denounced the cinema of that "vile traitor," the ousted Shah, as "a center of vice," but he refrained from banning cinema outright as a wicked modern invention.[1] For Khomeini immediately recognized the value of cinema, the possibilities for mobilizing it in the service of his grand scheme to reeducate the people in the ways of Islam.

Postrevolutionary Iran witnessed, then, not the tabooing but the flourishing of a heavily subsidized and officially promoted cinema, though one strictly regulated by the Ministry of Culture and Islamic Guidance, which explicitly forbade the smallest signs of foreign influence—such as the wearing of ties, the smoking of cigarettes, and the drinking of alcohol—and, more importantly, more globally, any infraction of the Islamic system of hijab. In its strictest sense, hijab is a veil or cloth covering used to obscure women from the sight of men to whom they are not related. In the widest sense, it is the entire "system of modesty" that demands the concealment of even the contours of a woman's body, which is always in danger of being revealed through her gestures and movements. Indeed, hijab seems to be motivated by the belief that there is something about women that can never be covered up enough, that does not stop threatening to bare itself even beneath the bedraped figure of the woman. Thus, the precautionary task of veiling is buttressed by architectural design and rigid social protocols that further protect women from exposing themselves and men from being exposed to the sight of them.

The impact of hijab regulations on cinema was massive,[2] as it was not just the figure and movement of the woman that required veiling but also the look directed at her. Strictures against the eros of the unrelated meant that not even religiously sanctioned forms of erotic engagement between men and women could be represented, since filming made women vulnerable to the extradiegetic look of the director, crew, and, of course, the audience. Thus, the look of desire around which Hollywood dominated cinema is plotted had to be forsaken, along with the well-established system of relaying that look through an alternating pattern of shots and countershots and the insertion of close-ups that could only have been shot through eyes that refused to remain downcast.

Besides restricting narrative situations and tabooing the most common style of editing, the system of modesty also obliged any filmmaker committed to maintaining a modicum of realism to shoot outdoors. Although, in real life, Iranian women need not and do not wear headscarves at home, in cinematic interiors they were forced to don them because of the presence, once again, of the extradiegetic look that exposed them to the view of unrelated men. But incongruous images of headscarves in scenes of family intimacy were more than unrealistic; they were oftentimes risible, and filmmakers thus tended to avoid domestic scenes as much as possible.

Ultimately, then, it was interiority that was the most significant cinematic casualty of hijab. Iranian cinema came to be composed only of exterior shots, whether in the form of actual spatial exteriors—the improbable abundance of rural landscapes and city streets, hallmarks of Iranian cinema—or in the form of virtual exteriors—interior domestic spaces in which women remained veiled and secluded from desire, outside the reach of any affectionate or passionate caress. The challenge facing all Iranian filmmakers, then, was to make credible and compelling films under this condition, namely the censorship of interiority, the tabooing of intimacy.

Revelations of American torture of Iraqi prisoners at Abu Ghraib brought to light an abusive reaction to the Islamic system of modesty. It turns out that *The Arab Mind*, a book first published in 1973 and reprinted only a few months before the US invasion of Iraq, got into the hands of pro-war Washington conservatives and became, in the words of one academic, "the Bible of the neocons on Arab behavior." Of special interest to these conservatives was a chapter on "Arabs and Sex," which argued that "the segregation of the sexes, the veiling of women . . . and all the other minute rules that govern and restrict contact between men and women, have the effect of making sex a prime mental preoccupation in the Arab world."[3] It was this sort of speculation that was responsible for planting in the heads of calculating conservatives the idea that shame would be the most effective device for breaking down Iraqi prisoners psychologically. According to a report in the New Yorker, two themes emerged as "talking points" in the discussions of the strategists: (1) "Arabs only understand force," and (2) "the biggest weakness of Arabs is shame and humiliation." In brief, shaming was chosen as the method of torture precisely because the torturers believed that Arab culture made the prisoners particularly vulnerable to it.

This belief was nourished on the banquet of that crude and—one would have thought—thoroughly discredited sociological division of the world into "guilt cultures" and "shame cultures." The distinction classifies guilt as an affect characteristic of advanced cultures, whose members have graduated to the stage where they possess an internal principle of morality, and shame as a "primitive" affect characteristic of cultures forced to rely, for want of such a principle, on the approving or disapproving gaze of other people to monitor morality. I will focalize my criticisms by offering my own curt and contrary thesis: the effects of shame and guilt are improperly used to define kinds of cultures; rather, what they define are different relations to one's culture. I use culture here to refer to the form of life we inherit at birth (not our biological birth but our birth into language), all those things—family, race, ethnicity, sex—we do not choose but that choose us, the entire past that precedes us and marks our belatedness. The manner in which we assume this inheritance, and the way we understand what it means to keep faith with it, are, I will argue, what distinguish shame from guilt.

Those who distance themselves from the dubious correlation of affects with stages of cultural and moral development rightly note that shame is marked by a kind of group sentiment, a feeling of solidarity with others.[4] This social sentiment is described as a feeling of shame for, or on behalf of, something other than oneself. One must proceed slowly here so as not to give shame an actual object. Strictly speaking, the syntagm "shame for" is a solecism; one feels shame neither for oneself nor for others. Shame is intransitive; it has no object in the ordinary sense. To experience it is to experience oneself as a subject, not as a degraded or despised object. I am not ashamed of myself; I am the shame I feel. Giorgio Agamben makes this point clearly when he designates shame as the "proper emotive tonality of subjectivity" and as "the fundamental sentiment of being a subject."[5] In shame, one encounters one's self outside the self, not integrated into but engaged with society.

Let us put this inquiry aside for a moment to return to the Islamic system of modesty, paying attention particularly to the films of Abbas Kiarostami, one of the most important and best-known directors to make films within this system. What gives the neoconservative association of shame and hijab its legs, of course, is the fact that both involve veiling. In the modesty system, as with shame, a curtain is always drawn, looks averted, heads bowed. On first approach, it would seem that no director was more in tune with the hijab system than Kiarostami, for his is a cinema of respectful reserve and restraint. This reserve is expressed most emblematically in his preference for what can be described as "discreet" long shots. Especially in moments of dramatic intimacy—a skittish suitor's approach to the girl he loves, the meeting between a man who impersonates another and the man he impersonates—Kiarostami's camera tends to hold back, to separate itself from the action by inserting a distance between itself and the scene and refusing to venture forward into the private space of the characters. So marked is the tactfulness of his camera that Kiarostami sometimes seems a reluctant filmmaker.

In light of this description of his overall film strategy, one sequence from The Wind Will Carry Us (1999) stands out as an aberration. The film's protagonist, Behzad, a documentary filmmaker, has traveled to the Kurdish village of Siah Darreh with his crew to film the ceremony of scarification still practiced by mourning villagers after someone from the village dies. In the sequence in question, Behzad—biding his time as he awaits the imminent death of Mrs. Malek, the village's oldest inhabitant—amuses himself by attempting to purchase some fresh milk from Zeynab, a young village girl and the fiancée of a gravedigger he has befriended.

Hamid Dabashi, author of a book on Iranian cinema and normally a great admirer of Kiarostami, excoriates the director for the utter shamelessness of this sequence in which, in Dabashi's view, an Iranian woman's privacy and dignity are raped by a boorish Iranian man, whose crime is all the more offensive for being paraded before the eyes of the world.[6] This is what Dabashi sees: Behzad descending into a hidden, underground space, penetrating the darkness that protects a shy, unsophisticated village girl from violation, and aggressively trying to expose her, despite her obvious resistance, to the light of his lamp, his incautious look, his lies, and his attempted sexual seduction.

ANXIETY AND THE "INEXPRESSIBLE FLAVOR OF THE ABSOLUTE"

The disdain for Behzad exhibited by Dabashi is heavily informed by his assessment of the protagonist as a mere Tehrani interloper adrift in rural Iran. This reading of Behzad's puzzled and sometimes combative disorientation—a disorientation he shares with many of Kiarostami's protagonists, screen doubles of the director—is a common one: geographically and culturally displaced, the modern urban sophisticate finds himself at a loss amid rural peoples and traditions. One is obliged to note, however, that it is as much the peri-urban character of these rural areas as their pristine primitiveness, notably in decline, which catches Kiarostami's eye. Cell phone reception may not always be good in the villages, but new telecommunications systems are already being installed, and the sight of random television antennae and satellite dishes atop thatched roofs assure us that no one in this part of the world need miss a simulcast soccer game. Regarding the traditional ceremony of scarification, for example, we learn in the film that it has been retrofitted, turned some time ago into a means of advancing oneself on the professional and financial ladder. Whenever a relative of one of the bosses dies, the workers compete for the distinction of being the most loyal mourner, exhibiting their self-scarred faces and bodies in hopes of impressing their bosses and being rewarded with a raise or promotion. Incipient capitalism is here in bed with traditional culture, exploiting it while eliminating it.

Without wanting to exonerate Behzad's rude behavior, I suggest that we abbreviate the distance that separates him from the villagers and look further for a more accurate explanation of his disorientation, one that goes deeper than the narrative alibi implies. Like other Kiarostami protagonists, Behzad behaves less like a rootless or deterritorialized modern man than like one who has been uprooted from his modern uprootedness to experience himself as *riveted* to a culture, a land, an ethnicity that remains inscrutable and that he tries to understand, without much success, by engaging in a quasi-ethnographic exploration of them. That modernity melted everything solid into air is an exaggerated claim, but it was expected that it would at least soften all that had once been solid to the consistency of clay, to render everything, including the subject, infinitely pliable.

Contrary to expectations, however, supposedly malleable modern man found himself stuck to something; something tore him away from the free-flowing current of modern life. It is as if a drain hole were inexplicably opened in the modern world, lending our fleeting "temporal existence . . . the inexpressible flavor of the absolute" and giving rise to "an acute feeling of being held fast."[7] That this riveting or reterritorialization is a confounding fact of modern life, and no mere theoretical abstraction, is evidenced most emphatically in all the stubborn outbreaks of national, ethnic, racial, and religious loyalties at a moment when such loyalties were expected to be dissolved by the deterritorializing thrust of global capitalism.

We know that modernity was founded on a definitive break with the authority of our ancestors, who were no longer conceived as the ground for our actions or beliefs. Yet the undermining of their authority confronted us with another difficulty; it is as if in rendering our ancestors fallible we had transformed the past from the repository of their already accomplished deeds and discovered truths into a kind of holding cell of all that was unactualized and unthought. Suddenly, it was the *desire* of our ancestors and thus the virtual past, the past that had never come to pass or had not yet been completed, that weighed disturbingly on us.

The theorization of this unfinished past was focused in the West around the concept of anxiety.[8] If it seemed necessary to come to terms theoretically with anxiety—as it did to Kierkegaard, Freud, and Heidegger, among others—this is because this affect bore witness to an altered relation to a past now conceived as incompletely actualized. The assumption that modern man would become pliable (to market forces or even to the force of his own will) rested on the belief that the break with the authoritative past placed a zero in the denominator of our foundations, rooted us in, or attached us to—precisely nothing. But anxiety, the affect that arises in moments when radical breaks in the continuity of existence occur, belies this assumption; rather, subjects find themselves to be "not without roots," which is significantly different from feeling rooted in the past, to a race or ethnicity that is transparent to us. For what is affirmed in the experience of being riveted is nothing that can be objectified or personalized as one's own.[9] On the contrary, it is the experience of being attached to a "prehistoric Other that it is impossible to forget," even if—in being without attributes—it offers us nothing to remember.[10]

It has been observed that anxiety often overtakes revolutionaries immediately after revolutions and seems not to free but to paralyze the hand that would draft a new constitution. What accounts for this curious phenomenon? While many psychoanalysts were insisting that anxiety was an affective response to loss or abandonment, Freud reasoned that this could not be so, since the proper response to loss would be mourning, not anxiety. Like Freud, the philosophers mentioned maintained that anxiety does not depend on any actual condition, albeit one of loss, but rather on "a condition that is not." Kierkegaard offers a clarifying illustration of the difference: the feeling of anxiety is not captured, he says, by the complaint "My God, my God, why hast thou forsaken me?" but rather by the entreaty "Whatever you are going to do, do quickly!"[11] Anxiety is not the experience of a loss that has occurred; it is the experience of some impending event, the anticipation of something that, while connected to what precedes us, has not yet happened. It is the looming of the unknown, the awakening of a possibility whose contours are indiscernible.

In other words, the break instituted by modernity did not render the past totally dead to us. It did not abandon us to a solitary present divorced from the past but handed us over to a present that felt overpopulated—not, as is usually said, because of the increasing density of cities or our bombardment by an increasing number of new stimuli but because we seemed to be parasitized by an excess that refused to disclose itself to us. Anxiety is the feeling of being stuck to an excess from which we can neither separate ourselves nor lay claim to, of being tied to a past that, not having happened, cannot be shed. Our implication in the past thus took on a different complexion. For while formerly a subject's ties to her past may have seemed rigidly binding, they were experienced as external, as of the order of simple constraint. One had to submit to a destiny one did not elect and often experienced as unjust. But one could—like Job or the heroes and heroines of classical tragedies—rail against one's destiny, curse one's fate.

With modernity, this is no longer possible. The "God of destiny" is now dead, and we no longer inherit the debts of our ancestors but become that debt. We cannot distance ourselves sufficiently from the desire of our ancestors to curse the fate it hands us but must, as Lacan put it, "bear as jouissance the injustice that horrifies us."[12] Jouissance—roughly equivalent to Freud's libido—names a capacity to alter our destiny. And yet this is not a capacity we can possess. It is something horrifying; a monstrous otherness not at our disposal but something to be suffered.

If we think once more of the revolutionary whose hand is paralyzed by anxiety, we will see how closely Lacan's account hews to Freud's account of anxiety. If, stricken by anxiety, my hand goes on strike, refuses to write, this is because it has become saturated with libido, gripped by jouissance. My hand behaves, Freud explains, like a maid who, having begun a love affair with her master, refuses to continue doing her household chores.[13] In the moment of anxiety, one loses one's taste for ordinary, routinized life: cooking, cleaning, all practical interests. It is this automatic way of life that is paralyzed by anxiety. However, this analogy is, as Freud himself says, "rather absurd," insofar as it fails to account for the real situation of the maid, who, while torn away from her mundane duties, is now bound to a terrible, inscrutable master: her own libido, or potentiality. Elsewhere, Freud will dispense with the analogy and define anxiety more straightforwardly as fear of one's own libido.[14] As with Melville's Bartleby—the scrivener who goes on strike, refuses to write—we are struck by the involuted refusal, "I would prefer not to," a flash of potentiality that will not unfold itself but manifests itself only in the paralysis.

Kiarostami's protagonists exhibit a paralysis of this kind, one occasioned by their inability to comprehend the desire of their ancestors and thus their own place in the very culture to which they nevertheless maintain a feeling of anonymous belonging. One of the primary locations in *The Wind Will Carry Us* is a cemetery to which Behzad continuously repairs to pick up a stronger cell phone signal and where Youssef, a gravedigger, continuously digs, remaining thus underground and invisible throughout most of the film. We surmise that the purpose of his efforts is ultimately the installation of a telecommunications tower, but since Mrs. Malek is on the verge of death, the digging simultaneously hints at preparations for her funeral. That a burial ground would become the site of telecommunication efforts bespeaks an anxiety attendant upon the loss of any clear signals issuing from a past that remains inscrutable.

Eventually, the earth caves in on Youssef, who must be dug out.

The unsteadiness of the ground is not unique to this film; it is a constant in Kiarostami's work, where the salient characteristic of the earth is its unsteadiness: it is always caving in, buckling, quaking.[15] The ground in many of his films is ungrounded, hollowed out—or more precisely, made to resemble catacombs. While earthquakes are a difficult geographical fact of life in Iran, Kiarostami's continuous reference to this datum in many of his films turns it into a fact of another order. No longer just an uncompromising truth of the terrain, it becomes a cultural fact whose meaning cannot be unearthed. Like the past buried in it, the ground turns out in Kiarostami's world to be active and shifting, an unsettled affair. It is as if the past itself were under construction in his films.

In *The Wind Will Carry Us*, it is not only Youssef who remains invisible to us throughout the film; several characters—eleven by Kiarostami's count—remain out of frame and thus unseen. Asked by an interviewer what these curiously insistent visual absences signified, Kiarostami replied that the film was about "beings without being."[16] In *Where Is the Friend's House?* (1986), "being without being"—that is, being that is not but which, remaining unrealized, perplexes characters by affixing itself to them—assumes the form of a notebook that a young schoolboy is certain is not his own, though it appears in all particulars exactly like his. He spends most of the film trying unsuccessfully to return it, mysteriously deciding in the end not to give it back to its ostensible owner. Effectively, the notebook has no exclusive owner but becomes the bond between the two students.

In *Taste of Cherry* (1997), the anxiety-provoking element fails to take the form of a putative object and instead infuses the film with a perplexing textual opacity. The film follows a middle-aged man, Mr. Badii, who has no discernible reason for discontent (far from it) and yet spends the entire film trying to find an accomplice to his suicide, one who will promise to cover him with twenty shovelfuls of dirt and double-check to make sure he is really and truly dead. From this, we suspect that Mr. Badii is bothered by a fear of being buried alive. It is as if he were trying not simply to kill himself but to extinguish some surplus of self that does not respond to his wishes and thus impresses him as capable of surviving even his death.

Speaking in an interview about *Taste of Cherry*, Kiarostami offered this comment: "The choice of death is the only prerogative possible [. . .] because everything in our lives has been imposed by birth [. . .] our parents, our home, our nationality, our build, the color of our skin, our culture."[17] Though Mr. Badii has no personal complaint, the thick presence of militia, the oppressive evidence of poverty, and the dust of industrialization visible in the urban perimeter through which he drives suggest choking. His suicide is thus readable as an attempt to escape the suffocation brought on by a world where one's identity is laid down by authorities who leave no room for freedom, no chance to choose what form one's life will take. And yet, if that which is imposed on us by birth is as enigmatic as Kiarostami's films tell us it is, then the rigidity of a life laid out by law must be read as a means of dodging a more primary experience, that of anxiety, which is stirred in us by an encounter with our capacity to break from this rigidity.[18] What Mr. Badii cannot abide is being riveted to the inscrutable desire of his ancestors, imposed on him by his birth into a culture that appears radically heteroclite. It is the incomprehensibility of "unrealized being," of his own potentiality, which suffocates him. He seeks through suicide to escape not the actual restrictions his culture imposes, but the overcrowded space in which he finds himself bound to its unreadable imperative.

THE AFFECTIVE TONALITY OF CAPITALISM

I have lingered on anxiety, which Lacan identified as the only affect, because I am interested tracing the various ways in which shame functions in Kiarostami's films. If Lacan is correct, one can only get to shame by familiarizing oneself with the workings of anxiety. I will thus treat anxiety as the "stem cell" of affects, which is transformed in different social theaters, to produce guilt and shame. Fundamental to affect is the sense of being unable to integrate or divorce oneself from a strangeness that remains "closer to [ourselves] than [our] jugular vein."[19] So similar are the affects of anxiety and shame (particularly) that Levinas, in his early work *On Escape*, differentiates them only by a tiny hiccup of hope that is present in anxiety and dashed in shame. Like others, including Freud and Lacan, Levinas characterizes anxiety as a confrontation with a state of emergency, a signal or imperative to flee, to escape an alarming strangeness that attempts to hold us in its grip. It is only when this imperative faces the impossibility of success that anxiety turns dejectedly to shame. But where Levinas takes for granted that it is the hope of flight that fades in shame, I will argue that what disappears is the imperative of flight.

We begin. The society of others performs a civilizing function not, as is usually said, because it tames primitive animal instincts but because it colonizes the savage, inhuman jouissance that parasites the human child. Unable to tolerate being alone with this inhuman partner, one is gratified to find less oppressive companions. This point prepares us to approach again the distinction often made between shame and guilt cultures. It would be better to argue that there are different ways of distancing ourselves from the stifling sense of foreignness imparted to us by our own culture.

The unctuous aggressiveness exhibited by Behzad toward Zeynab is only one episode of his generally insensitive behavior. As he hangs around Siah Darreh waiting for Mrs. Malek to die, he occupies himself not only with his pestering of Zeynab but also by trying to snap photographs of the villagers, who cover their faces and demand that he put down his camera. The film clearly indicts him for his rudeness and indiscretion, but in what precisely do his crimes consist, and why do the villagers not want their pictures taken? If every subject is in need of an image, why are Behzad's attempts to offer the villagers photographs of themselves greeted as acts of rudeness or malice rather than of kindness? One of the villagers in *Life and Nothing More* seems to respond directly to this question when he complains to Farhad, the film-director protagonist of that film, that the images of the villagers captured by his camera make the villagers appear "worse than they are."

It is not the taking of photographs per se but these particular photographs that are the problem. Behzad and Farhad travel to the villages to document a phenomenon on the verge of disappearing. Their mission is to capture a world in the process of being lost, people about to die or presumed to be buried in rubble; they want to preserve in archives ritual practices and ways of life on the edge of extinction. The imminence of loss, of death, licenses the rudeness of the photographers, justifying in their minds their indiscreet attempts to snatch from loss—from transitory, fleeting life—something lasting, images that can be stored in the memory banks of their culture. But it is not merely the race against time that powers their rudeness, for these nosey archivists believe they confront an additional obstacle in the villagers themselves, who refuse, they assume, to disclose to them the information they seek to record. In other words, what these diegetic film directors disregard while making their images is the subjectivity of the villagers, the fact that they are themselves curious about themselves. These colonizing directors seek to pry from the villagers secrets that elude them, secrets that are not theirs to disclose.

Is Behzad's obscene rudeness not of the same sort as that made scandalously evident in the Abu Ghraib photographs? The problem is not simply that the photographers in each case invaded the privacy of those they photographed; it consists rather in the same obscene denial that there is an obscene, an off-screen that evades every persistent, prying eye. The ultimate crime of both series of photographs, the source of their malicious abjuration of respect, is their assumption that the photographed subjects have no privacy to invade. This is the bottom line, the point on which I am insisting: privacy cannot be invaded, cannot be penetrated, either by the subject or by the most sophisticated, state-of-art photographic devices.

At the dawn of the twentieth century, Nietzsche expressed his scorn for that century's characteristic and misguided belief that it was possible to see through everything.[20] He protested the lack of reverence and discretion that fueled his contemporaries' tactless preoccupation with disclosing and unmasking everything. "Nothing is so nauseating in . . . the believers in 'modern ideas,'" he scoffed, "as their lack of shame, their complaisant impudence of eye and hand with which they touch, lick, and finger everything."[21] This frenzied desire to cast aside every veil, penetrate every surface, transgress every barrier standing between us and the real thing lying behind it installed in the modern world a new sort of "beyondness," a new untouchable, one that is in principle there for the grasping, even if in actuality it is always out of reach. This secularized sacred, which inspires a new, modern desire for transgression, does not originate in a belief in the existence of another world but in the belief that what we want in this world always lies just behind some roadblock preventing our access to it.

This new "beyondness" is held in place by a definable structure, that of guilt, which must be understood not in its limited, psychological sense but in the sense I proposed above: a specific form of relation to one's own culture. Agamben offers in passing a broader definition of guilt in line with our own. In *Homo Sacer*, he defines "the cipher of this capture of life in law" (e.g., the cipher of biopolitics) as "guilt (not in the technical sense . . . but in the originary sense that indicates a being-in-debt: *in culpa esse*), which is to say, precisely the condition of being included through an exclusion, of being in relation to something from which one is excluded or which one cannot fully assume."[22] It is the phrase "being in relation to something one cannot . . . assume" that first catches our attention because it happens to be the one Levinas uses to describe anxiety and shame, the complex feeling of being riveted to an inalienable and opaque surplus of being. Agamben sets Levinas's phrase alongside an apposite one of his own, "being in relation to something from which one is excluded."

The latter phrase absorbs and slightly alters the former and thereby defines guilt as a transformation of anxiety. Like anxiety, the feeling of guilt consists in a feeling of being unable to coincide with oneself by integrating a troubling surplus of being. In guilt, however, this inability is no longer experienced as being stuck to an inalienable alienness but as an inability to close the distance that separates us from something that excludes us. How does this transformation come about? How does one become excluded from a part of oneself with which one cannot quite catch up, rather than attached to what one cannot assume?

We find our answer in the Freudian theory of guilt, in the paradox of the superego (which punishes obedience with guilt) that is inextricable from the paradox of ego and cultural ideals (which we are simultaneously enjoined to live up to and forbidden to attain). Faced with the unbearable opaqueness we are to ourselves, with the unassumable excess that sticks to us, we unburden ourselves by allowing the ideals set up by society to become blueprints for our identity and action and thereby provide us with some clarity. Through cultural ideals, the question of what it means to belong to a culture is silenced and replaced by mesmerizing cultural goals that gather awestruck subjects. But because every ideal is sustained by a prohibition against attaining it, we are always in debt to them, always in arrears to our ego and cultural ideals, which insert us into our culture precisely by excluding us from its inner sanctum.

The very prohibition/exclusion that binds us to these ideals also invites transgression. What is forbidden lures us with its unattainability—if only we could summon the courage to disobey, the fortitude to step over the line. In short, ideals are the source of that secularized sacred deplored by Nietzsche, the just-beyond reach that ignores the impenetrability of one's own, as well as others', self-opacity. What was hidden and paralyzing is now tantalizingly close and urges transgression.

The Ego and the Id presents an argument about guilt, one that reads as profoundly tributary to the one just mentioned. Freud maintains that "reflection . . . shows us that no external vicissitudes can be experienced or undergone by the id, except by way of the ego, which is the representative of the external world to the id. Nevertheless, it is not possible to speak of direct inheritance in the ego. It is here that the gulf between an actual individual and the concept of a species becomes evident."[23] I understand this "no direct inheritance in the ego" as sanction to treat cultural inheritance as libido or jouissance excited by the brush with ancestral desire. Beyond particular historical facts, images, texts, or codes of behavior, we also inherit from the past a surplus of jouissance, an overwhelming sense of being taken up into something we do not understand. For this reason, the subject is never completely absorbed into her culture. This may take the form of guilt, a sense of failing to live up to cultural ideals. The sense of exclusion from some sacred core of existence can lead to acts of zealotry. It might also allow some to fall prey to systems that encourage greed. In The Wind Will Carry Us, for example, many of the villagers participate in the ritual of scarification that follows the death not as an act of bereavement but to attract the attention of their bosses. These villagers seem to have bought into the capitalist belief that there is nothing that is not ripe for exposure. They, too, have begun to acquire that immodest, capitalist taste for what C. S. Lewis referred to as a "very cheap [form of] frankness."[24]

Against this background, the Islamic system of modesty—with its volatile disdain for the modern passion for exposing everything, its loud protestations and rigid protections against the "touching, licking, and fingering" of everything—would seem to offer an welcome antidote to the global immodesty fashioned by Western capitalism. The system of modesty targets a worthy enemy; the question before us, however, is whether it adopts effective measures against its target, whether it succeeds or fails to protect a subject's modesty. With this question in mind, we return to the fresh milk sequence in The Wind Will Carry Us to determine if it deserves the tongue lashing Dabashi gives it.

SCENES OF SHAME

As Behzad descends into the subterranean chamber, the catacomb, where he will catch up with Zeynab, we are invited to wonder, "What sort of place is this?" One need not know anything about villages in Northern Iran to know that not even there do people milk cows in pitch black underground caves. This is no ordinary or actual location, no touristic glimpse of some of Iran's exotic or quixotic landscape; rather, it is an example of "visionary geography," a liminal space defined in Islamic philosophy as the place from which new forms emerge.[25] After Behzad crosses the threshold, the screen goes black for several long seconds, as if to mark the absolute separation of this space from the others in the film.

Holding on the black screen for an uncomfortably long time, Kiarostami also allows the depth of the blinding darkness in which Zeynab remains enshrouded to impress itself on us. From the bright sunlight outside, we pass into a place so luminous that nothing stands out against it; a place filled with a light so intense that nothing in it is distinguishable from anything else, a place of pure exposure, of dazzling blackness. While the screen is still black, the voice of Behzad inquires, "Is there anyone here?" Answerable in the negative, this question is more profound than it might first seem. For there is, in fact, no one here in this darkness, no "I," only the milking of a cow, the gerundive form of the action Zeynab is performing substantivized, lacking any subjective support.

In *Being and Nothingness*, Sartre describes a scene that is in many points similar to this one in *The Wind Will Carry Us*. A voyeur, crouched before a keyhole, peers through it intently. At this point, there is nothing but this pure act of looking, peering through a keyhole, the act that totally absorbs the voyeur.[26] The voyeur himself is not present. He is precipitated out from his act as a subject only at the point when a sudden rustling of leaves startles him and fills him with shame. The voyeur appears only as the experience of shame, as shame-full in the precise sense. It is only when he senses his being looked at by the "gaze" of an indeterminate other that the voyeur acquires a sentiment of self. The sentiment of self and the experience of shame are synonymous. The scenes from Kiarostami and Sartre are similar, then, in that in each the gerundive form of an act—milking a cow, peering through a keyhole—indicates the absence of a subject, whose emergence will be marked only later by the arousal of shame.

The apparent dissimilarity between the two acts may make my analogy seem far-fetched. I will thus address the hesitation that may remain by focusing first on the scene of peering through a keyhole. What does Sartre say about it? Surprisingly little. In fact, he seems remarkably intent on refraining from drawing too much attention to the act in which his Peeping Tom is engaged when interrupted by the gaze. This polite inattention is partly explained by the fact that Sartre does not want to distract from his point that he is not speaking of shame in the "civic" sense, as he says. By this, he seems to mean that sense in which, having already entered polite society and learned its rules, one is disgraced by being caught breaking one of them. Sartre is concerned, rather, with a more fundamental definition of shame; he regards it as an affect that attends the subject's awareness of being in a world among others. This awareness of being a social being precedes all measure and every rule by which a subject might find himself judged. It is not, therefore, the nature of his act—the fact that it is one of lascivious looking, which causes the voyeur shame—but the fact that the gaze makes him suddenly aware of the presence of others as such.

There can be no denying, however, that there is something more going on in Sartre's refusal to utter a peep about this peeping, his lack of curiosity about the voyeur's precise act of prurience. Plainly, he has sanitized the scene. Less discreet, Lacan returns to the scene to highlight the nature of the act. It is not by chance, he unblinkingly observes, that shame catches the voyeur in a moment of desire. He does not reject Sartre's argument that the gaze of the Other neither judges nor prohibits the act of the voyeur as socially unacceptable. But to deny the censoriousness of the gaze is not to deny any relation between it and desire. Lacan's point is precisely this: rather than condemn or prohibit, the gaze enflames desire; shame is a sexual "conflagration."[27]

Excising sex, Sartre produces a chaste reading of the shame scenario, which he turns into a bathetic drama wherein an abstract and sovereign act of looking is forced to confront its anchorage in the vulnerability of its bodily foundations. The rustling of leaves functions as a kind of index finger that picks out the voyeur, rendering him painfully conspicuous, a body too much in a scene where he thought himself bodiless and unobserved. The emperor of seeing is suddenly brought down, reduced to the dead weight of his body, his body as object. Sartre trades the censoring function that is usually ascribed to the gaze for an alternative function: limitation. In his interpretation, what the gaze exposes is the subject's finitude; it reminds us that others as such set limits on our freedom, impede our actions and get in the way of our plans. The body exposed by shame is thus nothing more than a figure for this limitation of the subject's freedom; it is a body that can be hurt by others, that remains ever vulnerable to all that is external to and opposes it.

From this point, we can begin to measure the consequences of Lacan's opposition to Sartre's sanitization of the scene, which is stated in the following counter-insistence: "It is not the annihilating subject; correlative of the world of objectivity, who feels himself surprised, but the subject sustaining himself in a function of desire."[28] If it is not the subject who experiences his freedom as limited by others who experiences shame, then neither is the body at stake in this experience the stupid, delimited object Sartre imagines.

One problem with the latter's reading is that it fails to capture the squirminess of shame, which is more clearly evoked in Kiarostami's sequence by the camera's exposure of the cow's udders as they are being milked by Zeynab. It is not the body as figure of limitation but the body as figure of one's nakedness that is exposed by shame. The nakedness of the body is not, however, a simple function of its being unclothed. As is attested in Kiarostami's scene and by the obsessive fears that, at its extreme, haunt the hijab system—which visualizes in the clicking of a woman's heels the place where her legs join her body, and in the cadences of her voice the softness of her skin—one can remain naked beneath yards of clothing. As we will see, the dialectic of shame eschews simple opposition (naked/clothed or exposed/concealed). For now, we can say that the body's nakedness is a function of its sexualization. Sexualized, the body is vulnerable not, as in Sartre's version of the story, to other subjects but to the savage otherness of its own libido. The sexualized body is one whose boundaries have already been breached, one that has suffered an irreparable and constitutive hurt.

Lacan's reintroduction of sexuality into the Sartrean account of shame paves the way for us to reconnect shame to anxiety, while reexamining Levinas's argument about their relation and the question of cultural inheritance they raise. Although Levinas does not explicitly conceive the surplus that rivets the subject as libido, his argument does broach the question of racial inheritance, and sexual pleasure does emerge in his discussion at the point at which shame is introduced.[29] Levinas's argument is that, while pleasure promises escape from anxiety, shame testifies to the inadequacy of sexual pleasure, which proves incapable of delivering on this promise. Earlier, I left hanging the question of the validity of this argument about shame's disappointment. I return to it now by examining one more scene of shame made famous by its theorization: I refer to the scene Agamben introduces in *Remnants of Auschwitz* to flesh out Levinas's theory of shame.

Originally recounted by Robert Antelme, the scene concerns a student from Bologna who is arbitrarily picked out of a line of students by an SS officer and thereby marked for execution.[30] Remarkably, the unfortunate student does not question his selection nor look over his shoulder in hopes of discovering that it was someone other than he who had been selected. No, the pink flush of his cheeks signals his recognition that it is he who has been designated and that he cannot escape this fact. The dead certainty that accompanies anxiety sticks, too, we see, to shame.

This common sense of certainty may in part be what leads Levinas to nearly conflate the two affects, with the small distinction that shame is certainty more emphatic as it is more fatalistic. Not only do I know beyond doubt that I am that, that which rivets me; I also know there is no escape from that. That is that. The reddening of the Italian student's face would seem to blurt out an

"I am here," a resigned surrender to the fate handed him by the SS officer. But is that really the end of it? Does the sudden surging up of the question of pleasure in Levinas's discussion of shame not betray a disavowed recognition that some difference is being overlooked? Is Levinas not guilty, in short, of the same error as Sartre, of de-eroticizing shame? The heat and glow that suffuses the face of the one shamed telegraphs this eroticization and their error.

On the elementary level of description, there is a common distinction between anxiety and shame that we must now consider. While anxiety manifests itself in an urgent impulse to flee, shame is manifested in an impulse to hide. Levinas's argument depends on our reading this transformation of the impulse as necessitated by the defeat of its first manifestation: because flight is hopeless, all I can do is try to hide. But this is not the proper way to read this transformation, which depends, rather, on an alteration of my relation to that which anxiety wants to escape.

To test this hypothesis, we must take a closer look at the relation between exposure and concealment, which may be said to substitute for the anxious relation between paralysis and flight. Although the relation is usually assumed to be sequential—exposure coming first, followed by the defensive attempt to conceal—the pink cheeks of the student from Bologna raise questions about this assumption. As much as his blush broadcasts his presence, it also seems like the lowering of a shade to shutter or shield him from view. It is as if in his very exposure, his very visibility, he were announcing his disappearance from view, his retreat.

If blushing, the most common visual manifestation of shame, is critical to understanding it, this is because this affect has a special relation to sight, to the gaze, in contrast to guilt, in which the relation to the voice is what matters. Even when it is a sound that occasions shame, the experience of it is one of being looked at, submitted to a gaze. This is how it happens that the question of shame intersects the question of the image in Kiarostami's cinema. What shame seeks is the same thing Kiarostami, as filmmaker, wants to create: an image capable of capturing the reflection of what has no image. Be attentive, for here is where the detour through anxiety repays its costs. Those who dispense with this detour are precisely those who end up regarding shame as a passive suffering of exposure to a look against which only a pathetic defense is available: cowering beneath covers.

Exactly what does the gaze expose? This is a question about which there is far too little reflection. It is easy to accept the description offered above—shame erupts in response to a rupturing of the circuit of communication-recognition—as supplying the following answer: the gaze exposes a different, less flattering image of ourselves than we previously held. But this is clearly a mistake, for what the gaze makes visible is that very thing that has no image, that unassumable, opaque surplus of self that anxiety wants to be rid of. In shame, however, the inalienable alienness that attaches itself to me no longer threatens me with its suffocating overpresence but comes to define the intimate distance that constitutes my sense of interiority, my sense of myself as subject.

I have, from the start, been trying to define shame as a sense of self. It might be helpful at this point to turn this strategy around by defining the experience of self through shame. A long philosophical tradition has taught that the subject experiences itself as an immediacy but as an unthinkable distance. While this account is not incorrect, it is anemic. We look to psychoanalysis, then, for a more robust account and locate it in the proposition that the subject's definitional noncoincidence with herself stems from an encounter with jouissance, which attaches itself to her not as something she is but something she has. The various affects—of anxiety, guilt, and shame—make plain a further inadequacy of the bald philosophical assertion that the subject experiences herself through this inappropriable excess. In anxiety—the only affect in Lacan's account, although I suggest that we think of it as the primitive affect—is experienced as a paralyzing and potentially lethal. A minimal distance, or delay is necessary to stave off anxiety's lethal threat. With guilt this minimal difference is experienced as a fault, a simple inability or permanent lagging behind one's goals. Shame is also a negative affect in the sense that it, once again, exposes me to my nontransparency and, like guilt, it alleviates the crushing burden of anxiety. But how to conceive this experience of self which is shame?

Imagine a young girl sitting contentedly at a soda fountain with her polite, well-to-do friends, sipping a milkshake as she looks distractedly into the mirror behind the counter. Suddenly, the image of her mother, who has just ambled into the drugstore, appears in the mirror. It is a ridiculous image of a preposterously festooned mother; upon looking up and seeing it, the daughter burns with shame.[31] If shame is the experience not of some object (in which the girl would see her mother shamefully objectified, exposed finally to the formerly loving daughter) but is rather the feeling of self, how is this truth exemplified in the scene? Why does the appearance of the mother's image cause shame? It is unlikely that the reflection in the mirror would have caused shame if it had been that of a stranger or an acquaintance to whom the girl was indifferent. It matters that there is a strong bond of love connecting the daughter to the mother, for without this there would be no shame. Something about the daughter that is normally hidden is exposed in the scene, but it is not that this silly woman is her mother, nor is it that she is more like her mother than her fine manners and tastes have so far let on.

What shame exposes is her love for her mother—though to state it this way is not yet to capture the feeling precisely. The daughter's love for her mother has been fully evident before this event, to others and to the daughter herself, just as the interest of Sartre's voyeur in what is happening on the other side of the keyhole is evident. But these experiences of love and intense curiosity are, up to the moment the gaze appears, consumed by the objects on which they are lavished and the actions they entail. The moment of shame arrives when the subject who loves or peers intently through the keyhole makes herself visible to herself and others as a subject, as the one who loves, who desires. The subject sees herself as desiring, as actively submitting to the passion of her attachments. It matters less what incident occasions the feeling or what else the subject is doing at the time; what matters is that, at the moment the gaze appears, the subject experiences herself as engaged in active submission to some passion.

To put this in terms of the proposal I made regarding the psychoanalytic invigoration of philosophy, this experience of self as subject is the same one philosophy describes, an experience of the void that prevents me from coinciding with myself, understood now as an encounter with jouissance. In contrast to the feeling of being parasited by a crushing presence or punishing superego, however, this feeling is one of *enjoying one's jouissance*. It may at first seem surprising that the experience of oneself as subject is not one of "pure activity" but one of "passivity," or the assumption of a "feminine attitude" (to use Freud's terms), but this is the description of the experience of self that shame makes available.

One of the finest illustrations of this psycho-philosophical point is found in Joan Riviere's justly famous case study.[32] The unnamed patient is a woman who constantly battles anxiety. Curiously, this does not manifest itself as performance anxiety; a political activist with a strong intellect and oratorical skills, she frequently delivers public lectures. Her problem is a postperformance anxiety that befalls her after these speeches, which she deals with through "compulsive ogling" and flirting with men from the audience and through the fantasmatic production of scenarios in which she submits herself sexually to Black men while plotting against them.

Riviere contends that the woman's anxiety is aroused by a fear that she will be caught in possession of something (the phallus) that is not rightly hers (but has been stolen from her father) and that her defense strategy is to pretend not to have it by concealing her possession of it. We know that anxiety is caused by a surplus that one feels is not rightly one's own, but that surplus possesses the subject, not the other way around. It is obvious that this woman desperately wants to make an appearance, to exhibit herself on the public stage to escape the oblivion anxiety threatens, but her public speechmaking seems inadequate to the task. The reason? Alienating herself in her professional role, she disappears into it; there is no remainder, no subject left over. She thus resorts to a different strategy: making herself visible in shameful scenes of degradation or the performance of demeaning tasks. That these are not scenes of simple passivity is evident in her plots to turn these men over to justice or to escape them. It is quite apparent that she is pulling the strings in these scenarios, actively passive within them.

A number of other questions spring from this; let us return to the fresh milk sequence (readable alongside the other scenes of shame we have looked at) and approach them from there. A simple village girl and a minor character in the narrative, Zeynab moves about her world without any particular self-awareness, absorbed by everyday chores. In the intimate grotto-like space in which the scene is set, however—a space associated with burial, unforgettable ancestors, and the pressure of their desire on her—she is foregrounded, drawn out of herself. It is not Behzad's impertinent look that disturbs her; she is relatively indifferent to him and his bad manners.

What interrupts her complacency, her full absorption in the world, is the erotic poem by Forugh Farrokhzad that Behzad reads to her as part of his bungled attempt at seduction. From the interior of the poem, the gaze emerges and is even explicitly mentioned: "the earth/ screeching to a halt,/ something unknown watching you and me beyond this window."[33] Visibly fascinated by this poem, the red-robed Zeynab is not entirely exposed (for this would render her simply passive) but rather exposes herself (an active passivity) as desiring.

It is important to reemphasize this distinction to prevent shame from being reduced, as it too often is, to a retiring shyness, even though some have correctly observed that this affect often manifests itself as a "bold . . . candor," in candid acknowledgments of the libidinal investments that ravish and surprise.[34]

In this imaginal "underground barn" scene, Zeynab to appear without losing herself in her appearance. This is the question we must finally answer: how can we appear without disappearing into our appearance? Think of the extreme poles of shame scenarios. On the one hand, there is the first horrified sight of the death camps by liberating armies, which was said to have aroused shame and thus to have forced witnesses to look away. On the other, there are "actions of love and extravagant generosity," in response to which Nietzsche once said, "nothing is more advisable than to take a stick and give any eyewitnesses a sound thrashing."[35] Why do we avert our gaze and feel shame in response to the inhumanly awful and the exquisitely beautiful? The first answer likely to be offered must be discarded, for shame involves no taboo against looking or touching. To distinguish this affect from guilt requires us to refuse taboo—which is uttered from a beyond to protect a beyond—any say in the matter. Declaring something untouchable, out of bounds, taboo not only creates a beyond, a sacred zone set apart from us; it also incites, as we noted, a counter-imperative to transgress the boundaries excluding us from that sacred place, to touch, finger, penetrate with our look all it would withhold from us.

Still, we cannot deny that shame often betrays itself in an averted look. The averted look is not, however, a sign of obedience to a stricture against looking but of the appearance of a new opportunity to look: inward. It is as if our attention were directed not to a parallel, transcendent space, but to an oblique one slightly detached from visibility—the space of a self into which we could withdraw from the scene that engages us. This simultaneous relation between exposure and concealment now needs to be formulated.

In contrast to guilt, which introduces through prohibition a division between the sensible world and an ideal world that transcends it, shame operates without recourse to prohibition, ideals, or a heterogenous realm outside the sensible; it operates, in other words, entirely within the sensible realm of vision, introducing there—within the visible—a slight separation of the visible and invisible. One could describe the experience of shame, in sum, as that of witnessing oneself hiding, as the sense that one has ducked behind one's appearance. Between the appearance and what remains invisible, no interdiction intervenes; nothing is prohibited from appearing. Rather, it is a question of an appearance that permits something to disappear.

What is it that thus permits me to disappear? What allows me to camouflage myself behind my visibility? It is that very thing that has dominated the scene while avoiding analysis up until now: the gaze. Sartre brings it into focus and makes a breakthrough in conceptualizing it. The gaze, he says, cannot be matched to an actual pair of eyes; it is not locatable in a person. The gaze has no bearer, belongs to no one. If, feeling a gaze rest upon me, I scan the subway car to try to pin it on some suspicious-looking person; the experience of the gaze will evaporate at each point on which my accusation alights. There is a fantasmatic dimension of the gaze that suggests it cannot be contained within an intersubjective dialectic. But in the end, Sartre does not follow-up on this suggestion and thus the a-personal dimension of the gaze serves in his account merely to enhance the power of the Other by effacing his limits. The fact that I cannot attach it to the actual eyes of an objectified other gives the gaze all the more power to objectify and limit me. This is a point Val Lewton, the legendary producer of horror films, well understood: do not show the horrible thing directly embodied in a person, for this will only have the effect of attenuating the threat.

Lacan reads the phantasmatic dimension of the gaze differently. There is no warrant, he argues, for Sartre's placement of the gaze exclusively on the side of an adversarial other. If one wants to understand the phenomenon of shame, the relevant difference is not between two different sets of eyes, but between and an eye and a gaze. To be ashamed is to place oneself in a passive position, become the brunt of an accusation. One regards oneself as exposable to oneself as well as to others. To *have* shame, on the other hand, is to adopt an intra-passive position toward what is not exposable in oneself, to assume responsibility for the latter, that is to say, for one's shadow self.

In Lacan's reading of Sartre's scenario, the voyeur, semi-detached from the wider world and caught up in a net of desire, is gifted with a gaze that permits him to see what he could not otherwise see: his own appearance – as appearance. This is not to say that he sees what others see when they look at him but that he sees his not-being-seen. His outward image takes on the role of disguise. He is able to appear in public while preserving his privacy. In a gesture of sleazy flattery, Behzad tries to establish some silly points of coincidence between Zeynab and Forugh, the leading Persian poet of the twentieth century. There is absolutely no sign, however, that Zeynab is interested in being like the poet. What interests Zeynab is dissimulation (the possibility of which is suggested by the poem), the possibility of being able to present herself in public while remaining concealed.

Unlike anxiety, shame is not a signal that one must seek cover from its threats. It is the sense of being undercover, of having found cover in one's appearance. Not "I am here" but "I lie here disguised." An SS officer may order me to step forward, and I may obey by presenting myself before him. But to experience shame in doing so is to stand a little to the side of one's appearance and to remain there, undetected. Make no mistake: I can have no shame or shield apart from my appearance, for my interiority or self-intimacy is the recurvant effect of a certain form of publicity. If one takes anxiety as the subject's primitive condition, one sees that the "gaze of the Other" serves to limit not my freedom but, instead, my devouring, limitless anxiety. The paradox of libido uncovered by Freud is that some limitation or obstacle is necessary, not to prevent it from spilling over into public space but to "raise its tide." This early insight is comprehensible as a way of accounting for the difference between anxiety and its limitation via shame. In this context the gaze appears as an obstacle, which sends my look, like a shuttlecock, back toward me. It sees me as part of the world but does not censor or judge. In fact, it acts as a prophylactic to protect us against any all-seeing Censor.

The point is often made that censorship does not merely negate but is also productive. Without the Hays code, for example, no one would ever have known the "Lubitsch Touch"; similarly, one might say that without hijab regulations, Iranian cinema might not have blossomed as it did. This flat dictum has a grain of truth, but never seemed satisfying to me. It is not simply censorship that produces great works of art, just as it is not every obstacle that raises the tide of libido. We know that some obstacles can never be overcome because acts of transgression only fortify them. For censorship to be productive, there must be some recognition that the Censor has a blind spot, and thus a positive belief must exist that the order of appearances is neither fully transparent to the Censor's look nor merely a realm of illusion and distortion. The gaze looks back at me not only at that point where my look encounters its limit but also where it encounters a fissure in the world or in the Censor's eyeball. I look into the eyes of an SS officer, and I encounter not just an obstacle to my look but also this fissure, this blind spot of the Other, from which point no destiny can be foreseen, not mine, not anyone's. For even if this moment marks the hour of my death, it is the accident of this death that shame highlights. My destiny finds harbor in my appearance and remains undisclosed, even to me.

A final point about the fresh milk sequence in Kiarostami's film. While I have attended only to the diegetic unfolding of shame in it, it is clear that a sense of shame pervades both the diegetic situation and the audience's relation to it. Extremely discomfiting, the scene does not allow us to sit unobserved in the darkness of the auditorium but instead forces us to experience our own uneasy, hidden presence on the scene. The final quarrel I have with Dabashi's outraged response to the sequence is that it declines Kiarostami's invitation; it refuses shame by instead expressing shame for, or on behalf of, Zeynab as if to distance Dabashi from the experience itself. I repeat my initial proposition: there is no such thing as "shame for." There is only shame, the experience of submitting to the gaze oneself. There are no spectators or witnesses to shame; one is always interior to the experience of it. Yet there is no denying that the gaze wounds; it severs the subject from herself and causes her to submit to an experience whose disturbing complexity is not adequately captured by the terms "pleasure" or "enjoyment." What happens, however, when one resists and tries through an alternative view of shame to defend oneself against the experience of it? In this case the gaze will be perceived, as in Sartre, as coming from without, from an annihilating other, and as falling on some poor others who are made to feel shame. From a safe distance, unaffected by its wounding, I will experience shame only secondhand, on behalf of these others. This is not, I would argue, a scenario of contagious sociality but of a false, self-protective chivalry.

I have deliberately placed this discussion of shame as a provocation at the point of conflict between Islam and the West. One of the most heated issues of this conflict centers on the forced wearing of the veil and the hijab system generally, which are met with violent condemnation in the West. The debate has thus far been too narrowly framed insofar as it has not (at least to my knowledge) been concerned with the ontology of shame. This approach would no doubt raise serious challenges to both sides of the argument.

The recurrent image in The Wind Will Carry Us of Behzad running about, trying to pick up a better signal for his mobile phone, brings to mind the historic debates over wiretapping in the United States. During these debates, it was argued that privacy was not localizable in a delimited space that might then be ruled out of reach to the state. Rather, it was attached to the subject and remained inviolable no matter where a citizen might be, in public or in private space. This argument exemplifies the ideology of freedom on which the West opposes the hijab system and regards itself superior to the Islamic world and its doctrine of submission. Yet the belief that the subject has property in the self, that property is privately held, is clearly untenable in the face of shame, which counts on publicity to dispossess the subject of that which it can never assume as property. A further question is raised by the apparent chivalry of the Islamic State, which strikes one as a defensive posture—though it would be wrong to attribute such suspicious chivalry to the Islamic State, since it is rampant across the globe.

In any case, we owe this entire speculation to the modesty system's strict regulation of cinema, which, by obliging filmmakers to film mainly exterior spaces, set Kiarostami the task of demonstrating that interiority is not only compatible with, but dependent upon, the existence of an all-exterior world.

7

THE SEXUAL COMPACT

THE NUMBERS GAME

In the mid-1970s, a global warming began to melt the icy resistance of feminists to psychoanalysis, thanks to the publication in England of Juliet Mitchell's *Psychoanalysis and Feminism*, the upsurge in France of a group of "New French Feminists," and the work in the United States of Shoshana Felman, who made a persuasive argument for a feminist-friendly "French Freud." For approximately a decade, psychoanalytic feminism flourished as one of the most exciting and productive discourses of its time. While never completely uncritical of Freudian theory, feminists nevertheless deeply appreciated the fact that it was unique in according a fundamental status to sexual difference and feminine sexuality. This made the experiences of women an issue of far-reaching importance, one capable of throwing into question some of the basic assumptions underlying philosophical theories of the subject and political theories of community.

By the mid-1980s, however, signs of a climate change in the relations between feminism and psychoanalysis were already apparent. Teresa de Lauretis telegraphed in the title of her ground-breaking book, *Technologies of Gender*, the key terms that would oversee the uncoupling of the two discourses and articulated in her highly prescient preface the slogan under which this uncoupling would effectively occur: "A feminist theory of gender . . . points to a conception of the subject as multiple, rather than divided."[1] The consequences of this formulation, and the growing interest it heralded in a rigorous interrogation of psychoanalysis, cannot be underestimated. There arose, however, in many of us an uneasy sense that something was being lost in this precipitous embrace of the newly defined category of gender. As "the end goal of the feminist revolution"—defined by Shulamith Firestone as "not just the elimination of male privilege, but of the sex distinction itself"—seemed to draw nigh, some wondered whether sexual difference was really as eliminable as class differences were and whether it was desirable to strip the former of significance.² In light of this uneasiness, I here list the salient and tightly interwoven features of the mid-1980s shift away from sexual difference:

(1) The psychoanalytic category of sexual difference was, from this date, deemed suspect and largely forsaken in favor of the neutered category of gender. Yes, neutered, I insist on this, for it was specifically the *sex* of sexual difference that dropped out when this term was replaced by *gender*. Gender theory not only thrust the term *sexual difference* out of the limelight but also removed the sex even from sex. For while gender theorists continued to speak of sexual practices, they ceased to question what sex is. No longer the subject of serious theoretical inquiry, sex reverted, then, to being what it was in common parlance: that which is involved in a highly restricted set of activities or in attachments to certain objects or persons. Or, within theory, a secondary characteristic that, tired of playing second fiddle, now asserted itself as impudent swagger or naughty voluntarism.

The turn away from the Freudian theory of sex and sexual difference meant that many important questions posed there would also be regarded as outdated and left unattended. Take, for example, the antiquated criticism of Freud's "pan-sexualism." This charge—that Freud overrated the importance of sex, seeing it as the ubiquitous cause of everything—is stunning in its obtuseness. Noting, correctly, that Freud was intent on thinking sex and cause together, his accusers neglected to consider that this reconceptualization of the two in light of each other would leave neither untouched but would, on the contrary, alter our commonsense notions of both.

The Freudian concept of overdetermination blurred this fact out, but it was ignored, with the response focusing only on the idea of a surfeit; that is, that the causes of our actions are never unique but always multiple. What ought to have been clear from Freud's exposition is that *overdetermination* cannot be adequately approached except as acknowledgment of the subject's *underdetermination*. As subjects, we cannot trace backward from condition to condition until we arrive at some "lonely hour of the last instance" (as Althusser would later put it), where a final cause operated alone to determine our actions. No external or internal necessity guides subjects, who are thus susceptible to endless enticements, to various stimuli, none of which is sufficient by itself to motivate us. It is precisely there where animal instinct is found to be lacking that Freud inserted his speculative concept of drive, which was never a drive to x, y, or z, never connected by necessity to a particular object, for sex has no domain. What is essential is not the substitution of a plurality of causes for a single one but the fact that sex as cause cannot be located in any positive phenomenon, word or object, but is manifest in negative phenomena exclusively: lapses, interruptions that index a discontinuity or jamming of the causal chain.

(2) The flight into the multiple, conceived as discrete instances, had, of course, a number of other adverse consequences on the theory of sex. If sexual difference became problematic for gender theory, this is because the former was presumed to be heterosexist. It divided subjects into two genres and implied a necessary and/or natural relation between them. (You see what happens when you ignore what I just said; sex is for psychoanalysis a theory of *underdetermination*.) Why—gender theory asks—must there be only two genres of persons, two sexes, rather than an infinite number of them? I like to think of this as the Oprah Winfrey theoretical gift of sex: "You get a sex, and you get a sex, and you get a sex," in which sex can be owned like a car. Refusing this gift, I will instead pose some questions of my own.

Is it automatically the case that many are superior to two? Many are more numerous, certainly, but what concerns me is that a precipitous multiplication pushes aside questions that need to be asked, that the proliferation of kinds of subjects (whereby each is her own kind) represents a retreat of thought rather than a theoretical advance. Here is an analogy: Freud conceived the drives as fundamentally antinomic, as divided in two. However, his enthusiastic contemporaries attempted to "improve" on his theory by multiplying the drives such that every action in which a subject might engage was explained by the existence of a separate drive. (Never mind, again, that drive was never conceived as a drive to x, y, or z.)

However, it quickly became evident that the question of what caused these actions was not answered by the ad hoc proliferation of drives; it was simply deferred. The proliferation of genders repeats this same mistake; it multiplies rather than thinks. That is, it shirks from thinking difference and simply adds another one to a previous one, indefinitely: $1 + 1 + 1 \ldots$ From where do all these individual ones come? What makes them individual? In large part they come from commonsense observation that there *are* individuals, there are differences, which observation turns into an ontological principle (the ontology of the multiple) to be defended, few questions asked. It is simply assumed that an individual comes from herself, that whatever makes a subject this particular subject makes her so, per se. This is the nominalist position, and gender theorists operate largely on this assumption.[3]

One sympathizes, God knows, with the reasoning behind their flight into the multiple, their attempt to get out from under an overarching, englobing one in which all differences would be included and greatly reduced to local and minor variations in the nature that unifies them. But this flight does not take us far, and it is thus necessary to plot another path. Fortunately, we have at our disposal a philosophical arsenal bequeathed to us by—this will surprise you—the extended elaboration of the central concept of monotheism: the concept of the One. The task of the monotheists was to credit—not just theologically but also philosophically—the possibility that one God could serve as the God of all peoples spread across the earth. It is easy to be cynical about this endeavor, to view it as nothing more than a doctrinal mask for the political ambitions of the one Church intent on consolidating its power and gaining dominion over foreign armies and lands. The philosophy of William of Occam and other medieval nominalists provided skeptics of the Church with a razor sufficient to shred this mask to bits. There is, they declared, no other unity than numerical unity, individual beings in themselves and of themselves. No need to posit a separate principle or another reality, for whatever makes an individual man a man makes him as concrete individual. There are no universals, no universal man, no species or genera; all such entities lack existence and are simply concepts fabricated by our minds—or, more cynically, by minds intent on gaining power over us by means of these fabrications.

This position was at war with that of Duns Scotus and other realists, who insisted that species and genera were not arbitrary groupings of individuals but real entities. Arguing passionately for the reality of universalia, realists insisted on defining their unity as nonnumerical, that is, unities or Ones could nevertheless not be counted as such inasmuch as they are not determinate but open and nonself-identical. Real universals are, for this reason, unable to determine the particular nature of any individual, and no individual could exhibit the nature of the principle, whether this be the principle of humanity or God.[4]

Medieval Islamic philosophers contributed to monotheism a compelling conceptualization of the real, nonnumerical unity of God, which it expressed succinctly in the formulation "There is no God but God." God appears in this formulation twice negated. The first negation completely removes Him from the order of living individuals, from human existence.[5] This negation produces the apophatic dimension of God as of all real universals, which are inaccessible to us in their nondeterminacy. The second negation announces the appearance of God in the human order, but it does so without canceling the first negation. Divine being appears in each individual being as that being's innermost core, as the eternal "thisness," the haecceity or Angel of its individuated being; in this way do individuals manifest God, but—again—negatively.[6] This means, as was said, that no individual can exhibit or incarnate God, who is the principle that exceeds the plurality of individuals as well as each, individually.

Consider Marx's famous quip that he never once encountered in the streets a universal man but met there only concrete men. On the contrary, Islamic philosophers and realists in the medieval sense would argue that the universal manifests itself in concrete men insofar as it forms a part of them. And yet this part is peculiar not only inasmuch as it is greater than the individual of which it is part but also in the sense that it manifests itself negatively as something withdrawn, as unassumable by the individual.

To all individuals subsumed by an abstract universal, we can attach predicates that identify them once more: he or she is (in his/her nature) X: *homo faber*; a political animal; a thinking being. However, the real universal does not respond to this model of essences and attributes, or predicates, which undergirds the abstract universal. Instead, the former throws such predicates into question. For if it were true that the nature of God, or man, or Polish people were really present in this person here and could also be present in that person there, we could not truly say—the realists argue—what the nature of God, or man, or Poles is. The real universal withdraws from individuated beings any predicate that might be universally applied to them, Still, the real universal is *not* a fugitive from the One, a flight into the multiple, a skeptic of group belonging. Rather, it posits a fugitive One, a One that flees from itself while multiplying its singular presences. We might say that the real universal is an insistent surplus able to negotiate with historical circumstances, not an abstraction added to on an already existing world.

Now, my proposal is that the concept of a real universal was redeveloped in a much expanded fashion in the Freudian/Lacanian theory of sexuality. It was through this theory, elaborated powerfully in the theory of the drive, that psychoanalysis universalized human nature as that which has no nature. Put differently, the nature of man was radically plasticized. This rethinking of the One was begun in the medieval period in an effort to dismantle Aristotle's abstract concept of the universal and, more generally, as part of the effort to replace the entire cast of mythological deities, and all their human foibles, with monotheism. These operations provoked heated discussions of the process of individuation, whereby every human individual maintained a relation with a single God. The philosophical attention given to this day to *Parmenides*, the Platonic dialogue devoted to the conception of the One, attests to the abiding importance of this conceptual challenge.

Freud is seldom given the credit due him for preempting the charge he knew would greet his foray into group psychology. The anticipated charge—psychoanalysis had no right to extend itself beyond its remit, its mandate and expertise—did not fail to arrive. But it arrived belatedly, since Freud had already answered it at the beginning of *Group Psychology and the Analysis of the Ego*, when he stated that a defining tenet of psychoanalysis had always been that the division between the individual and the group fell within the individual subject. This meant that the emergence and composition of the group was therefore the proper territory of his new science. The subject of psychoanalysis is a joint entity, psychic and social at once. Lacan's return to Freud famously stressed this point by decentering the stand-alone ego and critiquing the misguided goal of ego psychologists to shore up its autonomy. The subject of psychoanalysis cannot be understood outside its relation to its milieu. One should therefore read Lacan's brief definition of jouissance as "an inheritance you can enjoy," one that you can use but cannot "use up," as an endorsement and lynchpin of the Freudian concept of the subject.[7] The point is not that no one has an exclusive right to jouissance, for it must be shared. That is to say, it would be incorrect to assume that Lacan is saying that the right to this collective reality—that is, to jouissance—is not an exclusive right of any individual, for it belongs to the group. Jouissance is not something that can be shared; it is a factor of singularization. But it is also incorrect to say that jouissance belongs to singular subjects. Jouissance is not a possession; it can only be used, though no amount of use will deplete it. The point I am emphasizing here is that psychoanalysis is comprehensible as a modern inheritor of the concept of individuation, of the quest to understand how the many relate to the One. Its major contribution to this centuries-long quest is the concept of jouissance.

Lacan confesses in one of his seminars that his work should be understood as an antidote to nominalism. In the medieval debates over the question of the One, it was the realists who took up the charge against nominalism. Lacan insists, however, that his own realist position differs from that of the medievalists. He is no doubt correct, but only if we disregard the Muslim mystics, whose work informs the *Encore* seminar. In that seminar Lacan, like the realists of old, returns to Aristotle, this time to confront him with Freud. The argument of *Encore* approaches the question of sexual difference by offering a theory of the real One, which is paradoxical insofar as it is not at one with itself. From this starting point, it becomes evident that the two of sex does not conform to that limited number to which today's nominalists object. Sexual difference is inconceivable as a reduction of a large multiple to a smaller one—to a mere two—because the two is not just another one, a second one, added to the first. The two are too heterogeneous to be regarded in this manner.

(3) The two of sexual difference was pressured to surrender to the multiplicity of gendered positions to respect the historical variability and constructedness of the subject. Although it was acknowledged that sexual difference was conceived by psychoanalysis not as a biological given but as an effect of a specific technique, or apparatus—namely language—the new wave of feminists worried that the structuralist conception of language was ahistorical and produced invariant effects. For this reason, the apparatus (*l'appareil*) of language was dislodged from its role as the smithy of sex and replaced by historically variable technologies or *dispositifs*—that is, the complex machinery of social practices and knowledges, relations of power, norms and ideals—responsible for constructing gendered positions and relations.

However, the recourse to technologies of gender quickly confronted a problem: that of technological determinism. How can we ensure that what came out of the machine was not simply what was put into it, that the gendered subject was not completely stripped of autonomy? This problem was fixed by a well-recognized and anodyne truth: techniques had to be continually redeployed, repeated, but repetition always fails because nothing can be repeated in the same way twice. Or, there is no such thing as repetition.[8] It was on this denial of repetition that gender theory staked its hope, for the dooming of repetition meant that variation was inevitable and this margin of variation, this slim difference, was seized upon as the site of resistance, the launching pad of thousands of small differences.

The epilogue of *Fear and Trembling* relates an amusing anecdote to which Kierkegaard would implicitly respond in the book immediately following it, *Repetition*. "Heraclitus the obscure" had a disciple who was so inspired by his master's fine thesis that "one could not step in the same river twice" that he could not prevent himself from embellishing it further: "One cannot do it even once."[9] Somewhere, Lacan, speaking of Heraclitus, refers to the "muddy waters of [the latter's] occultism," thinking, perhaps, of both Jung and the ancient epithet attached to Heraclitus's name, for Lacan nods in affirmation of Kierkegaard's point in recounting the anecdote of the overzealous disciple. What exactly is Kierkegaard's point? It is that the disciple inadvertently undermined his master's purpose; for if one remains content with a dismissal of repetition as impossible, one cannot—as Heraclitus intended—affirm movement and change. What the flat denial of repetition obscures is an important fact; if there were no repetition, then the Eleatic denial of movement (with which Kierkegaard opens *Repetition*) would be valid. But it is not valid; there is movement, there is change, and these are possible because there is repetition.

Gender theory hangs its hat on the impossibility that something could ever be "repeated backward," that is, that an act or experience that had once taken place could occur or be experienced in the same way again. The Greeks called that which gender theorists deny *recollection*. However, Kierkegaard—and Freud, after him—distinguish recollection from repetition, which proceeds in the opposite way by "recollecting forward" an event that had never occurred or a memory that had not "aroused . . . an experience."[10]

One of Freud's first examples of this process clarifies what is at issue in repetition as opposed to recollection. Emma suffers from a phobia of entering stores by herself. The origin of the phobia, it turns out, lies not in a single incident but in two incidents taken together. In the first, a shopkeeper grabs her genitals through her clothes. An outside observer might say that in this incident she was sexually assaulted, but Emma is no outside observer, and she herself, too young to know anything about sex, could not and did not experience the assault as sexual. Some time later, having passed the age of puberty, Emma once again enters the store alone. This time, two shop assistants laugh at her clothes. While an outside observer would see in this incident no hint of sexual aggression, Emma, who recollects the previous scene forward, experiences that former scene as if for the first time and senses a sudden "sexual release."

This canonical example of repetition is also—and significantly—an illustration of what Freud calls the "diphasic onset of sexuality." What is remarkable about the example is the fact that sex seems to be locatable in neither of the scenes, or snapshots, presented in the analysis. In the first, sex is absent from experience, while in the second it is absent from the actions that transpire. One might be tempted to trot out the old pansexualist charge once again or to update it by accusing Freud of perpetrating a "cinematographic illusion" of sorts, not by stringing two still frames together on an abstract, homogeneous time line to create the illusion of movement but by doing something similar: stringing together two perfectly innocent scenes on the same time line to create the illusion of sex. One only needs to stop the projection and both—movement and sex—would disappear, like a mirage.

To save both, we need to follow the advice of Deleuze and recognize that the instants or "frames" are not static, immobile but rather mobile sections, snapshots, precisely, inasmuch as they are incomplete figures—"in the process of being formed or dissolving"—of transformation. This simple recognition makes the sequence of snapshots an "immanent analysis of movement" or—in the Emma example—of sex, wherein movement or sex appears as the active link *between* the instants or scenes.[11] This analysis is deemed immanent by Deleuze because it grasps the figures and scenes as they unfold in time, as finite figures and finite scenes. Or, perhaps we should say that it is so because it grasps the finite immanently. We propose this refinement to make the point that an immanent analysis regards the finite not as something that is limited to a specific length of time, or is circumscribed chronologically, but as what, in its ingoing singularity, has no term and as such repels circumscription.

If the finite, approached immanently, is not defined by a boundary that temporally demarcates it, it nevertheless, and for this very reason, becomes subject to another kind of limit. Not one that cuts it off as a segment from time ongoing but one that plunges it into its midst. The latter limit injects into finite being a heterogeneity that divides it internally or—better—de-phases it. The finite subject—subject to time—is subject to delay rather than to the immediacy of the all at once, to a *break*, then, in the all at once.

It is important to insist on this point to preempt the automatic assumption that intervals or breaks are only features of an abstract notion of time, which notion owes its abstract nature to the fact that it breaks the vital flow of time down into discrete segments of dead time. A nonabstract, immanent notion of time would, it is assumed, restore the continuous flow by eliminating the breaks. In truth, however, the finite subject is not immediately present to a continuous unfolding of events but to breaks, delays, obstacles, still points, to which Freud constantly drew our attention through his invention of a series of concepts. These include a "latency period" that divides the two scenes of sexuality in the Emma case, a "periodic nonexcitability" that interrupts psychic functioning, and a "memory system" that he famously installed between perception and consciousness, thus disjoining them, interrupting their continuity.

In his *Project for a Scientific Psychology* Freud describes perceptions as too ephemeral to leave any trace, meaning that the perception system remains unsullied, innocent, perpetually ready to receive further impressions, while consciousness is conceived as a belated defense against unconscious memories that have already been recorded. Although this model is altered a bit in "A Note upon the 'Mystic Writing-Pad,'" the disjunction between perception and consciousness retains its prominence and leads Freud to this firmly stated conclusion that "this discontinuous method of functioning of the system Pcpt-CS (perception-consciousness system) lies at the bottom of the origin of the concept of time."[12] (Given his early and continued commitment to these models of an out-of-joint time, it is surprising that Freud was ever associated with a theory of continuous biological development.)

The crucial point is this: Freud gives sexuality the same structure he gives to the temporality of psychic functioning. This relation is not founded on mere analogy; neither term—time nor sex—has priority over the other. The two are co-originary. The subject is sexuated inasmuch as she is finite, subject to time. Or, sex belongs not to the essence of the subject but to her historicity; it defines her life of pleasure/unpleasure inasmuch as she is finite, subject to time's vicissitudes.

In the temporal logic of psychic functioning as in the sexual logic brilliantly illuminated by the Emma case, two incidents or moments of time are divided by a break; the second repeats the first but not exactly. This noncoincidence is what triggers the naive, historicist denial of repetition; "not exactly" is not enough by historicist lights. For Freud, however, things are otherwise; it is noncoincidence, lack of synchrony that repetition repeats. Postpubescent Emma finds in the earlier scene something—namely sex—lacking, though her discovery is anachronistic since sex was not lacking to prepubescent Emma so much as to the distant observer whom the older Emma will come to be. Moreover, anachronism—or temporal heterogeneity—is doubled, for not only does the past come to be infected by the sense of a displaced present (thus introducing a premature sexuality that arrived too early to be felt), but the present also seems to be infected by a displaced sense of the past (creating a belated experience of sex as a kind of leftover of the former scene). Too early/too late: these are the times of sexuality as well as the times of time itself.

But why not simply see in this a double failure of repetition, rather than a successful repetition, the actual occurring of time and sexuation? Why assert—against the historicist denial of repetition and the Eleatic denial of movement—that the subject does actually become immersed in the waters of sex/time? These questions and denials all arise from the same source: the misguided assumption that breaks and flows are always antithetical. The Emma case belies this assumption. The anachronisms produced by the diphasic onset of time testify most assuredly to the persistence of a break rather than to a flowing into each other of the two scenes precisely because what is produced is not a homogenous stream of time. Emma does not make her older self present to what could not have been present to her younger self (there is no sense of a continuous maturation or education here), nor does she reconstitute what was not as what now is. Each scene is thus internally disrupted as Emma remembers forward what did not yet happen as what had already happened.

Rather than a double misfire, however, we witness here the actual onset of sexuality. Emma is sexed; the event of sexuated time passes, and to prove it, there is a sudden burst—a now—in the sexual release. This now, this burst, happens in a split second, a second that splits rather than gathers the two scenes. Meanwhile, the movement, the passage or flow, takes place not between the two scenes but within each. The two scenes in the shop remain the before and after of what divides them and prevents them from flowing together, yet each undergoes an alteration not by the other but in relation to the other. As a result of this, each scene opens up, loses its self-containment. Again, we must caution that this does not mean that one scene comes to contain the other. Instead, both of Emma's encounters—with the store owner in the first case and the shop clerks in the second—become irreducible to the present moment of their taking place. And this is precisely where continuity comes in, finds its footing, for the later scene will find in the earlier one its point of genesis—though this will be not in what happened there but in what did not happen.

To respect history is to remain mindful of the fact that not only does the past bear on the present but also that the present bears on the past. The two collude with each other, flow toward each other but never into each other. There is temporal continuity but only because there are temporal breaks. The subject is finite, in time, only because she is divided by it, out of sync with it. Staking so much on its denials of division and repetition, gender theory, I would submit, relies not only an abstract, neutered notion of the subject, but on an abstract notion of time as well.

FOUCAULT ENTERS THE MIX

Having stated some of my objections to what I regard as a "wrong turn" turn toward gender in the '80s, I would like to restart the discussion from a different historical moment: the period in the 1920s when heated debates erupted over Freud's theory of castration as essential for the formation of the sexed subject. What many in the fledgling field of psychoanalysis—including Ernest Jones, Helene Deutsch, Melanie Klein, and Karen Horney—found unpalatable was the universality of castration, its indifference to the anatomy of the subjects it was supposed to bring into being. If castration aims at the phallus and the little girl has none, so the reasoning went, then the theory does not do her justice and must be modified to account for her anatomical and biological differences from the boy. Juliet Mitchell summarized these early debates in the following way:

> The opposition to Freud saw the concept of the castration complex as derogatory to women. . . . Women, so to speak, had to have something of their own. The issue *subtly* shifts from what distinguishes the sexes to what has each sex got of value that belongs to it alone. In this context, and in absence of the determining role of the castration complex, it is inevitable that there is a return to the very biological explanation from which Freud deliberately took his departure.[13]

The first thing to note is that this early opposition to Freud was aimed specifically at his—let us call it for the moment—"monotheistic" conception of sex; that is, his thesis that there is only one libido and it is male.[14] Abandoning this counterintuitive thesis like the plague it seems to be, his opponents ended up reducing sexual difference to the prelinguistic, brute difference between the sexual organs of boys and girls. The second thing to note is that the shift from sex to gender that occurred during the debates of the late 1980s resulted in a symmetrical error. The elimination of sexual difference in favor of a study of the social technologies of gender construction left biology behind altogether and produced subjects without any vitality, subjects without bodies, or, more precisely, subjects without sexual organs. (I hasten to add that all organs are sexualized in psychoanalysis.)

Given the fact that so much of the work on the social construction of gender relied for its inspiration on Michel Foucault's argument against psychoanalysis in *The History of Sexuality, Volume* 1, a second look at the argument is fully warranted. Foucault, confronted with student demands for "sexual liberation" during and after the events of May '68, set out in this work to show that this demand for liberation was politically misguided, the rallying cry of a flawed revolt fueled, in significant part, by Freud's "repressive hypothesis." In the face of this harsh accusation, one must be precise about what the father of psychoanalysis actually said about repression. He said, specifically, that while ideas are susceptible to repression and once repressed seek to return into consciousness, this leaves open the question of whether or not sex is repressed.

In *The Other Side of Psychoanalysis*, the 1969–1970 seminar he delivered in response to these same May '68 demonstrations, Lacan pointed out that Freud's full claim was that in contradistinction to ideas, which alone can be repressed, affect is displaced.[15] We can extend this theoretical point to sex itself. What purpose does this distinction between ideas and affect/

jouissance/sex serve? It allows us to observe that the latter is not inaccessible to consciousness, or does not elude the subject, in the same way as a repressed idea does. For if there is always a chance that a repressed idea will gain entry and be recognized by consciousness, there is no chance that jouissance will ever be anything other than displaced in relation to consciousness; it will never find a place that is proper to it. Sex does not identify; it is not a predicate of the subject.

It is this crucial distinction between ideas and sex that prompts Lacan's warning that in parading their sexuality, the students were in fact "looking for a master," allowing themselves to become the helots of a regime that was pulling their strings.[16] If they sought sanction in Freud's theory of sex for these self-displays, for their attempts to "out" their jouissance, they were knocking at the wrong door. And so was Foucault when he attempted to lay a significant portion of blame for the troubling rise of *scientia sexualis* (the hygienic, confessional, let-it-all-out theory of sex) on the doorstep of Berggasse 19.[17] Sex can never be put on display because it is nothing other than that teetering, unsettling displacement that permanently throws the subject's identity off-balance. In short, Foucault attributed to Freud a position he never held and then attacked it, arguing that far from demanding release from the shackles of power, sex operates in solidarity with it; sex—the notion of sex, Foucault insisted—is saturated with power through and through.

In truth, Lacan and Foucault were on the same side in regard to the way sex had—incorrectly—become a political factor during this period and the role it was being made to play in the new paradigm of human domination. Both cautioned the students that the demand for sexual liberation did not oppose power but, on the contrary, played into its hands. What they disagreed on was the definition of sex, how it was conceived in psychoanalysis. Lacan argued forcefully that sex is not repressed, that the mechanism of repression does not apply to it, and for this very reason, it made no sense to say that sex sought to be liberated from repression. Sex is not hidden, it is displaced. Lacan thus enjoined the students not to sacrifice their enjoyment to those in power by parading it, exposing it as if it were a predicate—more: the major one—of their identity.

In Foucault's view, sex was nothing more than a fictional construct of power that serves to bind subjects to unified, determinate, and normative identities. Political opposition to biopower must take the form, therefore, not of liberating suppressed sexual identities but of liberating oneself from them, freeing oneself from classification by their categories. Thus, while Lacan and Foucault were allied in their opposition to the demand for the liberation of sex, on the grounds that this demand was a ruse of power, Lacan put all his energy into showing that sex, or jouissance, was not answerable to the opposition liberation/repression. He castigated the idea that jouissance needed to be liberated as a sham, while Foucault pursued the idea that sex and the demand to be liberated—to be known, to assert one's identity—were inextricably intertwined.

But the original historical claim for which The History Sexuality is now best known is this: a mutation took place at the end of the eighteenth century that culminated in what Foucault named at the end of that book "biopower." The specific mutation that gave rise to this new regime occurred, in his words, in the "mode of relation between history and life." For while life had previously been viewed as outside history, "in its biological element" it was now also placed "inside human historicity, [where it was] penetrated by the latter's techniques and powers."[18] The author of an introduction to Ludwig Binswanger's "Dream and Existence," Foucault endorsed the argument Binswanger put forward, specifically that "life considered as function [as instinct] is not the same as life considered as history"; by their very nature, the two are incommensurable, and "it is their incommensurability that justifies the existence of both concepts, each within its own sphere."[19] This "each within its own sphere," the absolute separation of the terms, is placed in jeopardy whenever their incommensurability is ignored, for at this point, one of the terms begins inexorably to annex the other. Foucault essentially provides an historical illustration of Binswanger's thesis in The History of Sexuality when he argues that biopower is the annexation of life by power and that this particular denial of the incommensurability of life and history was "an indispensable element in the development of capitalism."[20]

The takeover of vital functions by human history (the latter consisting not only of technologies and power but also language and meaning, everything that constitutes the lived experience of life) is the inevitable result of the "new mode of relation" that effaces the radical distinction between vital functions and lived experience. But because there is, in fact, a radical split, because the terms are incommensurable—as Foucault, following Binswanger, asserts—that which pretends to forge a relation between the terms, or forges a fraudulent relation, must itself be fraudulent or, as Foucault puts it, "a mirage."[21] In Foucault's account, the "mirage" that allows us to remain blind to the incommensurability of life and human history is precisely sex, which thus performs a synthetic function: "[T]he [bio-political] notion of 'sex' made it possible to group together, in an artificial unity, anatomical elements, biological functions, conducts, sensation, and pleasures, and it enabled one to make use of this fictitious unity as a causal principle, an omnipresent meaning, a secret to be discovered everywhere."[22] (Once again, the misunderstood notion of pansexualism is treated with contempt.)

Foucault is claiming in effect that scientia sexualis, the science of sex, attempted to make a science of relations, of the knotting together of incommensurable, disjunct terms. If the fictitious entity, sex, was conceived as a "thing with intrinsic properties and laws of its own,"[23] these properties were those that defined a supposed commonality among otherwise distinct and incompatible terms, and its laws were those that rendered the relations among them predictable. The establishment of a commonality, and of predictable relations, supported the belief that life could be managed and made to yield greater gains. They also undergird the development of the techniques that put this belief into practice.

This historical thesis, as bold as it is complex, relies nevertheless on an observation that is common enough. It has often been noted that binary oppositions, while purporting to oppose disjunct terms, tend in fact to negate the negating power of one of these terms. Thus neutralized, the second, or unmarked, term loses its independent value and is taken up, sublated by the first, unmarked term. We saw that in the debates over feminine sexuality that occurred in the 1920s, the opposition between biology and symbolic forms collapsed in favor of biology, while the reverse happened in the gender theory debates of the 1980s: biology, or life, was sublated into symbolic forms and produced decorporealized subjects or bodies without sexual organs. One scarcely needs to add that the opposition male/female is the best-known example of this, for in this supposed opposition, the female term has often been shown to have the value only of a minor exception, one that is easily absorbed by the unmarked, male term that stands in for both.

What was new or unique to biopolitics, then, was the invention of something called *sex*, which permitted life to be sublated by history. Before this, blood, consanguinity, had played a major role in the machinations of power, but with the invention of the sexual mirage, hereditary allegiances and consanguine loyalties tended to be downplayed—if not completely eliminated. The species being promoted by biopower and the globalized economy of capital came to depend on a more individualized notion of the subject, one less encumbered by the older order of hereditary allegiances. The invention of sex, Foucault is saying, aided the construction of a completely individualized notion of the subject. Individualized! Not individuated or singularized.

In an interview he gave on French television just a few years before the publication of *The History of Sexuality*, Lacan made a claim so diametrically opposed to Foucault's that it stops one cold: "Back to zero, then, for the issue of sex, since anyway capitalism, that was its starting point: getting rid of sex."[24] (Stated otherwise, as I will argue, Lacan's message is this: capitalism made sex—that in the subject which is more than the subject—disappear.) The television interview aired during the time Lacan was himself returning to zero, going back to basics in his (1972–1973) *Encore* seminar on sex, sexual relation, and feminine sexuality. In retrospect, the entire seminar can be read as a preemptive strike against Foucault's misconstruction of the Freudian problematic of sex.

Responsible for triggering much of the French and, later, Anglo-American feminist interest in psychoanalysis in the 1970s, the seminar is filled with conceptual breakthroughs that were not so much challenged in the 1980s rejection of both psychoanalysis and sexual difference by gender theorists as they were ignored or left unmined. The formulation for which Encore became notorious is the one that stated "There is no sexual relation [Il n'y a pas de rapport sexuel]" even though the meaning of this statement was immediately trivialized, thus rendering it unworthy of the attention it received. The statement was taken to be a refutation of the Hollywood-style fiction of the romantic couple and an effort to expose the fact that actual sexual relations are inevitably freighted with compromise and disappointment, ultimately with failure. The famous observation of Freud, that "men and women are a phase apart psychologically," was embraced as a pessimistic, incontrovertible truth, and the admission of failure was celebrated as sober political wisdom.

Still, one has to be a little surprised that the impulse to trivialize did not check itself by pausing to wonder why such dime-store psychology would choose to express itself in this particular way, that is, as a negation of the impersonal phrase il y a (there is), a phrase alive with philosophical resonance. In philosophy, this phrase is regularly employed to state not something but the fact that this something is, that it exists. In its very structure, then, the phrase appears to append to beings a supplement of Being. Everything happens as if the verb "to be" had so atrophied that it required propping up by a prosthetic support of Being. Given this philosophical perspective, it becomes clear that Lacan's declaration that there is no sexual relation does not deny that such relations exist; rather, it kicks away the prop of Being, which serves to "precomprehend" these relations, turning them into prescriptions or formulas.

If there is no prop or support, no "ontological precomprehension" of being, no Being common to all, this means—in this case—that the sexes are incommensurable. They have nothing, no Being, that is common to them. The notion of their complementarity, which would conceive them as two halves of a common humanity, is thus firmly rejected, and Freud's statement about their being out of step with each other psychologically is confirmed, in a nontrivial sense.

Moreover, one must note that the casting aside of prosthetic Being is related to a second gesture that Lacan refers to explicitly as a "lopping off of the predicate."[25] Lacan's text is particularly recondite at this point, although the argument remains intact. Here, with a bit more elaboration, is what it says. Refusing in the first gesture the support of a common being—or in refusing to say that "a being is," which would imply that "its being is a thing which is, that its existence is a thing which exists"[26]—we are thereby permitted to "lop off the predicate," to say, for example, that "man is" without saying what.

Now, if "man is" can be considered a complete statement, one that requires no predicate to complete it, this is because the verb "to be" is no longer understood as merely a copula linking a subject to a predicate term. The lopping off of the predicate, testifies to the fact that the proper status of the verb "to be" is verbal, active; to be is an act. To say "man is" without feeling one has to say that he is something or other is to acknowledge that he brings himself into being. Those who think that Lacan has wandered off the Freudian reservation into some foreign philosophical territory would do well to reread Freud's essay "Femininity," where the same point is made: "In conformity with its peculiar nature, psycho-analysis does not try to describe what a woman is—that would be a task it could scarcely perform—but sets about enquiring how she comes into being."[27] How she comes into being, not how she is constructed as a woman by society, as this remark has, mistakenly, been read.

THE MYTH OF THE THIRD SUBSTANCE

Aristophanes's infamous myth of the two sexes as two halves of a whole, forever in search of one another, is mocked and dislodged by Lacan in the *Encore* seminar by an antic counter-myth of "the third substance." Lacan begins, seemingly resignedly, by noting "Nowadays, well, we just don't have that many substances. We have thinking and extended substance."[28] This statement is uncontroversially true; Descartes reduced the number of substances to two only, and the inheritors of his streamlining have been puzzling ever since over the problem of how to put them together. Having made this anodyne observation, however, Lacan grows more audacious, declaring next that for psychoanalysis, two substances are simply not enough. To make up for this deficit, he therefore postulates a third, which he baptizes enjoying substance (*la substance jouissante*).

Had he had not preceded this myth with a warning against automatically turning nouns into substances, had he not just effectively argued that being is not a substance but an act, we might have been tempted to think that Lacan was stating here that jouissance is a substance that can be added to the other two to form a link between them, the one that has gone missing at least since Descartes. Lacan would then be performing before our eyes the crime with which Foucault was even then preparing to charge psychoanalysis: the crime of inventing something called *sex* that would function as a mirage, as a vanishing point where the radical incommensurability between what can be thought, experienced, lived historically and the vital functioning of our bodies was obfuscated. But Lacan did try to inoculate us against this misreading of jouissance (his own preferred term) or of sex, in the Freudian sense. Freud, we know, did claim that the sex of the subject was determinable neither by physical science nor by a psychological study of social behavior; sex in the Freudian sense is not graspable either as an anatomical or conventional difference.[29] Neither one nor the other, sex is not, however, a third thing, the missing link that sutures the two.

The counter-myth of the "third substance" challenges the myth of the severed sexes who longed to be reunited by invoking Freud's own counter "mythology" of the drive. In a superficial reading, Freud's speculative and widely dismissed "drive theory" would seem less to challenge than to satisfy the longing to reunite what had been torn asunder, would seem to confirm Foucault's thesis that the concept of sex was just the sort of legerdemain biopower needed to sublate vital functions into political life. Listen, with Foucault's accusation in mind, to this familiar definition of drive given to us by Freud: drive "appears to us as a concept on the frontier between the mental and the somatic, as the psychical representative of the stimuli originating from within the organism and reaching the mind, as a measure of the demand made upon the mind for work as a consequence of its connection with the body."[30] This definition might be misconstrued to suggest that the drive, which occupies the frontier, between the psychical and the somatic, is the missing link connecting them to each other.

The Freudian myth of the third substance, however, resigns the above misreading of the Freudian drive to the museum of curios and demolishes the notion that sex is a separate, third term that causes the incommensurability of the binary terms to vanish. If we seriously credit Freud's positioning of drive as archaic, we are obliged to take enjoying substance as operating before the "substances" that emerge along its frontier. In other words, the rupture traced by drive precedes and gives rise to that which it ruptures. But sex, or enjoying substance, accounts not only for the radical disjunction of the two from each other but also for the internal disjunction of each. In this way, sex purloins the substantial, or self-enclosed, dimension of each of the so-called substances. Before proceeding, however, I want to state again as clearly as possible the argument thus far: Foucault argues that biopower, abetted by the Freudian theory of sex, eliminated the difference between life as function and life as historical experience, or between life and law, and thus eliminated the political space or space of possibility of human action. Lacan argues the opposite: Freud conceives sex as that which takes place in, and holds open, the space of human action.

If being as such is sexed, if being—defined as an act—is bound up originarily with jouissance, as Lacan maintains, we must look for evidence of this claim in each of the two substances that are "nowadays" assumed to exhaust the field of being. Lacan turns first to thinking substance to examine what becomes of it once Freud appears on the scene peddling his theory of sexuality. Descartes, who baptized it *res cogitans*, defined the function of "thinking substance" as the formulation of clear and distinct ideas, a fact that makes Freud's instructions to his patients—not that they should think clearly about what troubles them but should instead say whatever stupidity pops into their heads—appear scandalous. Indistinct ideas and unsorted nonsense acquire with Freud a value that would have dumbfounded Descartes. But why? In *The Project for a Scientific Psychology* (1896), in a statement that profoundly alters the conception of *res cogitans*, Freud asserted that "it is in relation to a fellow human-being [Nebenmensch] that a human-being learns to cognize."[31] Freud's premise is that the occasion of thinking, the incentive for the activity we call thought, is associated with this fellow human being, who was—Freud claims—the first object of our satisfaction. However, this primal object is enigmatic, for it stays with us forever not as a familiar and fond memory but as a thing, as a residue that evades judgment.

This thing, this *res*, is the very thing that will desubstantialize thinking substance. As with the classical notion of an underlying substance, this thing, too, is said to stay with us forever, never to abandon us, and thus to be the condition of our permanence or persistence as a thinking subject. And yet, while underlying substance guarantees the subject's self-identity, this thing is, on the contrary, the source of the continuous *aphanisis* of identity, its continuous obliteration. It is a strange fellowship we have with the *Nebenmensch*, for by evading apprehension, it refuses to offer any criteria for fellowship. This raises a key question, which Freud himself will try to tackle only later in his essay "The Unconscious." Why do we experience this fellow human being as a fellow, as uncannily close, as inalienably internal, rather than as simply alien? Why do we experience it, Freud asks in the essay, not as a second consciousness but as we do, that is, as such an intimate (if inassimilable) part of our own consciousness that it can only occur to us as a surplus of ourselves rather than as separate from us? Why do we count ourselves in our difference from ourselves not as two, but as one, albeit a paradoxical one, a more-than-one?

We should not let the answer Freud gives to this question distract us from the radical thinking behind his proposing it in the first place. For not only does Freud make the question proceed from the point Lacan will emphasize in the *Encore* seminar and elsewhere—that reason, for psychoanalysis, is not divorced from but intimately "concerns jouissance"[32]—he also immediately understands this "first object of satisfaction" as an unsettling of any easy distinction between the other consciousnesses, the community of thinkers, with which thinking puts us in touch, and the singularity of our thinking process. By answering that we experience the reality of the unconscious—sex or jouissance—as a part, however alien, of ourselves, Freud posits the "sense of self" as internal to our sense of being in relation to something other and greater than ourselves.

Encore's infamous pronouncement, "There is no sexual relation," stands little chance of being understood in isolation from its companion, *y a d'l'Un* ("there is [some] One").[33] Sex, we might say, is an exotic force; it pushes us away or severs us from ourselves. Sex is, in this sense, the enemy of relation conceived as an unbroken link (just as it separates the sexes from each other) as much as it is the enemy of a certain One, a unifying One. It is for this reason that Freud found himself unable to countenance the existence of what his friend, Romain Rolland, described as an "oceanic feeling," that is, "a feeling of an indissoluble bond, of being one with the external world."[34] Rather than a feeling, Rolland's description of the oceanic struck Freud as being "of the nature of an intellectual perception."[35] Like all abstractions, Rolland's notion of an oceanic oneness carries no conviction of existence; nothing in the concept necessitates its existence.

Refusing, therefore, to acknowledge its existential validity, Freud turned to his own theory to show how such an illusion might mistakenly claim to find support there, first of all in its discrediting of the purported autonomy of the ego. Specifically, the psychoanalytic claim is that the boundaries between the ego and its outside are weakened insofar as the ego is "continued inward, without any sharp delimitation, into an unconscious entity . . . designated as the id."[36] Freud implies, without pressing the point—no doubt out of a desire to find some common ground between his ideas and those of his friend—that this weakening of the ego's boundaries does not authorize the existence of an oceanic feeling. Why not? The answer lies in the problematic "continuity" Freud too quickly asserts. For: between the unconscious and consciousness, between the ego and the id, there is no continuity (in the common sense); there is only discontinuity, disruption, displacement. The "inner sense" I have of myself as other than myself—thanks to the unconscious and to the "first (ungraspable) object of satisfaction"—precisely prevents the oceanic feeling, the feeling of being immersed in the One, from overtaking us.

Countless paradoxes attest to this primary psychoanalytic insight, inscribed in Lacan's formulas of sexuation as the antinomic relation between the universal and existential quantifiers, the all and its exceptions. This antinomy is also acknowledged by Freud when he insists that each of us unconsciously denies our own mortality even though we accept the elemental fact that man is mortal. Individual subjects view themselves as exceptions, albeit exceptions that do not contest the validity of "the One" to which we belong. "I" and "we" are forever antinomic, in tension by definition, though this tension does not amount to a contradiction: to an "I" or "we." This is further confirmation of the point we have been making all along: the One of psychoanalysis is paradoxical, prenumerical, a One that is more than—and simultaneously, as we will see—less than one.

COMPACTNESS: THE EROGENOUS ZONE

Zeno's paradox of Achilles and the tortoise enters into Lacan's discussion of sexual difference in *Encore*, as if to illustrate the radical differences that divide men and women: swift versus slow, incremental half-steps versus continuous movement, man versus beast. But this somehow misses the point, for however different Achilles and the tortoise are from each other, they do not simply go off in their own directions, diverge. On the contrary, they constitute converging series, since each progresses toward the same limit, which they eventually reach—even if they do not meet there. At the limit, Achilles will not catch up with the tortoise but surpass her. So much for our romantic hopes of an ecstatic fusion! Instead, the two remain a phase apart, retain their differences from each other. What, then, is the point of noting their convergence?

Since Zeno, we have been accustomed to conceiving the limit only negatively, as unreachable, as defining an impossibility of movement. Yet Deleuze, in his book on Leibniz, speaks of convergent series (which tend toward a limit but do not always possess a final term) in a positive way, as entailing intensities.[37] Convergent series, which tend toward a common limit without meeting because there always remain an infinite number of points between them, create a positive condition that has a technical name: compactness. In *Encore*, Lacan invokes this condition: "I will posit here the term 'compactness.' Nothing is more compact than a fault."[38] What Lacan refers to as a "fault" is what we have been calling a limit. A fault or limit defines a locus or tight space, as Lacan acknowledges when he asserts that "the space of jouissance . . . proves to be compact."[39] A compact space, we could therefore say, is an erogenous zone, or compactness serves here to explicate the notion of erotogeneity. Lacan makes this argument more or less explicitly when he speaks in a rather strange way about a bed, as if he were not talking merely about a mundane object but a psychoanalytic concept. Indeed, we must read this seminar as his conversion of a bed, as a space of erotic encounter, into a concept by describing it precisely as compact—a space in which two people "squeeze each other tight," or experience jouissance.[40]

The first thing to note is that compactness is a space of impossibility, the impossibility of union or encounter, and at the same time it is a place where something out of the ordinary happens: jouissance. This draws attention to a truth on which psychoanalysis has always insisted: sexual enjoyment—jouissance—emerges from an encounter with the impossible, depends on a limit. Freud, for example, says "an obstacle is required to heighten libido."[41] This Freudian insight is irreducible to the simple observation that libido is often incited by an obstacle whether mounted by the other's coyness, social or familial taboo, or mere happenstance. For these observations often go on to focus on the overcoming of the obstacle via jouissance. The profound point Freud and Lacan make is that jouissance is manifest not in the overcoming of the limit or obstacle, or is not manifest as the shattering of the limit. Jouissance is, instead, a shattering *at* the insurmountable limit. The obstacle or separation remains intact.

This point can be brought back to our earlier reference to the *Nebenmensch*, the Thing, mentioned in *The Project*. Freud inadvertently blocks our theoretical curiosity and thus our understanding of this concept by defining it prematurely in the text as the first object of our satisfaction. According to the theory he will develop here and elsewhere, however, there is no object of satisfaction prior to its loss, no mother before her withdrawal. The first object of our satisfaction is not later lost, but becomes a lost object retrospectively. From this, we conclude that it is the object's status as inexistent that causes satisfaction or jouissance. In the terms used in *The Project*, the *Nebenmensch* (or Thing) evades judgment; thinking encounters a limit, an impossibility beyond which it cannot go. On the other side of this limit, there is nothing—no existing thing, nothing to think. However, on this side, there is not merely an experience of absolute impasse, of thought's negation. There is also affirmation in the form of satisfaction in an inexistent object, in an object that escapes the judgment of existence.

Deleuze attributes to Leibniz an argument that lights the path Freud will take: "I must have a body because an obscure object lives in me. . . . Leibniz's originality is tremendous. He is not saying that only the body explains what is obscure in the mind. To the contrary, the mind is obscure, the depths of the mind are dark, and this dark nature is what explains and requires a body."[42] Mind encounters a limit, an obstacle, which is nothing more (or less) than an inexistent object, a darkness. Yet this obscure object does not merely check the powers of mind; it also incites an unshakable conviction: there must be a body. Body does not impinge on mind and thereby obstruct it, nor for that matter does the mind collide with the body in its impenetrable density. Mind and body do not encounter one another; rather, mind encounters an obscure object that is neither purely internal nor purely external to it, and it is this object that persuades mind that something other must exist.

Leibniz does not define this obscure object as "satisfying" or as the object-cause of jouissance. It will be left to psychoanalysis to elaborate this dark spot in the mind in terms of libido or drive, as the frontier between lived experience and biological life. However, one can find among earlier philosophers—namely the medieval followers of Avicenna, for whom the concept of just such a frontier or *barzakh* (in Arabic) played a major role in their thinking—a certain precedent for the direction in which Freud would develop the Leibnizian notion of a mental darkness. For those medieval philosophers, the limit disjoined/linked the divine and the sensible worlds, but precisely because this limit passed not simply between these two worlds but also through the sensible, it (the limit or *barzakh*) was often conceived in terms of a dialectic of erotic love, as the disjoining/linking of lovers.

And for Ibn 'Arabi, at least, the real object of love was considered to be not what was obtained—that is, not the beloved as such—but rather "something nonexistent. . . . The object of loving adhesion in the moment when the lover has achieved union . . . is again something nonexistent, namely, the continuation and perpetuation of that union."[43] That is, what one loves in the other is "not a datum existing in *actu*" but not a mere nothing either.[44] Ibn 'Arabi brings this insight even closer to the Leibnizean dark spot by insisting that "Love [which] is closer to the lover than is his jugular vein" is so "excessive in its nearness that it acts . . . as a veil."[45]

In that compact space in which lovers, the sexes, *res cogitans* and *res extensa* "hold each other tight," what one adheres to is not something one obtains or grasps but that which escapes one's grasp inasmuch as it inexists, has not yet happened. However long it lasts, real love is enduring. It unites itself with a future that is not merely a receding horizon—if not now, perhaps tomorrow—but the future's proleptic event in the form of a surplus pleasure or (in Freud's phrase) an "incentive bonus" that promises more (encore) to come. This future, which arrives before it is actualized, is instigated by an encounter that is contingent, by a meeting with chance, with the unexpected. Here, clearly a distinction is registered between a future that is anticipated, awaited but forever put off—a future always incompletely achieved; let us call it capitalism's future—and the amorous future, which overtakes us (and the chronological order of things) by surprise, as fore-pleasure.

In his work on jokes, Freud defines the incentive bonus or fore-pleasure as a pleasure that slips through or hoodwinks the censor. However, it makes more sense in terms of his own theory to interpret fore-pleasure as an affirmation at the limit, an indication of a relaxing of the impossible. There is something I can neither know nor ultimately control. And yet, through the veils and dark spots, the obscurity in the depths of my mind, a truth speaks. Not in words or concepts, but as the not yet heard or seen.

THE RETURN TO TWO

The two of sexual difference must also be thought this way. Not as two separate and opposed ones, not "that binary partition one most spontaneously thinks of [as] 'sexual difference,'"[46] but as a "predual" sexuality, "more originary than the dyad" to which sexual difference is commonly reduced.[47] More originary than the dyad is the cut, the split, which is not a) a split into two "determinities [*Bestimmtheiten*]"[48] (i.e., not two determinate one's) nor an intervention in an originary One. For the One is not that which is split but rather that which is formed from the splitting. Thus formed, the One is paradoxical, a severed One, detached from some (surplus) part of itself from the start: $1 = a$.[49]

Derrida's argument in "*Geschlecht*: Sexual Difference, Ontological Difference" is that Heidegger chose the neutral term *Dasein* rather than man (*Mensch*) not in order to disavow the ontological status of sexual difference, but to distinguish sexual difference from the commonplace conception of it as dyadic. This would bring Heidegger's position in line with that of Freud, who adamantly maintained (against feminist protests) that there was only one libido and it was male. To insist that being and libido are not divided into two is not to assert that the male term absorbs, dispels, or neutralizes a second, female term. In other words, it does not end with the triumph of One. It acknowledges a paradoxical One, split from itself but not into another. Feminine sexuality, that dark continent of psychoanalytic thought, is not Leibniz's dark spot in the mind, but it is not unrelated to it. While Freud maintains that there is only one libido and it is male, the surety this affords does not prevent him from puzzling over the question of that libido which cannot be counted as male nor as another one.

NOTES

INTRODUCTION

1. Youssef Ishaghpour, *Le reel, face et pile: Le cinema d'Abbas Kiarostami* (Tours: Farrago, 2000), 66. "States" in Islamic philosophy are predicaments or conditions in which one is faced with an unknown.

2. This term was coined by one of Kiarostami's first and most avid supporters of the director in the US, Jonathan Rosenbaum. It appears in his review of *Taste of Cherry*, "Fill in the Blanks," published in *The Chicago Reader* on May 29, 1998.

3. Kiarostami's use of repetition is widely commented upon. See, especially, Laura Mulvey, "Repetition and Return: The Spectator's Memory in Abbas Kiarostami's Koker Trilogy," *Third Text* 21, no. 1 (2007): 19–29.

4. Christian Metz, *The Imaginary Signifier: Psychoanalysis and Cinema*, trans. Celia Britton, Annwyl Williams, Ben Brewster, and Alfred Guzzetti (Bloomington: Indianapolis University Press, 1882).

5. Jean-Luc Nancy, *The Evidence of Film Abbas Kiarostami* (Brussels: Yves Gevaert Editeur, 2001). Published in English, French, and Farsi, this book remains one of the most penetrating analyses of Kirarostami's cinema.

6. The Arabic term, *mazur*, "manifestation" or "epiphanic form," is discussed at length throughout the book.

7. This remark was made in an interview with Miguel Mora in 2004 and quoted by Alberto Elena in *The Cinema of Abbas Kiarostami*, trans. Belinda Coombes (London: SAQI, 2005), 183.

8. Sigmund Freud, "On Psychotherapy," in *The Standard Edition of the Complete Psychological Works of Sigmund Freud*, trans. James Strachey (London: The Hogarth Press and the Institute of Psycho-Analysis, 1953–1974), 7:260–261.

9. Freud, "On Psychotherapy," 261.

10. Youssef Ishaghpour, "True and False in Art," *Una poetica de lo real* (Buenos Aries: Malba, Coleccion Costantini, n.d.), 268. (This well-known phrase was translated un-idiomatically as "so I exist.") Published in Spanish and English, this collection of essays coincided with an exhibition of Kiarostami's film corpus, photographs, and installations at the eighth Buenos Aires International Independent Film Festival.

11. Henry Corbin, *Alone with the Alone: Creative Imagination in the Sufism of Ibn 'Arabi* (Princeton, NJ: Princeton University Press, 1990), 156.

12. Michel Chodkiewicz, *An Ocean without a Shore*, trans. David Streight (Albany: SUNY Press, 1993), 25.

13. Henry Corbin, *Avicenna and the Visionary Recital*, trans. Willard R. Trask (Irving, TX: Spring Publications, 1988).

14. Henry Corbin, *Avicenna and the Visionary Recital*, 3–4.

15. Henry Corbin, *Avicenna and the Visionary Recital*, 7–8, 30.

16. Hubert Damisch, *The Origin of Perspective*, trans. John Goodman (Cambridge, MA: MIT Press, 1995), 93–94.

17. Laura Mulvey, "Kiarostami's Uncertainty Principle," *Sight and Sound* 8, no. 6 (June 1998): 25, 26.

CHAPTER 1

1. An earlier version of this text, titled "The Fate of the Image in Church History and the Modern State," appeared in the open access journal *Politica Comun* 1, no. 2 (2012).

2. Henry Corbin, *Spiritual Body and Celestial Earth: From Mazdean Iran to Shi'ite Iran*, trans. Nancy Pearson (Princeton, NJ: Princeton University Press, 1955), 31.

3. Corbin, *Spiritual Body and Celestial Earth*, 30.

4. Corbin, *Spiritual Body and Celestial Earth*, 20.

5. Henry Corbin, *The Voyage and the Messenger: Iran and Philosophy*, trans. Joseph Rowe (Berkeley, CA: North Atlantic Books, 1998), 128.

6. Christian Jambet, *The Act of Being: The Philosophy of Revelation in Mulla Sadra*, trans. Jeff Fort (New York: Zone Books, 2006), 284.

7. Christopher Bamford, "Introduction," in *The Voyage and the Messenger*, xxi. Although he says that he is quoting Corbin directly, Bamford does not provide references to specific texts in this introduction.

8. A troubling, if humorous, illustration of this demotion of the imagination is given in Barry Mazur, *Imagining Numbers* (New York: Farrar, Straus, and Giroux, 2003), which quotes an editor at McGraw-Hill: "We were told [while composing high school history textbooks] to avoid using the word 'imagine' because people in Texas felt it was too close to the word 'magic' and therefore might be considered anti-Christian," 15.

9. Henry Corbin, *Alone with the Alone: Creative Imagination in the Sufism of Ibn 'Arabi* (Princeton, NJ: Princeton University Press, 1990), 71.

10. Henry Corbin, *Le paradoxe du monotheism* (Paris: L'Herne, 1981); it consists of three essays that lay out the paradoxes of Islamic monotheism, the importance of its angelology, and the main tenets of its apophatic theology. In a conversation with Fethi Benslama titled "Tranductions des monotheismes" (*Cliniques mediterraneennes* 73 [2006]: 213–230), Jean-Luc Nancy represents monotheism as a mutation of cosmology. This essay was translated by Ed Pluth as "Translations of Monotheism" and published in the online journal S in a 2009 special issue devoted to Islam and psychoanalysis, edited by Sigi Jöttkandt and Joan Copjec. See also *Imago Dei: The Byzantine Apology for Icons* (New Haven, CT: Yale University Press, 1990), where Jaroslav Pelikan discusses the conception of Christ as the creation of a "new being."

11. St. John of Damascus, *Three Treatises on the Divine Images*, trans. Andrew Louth (Crestwood, NY: St. Vladimir's Seminary Press, 2003), treatise III, 95.

12. St. John of Damascus, *Three Treatises on the Divine Images*, 96.

13. Henry Corbin, "Theophanies and Mirrors. Idols or Icons?," *Spring* 2 (1983): 2.

14. Relevant discussions of the widely observed distinction between lumen and lux can be found in Hans Blumenberg, "Light as a Metaphor for Truth: At the Preliminary Stage of Philosophical Conception Formation," in *Modernity and the Hegemony of Vision*, ed. David Michael Levin (Berkeley: University of California Press, 1993), 30–62; and in Tom Cheetham, *After Prophecy: Imagination, Incarnation, and the Unity of the Prophetic Tradition* (New Orleans: Spring Books, 2007), 90, 95.

15. William Chittick, *The Sufi Path of Knowledge: Ibn al-'Arabi's Metaphysics of Imagination* (Albany: SUNY Press, 1989), 11.

16. Cheetham, *After Prophecy*, 90.

17. Blumenberg, "Light as a Metaphor for Truth," 50.

18. Corbin, *Alone with the Alone*, 276.

19. Leo Steinberg, *The Sexuality of Christ in Renaissance Art and in Modern Oblivion* (New York: Pantheon, 1983), 9, 63; this book was originally published as a special issue of *October* 25 (Summer 1983). The *New York Times* praised the book as "one of the most provocative art-historical studies of the 20th century" (March 15, 2011).

20. Steinberg, *The Sexuality of Christ*, 9.

21. Steinberg, *The Sexuality of Christ*, 63.

22. Henry Corbin, "Comparative Spiritual Hermeneutics," in *Swedenborg and Esoteric Islam* (West Chester, PA: Swedenborg Foundation, 1999), 130.

23. For an extensive discussion of this issue, see Todd Lawson, *The Crucifixion and the Qur'an* (Oxford: OneWorld Press, 2009).

24. Corbin, *Alone with the Alone*, 207.

25. Corbin, *Alone with the Alone*, 203.

26. Corbin, *Alone with the Alone*, 244.

27. Steinberg, *The Sexuality of Christ*, 72.

28. Renaissance art, we would be safe in saying, narrowed the incarnationist dictum "this is my body" to the pictorial *ostentatio genitalium*, "This is His penis." This raises a host of questions and objections that cannot be addressed here, although they underwrite much of our argument and motivate our interest in the docetic alternative to the incarnationist position. The Hellenic, or pagan gods, were always demonstrably sexed, endowed with features and foibles that were correlated with their visibly sexed bodies. Monotheism, in ridding God of all attributes, obviously rendered Him bodiless and sexless. In taking on human form, God—in Christ's form—took on a body, one that was anatomically differentiated. Our claim is not that Renaissance artists inaccurately illustrate the dogma of incarnation but that their faithfulness to it highlighted the problems we find here.

29. Henry Corbin, ed. "Divine Epiphany and Spiritual Birth in Ismailian Gnosis," in *Cyclical Time and Ismaili Gnosis* (New York: Routledge, 1983), 106.

30. Steinberg, *The Sexuality of Christ*, 16.

31. Quoted by Catherine Malabou in *The Future of Hegel: Plasticity, Temporality and Dialectic*, trans. Lisabeth During (London: Routledge, 2005), 110.

32. See Corbin, *Alone with the Alone*.

33. Steinberg, *The Sexuality of Christ*, 46–47.

34. Corbin, "Divine Epiphany," 149.

35. Corbin, *Alone with the Alone*, 80.

36. Marie-José Mondzain, *Image, Icon, Economy, the Byzantine Origins of the Contemporary Imaginary*, trans. Rico Franses (Redwood City, CA: Stanford University Press, 2005), 13, 14. Mondzain refers in her introduction to the economy as a "universe of guile, which should remind us of what Islamic tradition knew and developed under the term, *hila*" (6).

37. Mondzain, *Image, Icon, Economy, the Byzantine Origins*, 14.

38. Mondzain, *Image, Icon, Economy, the Byzantine Origins*.

39. Christian Jambet, *La logique des orentaux. Henry Corbin et la science des forms* (Paris: Seuil, 1983), 189.

40. Corbin, *Alone with the Alone*, 186.

41. I am here borrowing the formulations Lacan uses for the necessary ("that which does not stop writing itself") as opposed to the impossible ("that which does not stop not being written"). The formulation of the contingent or conditional most often attributed to him is "that which stops not writing." See Jacques Lacan, *The Seminar of Jacques Lacan: Book XX, Encore*, ed. Jacques-Alain Miller, trans. Bruce Fink (New York: Norton, 1998), 58–60. Compare Chittick's explanation: "According to the principles of Peripatetic philosophy, the 'impossible' . . . cannot come into existence, in contrast to the 'possible,' which may or may not come into existence, and the Necessary, which cannot not exist. But 'imagination' is a domain in which contraries meet and impossible things take place" (123).

42. Chittick, *The Sufi Path of Knowledge*, 123.

43. Corbin, *Alone with the Alone*, 152.

44. Blumenberg, "Light as a Metaphor for Truth," 54.

45. For a superlative development of this thesis, see Gerard Wajcman, "Intimate Extorted, Intimate Exposed," trans. Ron Estes, Jr., *Umbr(a)* (2007): 37–57.

46. Jacques Lacan, *The Four Fundamental Concepts of Psycho-Analysis*, ed. Jacques-Alain Miller, trans. Alan Sheridan (London: Hogarth Press and Institute of Psycho-Analysis, 1977), 194–195.

47. David Sterritt, "Taste of Kiarostami," Senses of Cinema, September 2000, https://www.sensesofcinema.com/2000/abbas-kiarostami-remembered/kiarostami-2/. For Ibn 'Arabi on the concept of "seeing with two eyes," see Chittick, *The Sufi Path of Knowledge*, 356–381.

48. Corbin, *Alone with the Alone*, 199.

49. Corbin, *Alone with the Alone*, 184.

50. Corbin, *Alone with the Alone*, 245.

51. Chittick, *The Sufi Path of Knowledge*, 356.

52. Chittick, *The Sufi Path of Knowledge*.

53. Henry Corbin, "Apophatic Theology as Antidote to Nihilism," trans. Roland Vegso, *Umbr(a)* (2007): 64–65. This essay is a translation of an essay from Corbin's work *Le paradoxe du monotheism*.

54. Chodkiewicz, *An Ocean without a Shore*, 40.

55. Chodkiewicz, *An Ocean without a Shore*, 50.

56. Corbin, *Alone with the Alone*, 156; the phrase is from Ibn 'Arabi, "Love is closer to the lover than his jugular vein."

57. Corbin, *Alone with the Alone*, 145.

58. Gilles Deleuze, *Cinema 1: The Movement Image*, trans. Hugh Tomlinson (Minneapolis: University of Minnesota Press, 1986), 96.

59. The first quotation is from Lacan, *The Four Fundamental Concepts*, 63; the second is from Deleuze, *Cinema 1: The Movement Image*, 96.

60. Hamid Dabashi, *Close Up: Iranian Cinema. Past, Present, and Future* (London: Verso Press, 2001), 14.

61. Corbin, *Alone with the Alone*, 300, fn. 25.

62. Corbin, *Alone with the Alone*, 151.

63. Lacan, *The Four Fundamental Concepts*, 62.

64. Lacan, *The Four Fundamental Concepts*.

65. Lacan, *The Four Fundamental Concepts*, 62. Here, for convenience's sake, is the passage: "This reel is not the mother reduced to a little ball . . . it is a small part of the subject that detaches itself from him while still remaining his, still retained. This is the place to say, in imitation of Aristotle, that man thinks with his object. It is with this object that the child leaps the frontiers of his domain, transformed into a well, and begins the incantation. . . . To this object we will . . . give the name . . . the *petit a*."

66. Lacan, *The Four Fundamental Concepts*.

67. Chittick, *The Sufi Path of Knowledge*, 117–118.

68. Chittick, *The Sufi Path of Knowledge*, 118.

69. Aristotle, *De anima*, 2:11, 423b, translated as "On the Soul," in *The Basic Works of Aristotle*, ed. Richard McKeon (New York: Modern Classics, 2001), 7.

70. Aristotle, *De anima*.

71. Aristotle, *De anima*, 2:11, 423b, 23–24; my emphasis.

72. Aristotle, *De anima*, 2:11, 423a, 32.

73. John of Damascus, 91.

74. Jacques Lacan, *The Seminar of Jacques Lacan: Book VII: The Ethics of Psychoanalysis*, trans. Dennis Porter, ed. Jacques-Alain Miller (London: Tavistock/Routledge, 1992), 93.

75. Lacan, *Seminar VII*.

CHAPTER 2

1. Henry Corbin, *Alone with the Alone: Creative Imagination in the Sufism of Ibn 'Arabi* (Princeton, NJ: Princeton University Press, 1990), 187; see also Chittick, *The Sufi Path of Knowledge: Ibn al-'Arabi's Metaphysics of Imagination* (Albany: SUNY Press, 1989), 125, 134.

2. Harold Bloom, "Preface," to Corbin, *Alone with the Alone*, x–xi. In Henry Corbin, *Spiritual Body and Celestial Earth: From Mazdean Iran to Shi'ite Iran*, trans. Nancy Pearson (Princeton, NJ: Princeton University Press, 1977), Corbin cites Ibn 'Arabi's complete account of the myth (135–136).

3. Corbin, *Alone with the Alone*, 185.

4. Henry Corbin, "Mundus Imaginalis, or The Imaginary and the Imaginal," *Swedenborg and Esoteric Islam*, trans. Leonard Fox (West Chester, PA: Swedenborg Foundation, 1999), 32.

5. Corbin, *Alone with the Alone*, 135.

6. Christian Jambet, *The Act of Being: The Philosophy of Revelation in Mulla Sadra*, trans. Jeff Fort (New York: Zone Books, 2006), 27.

7. Jacques Lacan, "The Freudian Thing: Or the Meaning of the Return to Freud in Psychoanalysis," in *Écrits*, trans. Bruce Fink (New York: W. W. Norton, 2006), 337. This essay is a version of a lecture Lacan delivered in Vienna in 1955 in which he announces his "return to Freud" as a return to the truth that speaks in Freud's discourse.

8. Emmanuel Levinas, "Meaning and Sense," in *Collected Philosophical Papers*, trans. Alphonso Lingis (Pittsburgh, PA: Duquesne University Press, 1998), 75–107.

9. In Christian Jambet, "The Constitution of the Subject and Spiritual Practice: Observations on L'Histoire de la sexualité" (in *Michel Foucault, philosophe*, ed. Francois Ewald, trans. Timothy Armstrong [New York: Routledge, 1992]), the author attempts to establish a rapport between Foucault (who became infatuated with Iranian thought in the wake of the Iranian Revolution) and the work of Corbin.

10. Jean Laplanche, *Après-Coup*, trans. Jonathan House and Luke Thurston (New York: Unconscious in Translation, 2017), 130.

11. Jacques Lacan, "Position of the Unconscious," in *Écrits*, trans. Bruce Fink (New York: W. W. Norton, 2006), 711–712.

12. As part of his attempt to discredit Corbin, primarily, and Mircea Eliade, to a lesser extent, Wasserstrom claims that these two "brothers in arms" identified themselves with "secret militant orders," among which the Fedele d'Amore is singled out by name. See Steven Wasserstrom, *Religion after Religion: Gershom, Scholem, Mircea Eliade, and Henry Corbin at Eranos* (Princeton, NJ: Princeton University Press, 1999), 16. Lacan discusses this group in his Encore seminar; they are, in fact, the courtly love poets, militants of love.

13. While some of Jung's concepts—archetype being the most noteworthy—appear in Corbin's work, they are developed quite differently in the latter. In Corbin's elaboration, an archetype is much closer to Lacan's object than to Jung's concept.

14. For example, Wasserstrom suggests in *Religion after Religion* that the fact that the Bollingen Foundation published and subsidized Corbin's research is evidence that his work served a petro-political agenda (149, 150–151); that, although trained as a "mere philosopher, Corbin thought of himself as a prophet" (154); that "it [is not] inconceivable that Corbin supported Vichy" (146); and even though there is no evidence that Henry Corbin was anti-Semitic," he practiced "a kind of philosophical anti-Judaism" (179, 177).

15. Wasserstrom, *Religion after Religion*, 10.

16. Wasserstrom, *Religion after Religion*, 181.

17. Corbin, *Spiritual Body and Celestial Earth*, xxix.

18. In his fine book, *The Sufi Path to Knowledge: Ibn Al-Arabi's Metaphysics of Imagination* (Albany: SUNY Press, 1989), Chittick respectfully contends that Corbin overemphasized the concept of the imaginal world to the detriment to the cornerstone concept of Islamic teachings, "tawhid, the declaration of God's Unity" (x). For a measured account of Corbin's interventions in the field and the criticisms voiced against them, see also Hermann Landolt, "Henry Corbin, 1903–1978: Between Philosophy and Orientalism," *Journal of the American Oriental Society* 119, no. 3 (July–Sept. 1999): 484–490.

19. Corbin, *Alone with the Alone*, 207.

20. Chodkiewicz, *An Ocean without a Shore*, 56.

21. Wasserstrom, *Religion after Religion*, 56–57.

22. See Nicholas Halmi, "Coleridge on Allegory and Symbol," *The Oxford Handbook of Samuel Taylor Coleridge*, ed. Frederick Burwick (Oxford: Oxford University Press, 2009), 50.

23. Halmi, "Coleridge on Allegory and Symbol." It should be noted that it was Coleridge's essay "On the Prometheus of Aeschylus" that caught the attention of Schelling, who insisted that Coleridge may not have pushed the notion of "tautegory" far enough.

24. Henry Corbin, "The *Imago Templi* in Confrontation with Secular Norms," *Temple and Contemplation*, trans. Philip Sherrard (London: Kegan Paul International, 1986), 308.

25. Wasserstrom, *Religion after Religion*, 64; italics in original.

26. Wasserstrom, *Religion after Religion*, 63. For a superb corrective of Wasserstrom's misguided criticism, see Henry Corbin, "Apophatic Theology as Antidote to Nihilism," trans. Roland Vegso, Umbr(a) (2007): 59–83, an essay on the crucial concept of individuation.

27. Christian Jambet, "The Paradoxical One," trans. Michael Stanish, special issue on Islam, Umbr(a) (2009): 150.

28. Corbin, "Apophatic Theology," 69.

29. Corbin, *Alone with the Alone*, 114.

30. Gilles Deleuze, "Phantasm and Modern Literature," *The Logic of Sense*, ed. Constantin V. Boundas, trans. Mark Lester (New York: Columbia University Press, 1990), 300.

31. Corbin, *Alone with the Alone*, 154.

32. Corbin, *Alone with the Alone*, 114.

33. Corbin, *Alone with the Alone*, 199; see F. W. J. Schelling, *Historical-Critical Introduction to the Philosophy of Mythology*, trans. Mason Richey and Markus Zisselsberger (Albany: SUNY Press, 2007), 124.

34. Corbin, *Alone with the Alone*.

35. Tyler Tritten, "The Trace as Tautegorical: An Account of the Face in Levinas," *Canadian Journal of Philosophy* 18, no. 4 (2014): 256–273.

36. Corbin, *Alone with the Alone*, 124.

37. Corbin, *Alone with the Alone*.

38. Corbin, *Alone with the Alone*, 125.

39. Corbin, *Alone with the Alone*, 126.

40. Jambet, *The Act of Being*, 420–423.

41. Jambet, "The Paradoxical One," 141.

42. Christian Jambet, "The Death of Epiphany," trans. Robert Bononno, special issue on Islam, Umbr(a) (2009): 142.

43. Slavoj Zizek, *The Indivisible Remainder: An Essay on Schelling and Related Matters* (New York: Verso Press, 1996), 8.

44. Jambet, "The Death of Epiphany," 158.

45. Jacques Lacan, *Seminar XI: The Four Fundamental Concepts of Psychoanalysis*, ed. Jacques-Alain Miller, trans. Alan Sheridan (London: Hogarth Press and the Institute of Psychoanalysis, 1977), 46.

46. Jambet, "The Paradoxical One," 160.

47. Lacan, *Seminar XI*, 22; Jambet, "The Paradoxical One," 160.

48. Tritten, "The Trace as Tautegorical," 240.

CHAPTER 3

1. Wasserstrom, *Religion after Religion: Gershom, Scholem, Mircea Eliade, and Henry Corbin at Eranos* (Princeton, NJ: Princeton University Press, 1999). While I strongly disagree with Wasserstrom's assessment of Corbin, I also want to acknowledge it as a serious, learned, and useful book. It provides invaluable historical information and many fine arguments. Many of my disagreements stem from the fact that Wasserstrom's historicist stance is radically at odds with Corbin's as well as my own. He regards the Eranos scholars as products of their time. It is this notion of the homogeneity of "one's time" that is frontally attacked by the Gnostics whom Corbin defends.

2. Wasserstrom, *Religion after Religion*, 109–110.

3. Roxanne Varzi, an artist, filmmaker, playwright, and professor of anthropology, has written and staged a play, *Splinters of a Careless Alphabet*, about the influence of Western philosophy on the Iranian Revolution. In one scene a heated debate is staged between young Iranians who have adopted opposing positions on the question of whether Corbin or Khomeini offered the correct radical agenda.

4. Wasserstrom, *Religion after Religion*, 110. Every August from 1949 to 1978, Scholem, Eliade, and Corbin (the core of the Eranos group) met with several other religious scholars in Ascona, Switzerland to debate religious questions. As Wasserstrom points out, these dates mark the beginning of the Cold War and a new program of "Islamicization" that would spread throughout the Arab-Islamic world to challenge the hegemony of the West.

5. Christian Jambet, *The Act of Being: The Philosophy of Revelation in Mulla Sadra*, trans. Jeff Fort (New York: Zone Books, 2006), 21.

6. Henry Corbin, "Apophatic Theology as Antidote to Nihilism," trans. Roland Vegso, *Umbr(a)* (2007): 59–83.

7. Corbin, "Apophatic Theology," 60.

8. Giorgio Agamben, *Profanations* (New York: Zone Books, 2007), 77. I have chosen to quote from Agamben, rather than Corbin directly, because it is a succinct statement of the latter's argument and highlights the ties that Agamben's work has to Corbin's.

9. Agamben, *Profanations*, 75.

10. Jambet, "Four Discourses on Authority in Islam," trans. Sigi Jottkandt, *S: Journal of the Jan Van Eyck Circle for Lacanian Ideology Critique* 2 (2009): 8.

11. This notion of the effacement or "clouding over" of the dimension of the Cloud is very close to Badiou's concept of "covering over" and resonates throughout my argument. See Alain Badiou, *The Immanence of Truths*, trans. Susan Spitzer and Kenneth Reinhard (London: Bloomsbury Academic, 2018).

12. These are the most familiar translations of the term *Gharbzadegi*, first coined in the 1940s but made famous by Jalal-e-Ahmad's book *Westoxification: A Plague from the West* (self-published, 1962) and its subsequent use by the famous Marxist Islamic activist, Ali Shariati.

13. Corbin, "Apophatic Theology," 61.

14. Corbin, "Apophatic Theology," 60.

15. For a contemporary discussion of this question of the nonpaternal God of Islam, see Fethi Benslama, *Psychoanalysis and the Challenge of Islam*, trans. Robert Bononno (Minneapolis,: University of Minnesota Press, 2009).

16. In *Omens of Millennium: The Gnosis of Angels, Dreams, and Resurrection* (New York: Riverhead Books, 1996), Harold Bloom mentions this felicitous translation penned by his friend and fellow Gnostic, Bentley Layton.

17. See, for example, these wonderfully complex sentences from Alenka Zupančič's *What Is Sex?* (Cambridge, MA: MIT Press, 2017): "What distinguishes the human animal is that it knows (that it does not know). Yet at stake here is not simply that humans are aware, conscious of this lack of sexual knowledge in nature; rather, the right way of putting it would be to say that they are unconscious of it (which is not the same thing as saying that we are not conscious of it)," 16.

18. Wasserstrom, *Religion after Religion*, 128.

19. Henry Corbin, *The Visionary Recital*, trans. Willard R. Trask (Irving, TX: Spring Publications), 24.

20. Corbin, *The Visionary Recital*, 25.

21. Imam Khomeini, "Address at Bihishti-i-Zahra," in *Islam and Revolution: Writings and Declarations of Imam Khomeini*, trans. Hamid Algar (Berkeley, CA: Mizan Press, 1981), 258. See also Imam Khomeini's *Last Will and Testament* (Washington, DC: Interests Section of the Islamic Republic of Iran, 2007).

22. See the excellent essay by Negar Mottahedeh, "Iranian Cinema in the Twentieth Century: A Sensory History," *Iranian Studies* 42, no. 4 (2009): 531–532. I see Khomeini's position on the question of technology in a darker light than Mottahedeh.

23. Jambet, *The Act of Being*, 39.

24. "What exactly is Iranian cinema? . . . It is simple. Its exoticism is accessible . . . aesthetically ascetic, minimalist in its narrative construction, to the point of pictorial nominalism," Hamid Dabashi, *Masters and Masterpieces of Iranian Cinema* (Washington, DC: Mage Publishers, 2007), 329.

25. Jacques Lacan, *Le séminaire, livre XVII: D'un autre à l'autre* (Paris: Seuil, 2006), 28.

26. For an extensive discussion of Foucault's relation to this event, see Janet Afary and Kevin B. Anderson, *Foucault and the Iranian Revolution* (Chicago: Chicago University Press, 2005). The invaluable appendix contains essays by Foucault and his critics, published during the period in question.

27. Christian Jambet, "The Constitution of the Subject and Spiritual Practice: Observations on *L'Histoire de la sexuality*," in *Michel Foucault: Philosopher*, ed. Francoise Ewald, trans. Timothy Armstrong (New York: Routledge, 1992), 244.

28. Henry Corbin, *Alone with the Alone: Creative Imagination in the Sufism of Ibn 'Arabi* (Princeton, NJ: Princeton University Press, 1990), 114.

29. Corbin, "Apophatic Theology," 71.

30. I am, of course, alluding to Anselm's famous phrase "God is that than which none greater can be conceived."

31. Corbin, "Apophatic Theology," 67.

32. Chittick, *The Sufi Path of Knowledge: Ibn al-'Arabi's Metaphysics of Imagination* (Albany: SUNY Press, 1989), 148.

33. Corbin, "Apophatic Theology," 73.

34. Corbin, "Apophatic Theology," 76.

35. Jacques Lacan, *Seminar XI: The Four Fundamental Concepts of Psychoanalysis*, ed. Jacques-Alain Miller, trans. Alan Sheridan (London: Hogarth Press and the Institute of Psychoanalysis, 1977), 23, 24. A few pages later (30), Lacan explicitly links this state of "limbo" to the Gnostics.

36. Chittick, *The Sufi Path of Knowledge*, 149.

37. Chittick, *The Sufi Path of Knowledge*, 132.

38. Corbin, "Apophatic Theology."

39. Forough Farrokhzad is regarded as the greatest Persian poet of the twentieth century, and her film, *The House is Black* (1963) is revered by Iranian filmmakers as the precursor of new Iranian cinema. Kiarostami pays homage to her by borrowing the title of his film, *The Wind Will Carry Us*, from one of her most famous poems. The title of this section of my argument, "Listen!," is the imperative refrain of that same poem.

40. Dabashi, *Masters and Masterpieces*, 57.

41. Henry Corbin, "From the Gnosis of Antiquity to Ismaili Gnosis," in *Cyclical Time and Ismaili Gnosis* (London: Kegan Paul International, 1983), 174.

42. Corbin, "From the Gnosis of Antiquity to Ismaili Gnosis."

43. On the notion of the echo in Leibniz, see Gilles Deleuze, *The Fold: Leibniz and the Baroque*, trans. Tom Conley (Minneapolis: University of Minnesota Press, 1993); and Giorgio Agamben, *The Use of Bodies*, trans. Adam Kotsko (Redwood City, CA: Stanford University Press, 2016).

44. Christian Jambet, "A Philosophical Commentary," in *Paradise of Submission: A Medieval Treatise on Ismaili Thought*, ed. and trans. S. J. Badakhchani (London: I. B. Tauris in assoc. with the Institute of Isma'ili Studies, 2005), 45.

45. Corbin, *Alone with the Alone*, 290; Corbin quotes from Etienne Souriau, *L'ombre de Dieu* (Paris, 1955).

46. Sigmund Freud, "Instincts and Their Vicissitudes," in *The Standard Edition of the Complete Psychological Works of Sigmund Freud*, trans. James Strachey (London: The Hogarth Press and the Institute of Psycho-Analysis, 1953–1974), 14:121–122.

47. Jacques Lacan, *The Sinthome: The Seminar of Jacques Lacan, Book XXIII*, ed. Jacques-Alain Miller, trans. A. R. Price (Cambridge: Polity Press, 2016), 9.

CHAPTER 4

1. This statement is taken from an interview with Abbas Kiarostami by Michel Ciment and Stephane Goudet, who quote it in the essay "Le Goût de la cerise . . . et la saveur de la mure," *L'Avant Scene* no. 471 (April 1998): 2 (my translation).

2. Emmanuel Levinas, *Existence and Existents*, trans. Alphonso Lingis (Pittsburgh, PA: Duquesne University Press, 2001), 11–12.

3. Levinas, *Existence and Existents*, 4.

4. Henry Corbin, *Spiritual Body and Celestial Earth: From Mazdean Iran to Shi'ite Iran*, trans. Nancy Pearson (Princeton, NJ: Princeton University Press, 1955), 82.

5. Anson Rabinbach, *The Human Motor: Energy, Fatigue, and the Origins of Modernity* (New York: Basic Books, 1990).

6. In *24/7: Late Capitalism and the Ends of Sleep* (London: Verso 2013), need is italicized in reference to the "the scientific quest . . . to reduce the body's *need* for sleep," 4. I am assuming from this and other evidence that Crary wishes to distinguish from this scientific notion another relation to sleep, more like desire.

7. Sigmund Freud, *The Standard Edition of the Complete Psychological Works of Sigmund Freud*, trans. James Strachey (London: The Hogarth Press and the Institute of Psycho-Analysis, 1953–1974), 5:570.

8. Jacques Lacan, Seminar XI: The Four Fundamental Concepts of Psychoanalysis, ed. Jacques-Alain Miller, trans. Alan Sheridan (London: Hogarth Press and the Institute of Psychoanalysis, 1977), 51.

9. Lacan, Seminar XI, 67.

10. Levinas, Existence and Existents, 10.

11. Michel Foucault, The History of Sexuality, Volume I, trans. Robert Hurley (New York: Pantheon, 1978), 138.

12. Jacques Derrida, Aporias, trans. Thomas Dutoit (Redwood City, CA: Stanford University Press, 1993), 63.

13. Martin Heidegger, Being and Time, trans. John Macquarrie and Edward Robinson (London: Harper Perennial, 2008), 310.

14. Levinas, Existence and Existents, 36. Compare, also, Existence and Existents, 10: "the notion of the struggle for existence . . . taken at the level of the . . . economic order . . . appears as struggle for a future, as the care that a being takes for its endurance and conservation. It is the struggle of an already existent being for the prolongation of its existence" to Lacan: "Man, being but an object, serves an end. He is founded on the basis of his final cause . . . which in this case is to live or, more precisely, to survive . . . to postpone death and dominate his rival," in Lacan, The Seminar of Jacques Lacan: Book XX, Encore, ed. Jacques-Alain Miller, trans. Bruce Fink (New York: Norton, 1998), 105.

In an interview Philippe Nemo conducted with Corbin, "From Heidegger to Sohravardi," Corbin discusses both his initial interest in Heidegger's work and his strong opposition to the German philosopher's notion of dissatisfaction with this notion of being toward death.

15. Jonathan Crary, 24/7: Late Capitalism and the Ends of Sleep (London: Verso 2013), 126 and 109, where he indicts "the psychoanalytic reduction" of dream wishes to a matter of "individual desire and acquisitiveness," which rendered unthinkable any other than "wishes for a dream house, a dream car, or a vacation."

16. Levinas, Existence and Existents, 37.

17. Levinas, Existence and Existents.

18. Otto Friedrich, The Kingdom of Auschwitz, 1940–1945 (London: Harper Perennial, 1994), 2–3.

19. Levinas, Existence and Existents, 22.

20. Levinas, Existence and Existents, 14. See my "Cinema as Thought Experiment: On Movement and Movements," Differences no. 1 (2016): 143–175, in which I try to show the way the mother in Ten attempts to negotiate the conflicting pulls of the piety movement and a naïve, idealist feminism.

21. Levinas, Existence and Existents, 36.

22. Levinas, Existence and Existents.

23. Lacan, The Seminar of Jacques Lacan, Book II. The Ego in Freud's Theory and in the Technique of Psychoanalysis, ed. Jacques-Alain Miller, trans. Sylvana Tomaselli (New York: Norton, 1988), 89.

24. Henry Corbin, Alone with the Alone: Creative Imagination in the Sufism of Ibn 'Arabi (Princeton, NJ: Princeton University Press, 1990), 116.

25. Lacan, Book II, 89.

26. Lacan, Book II, 114.

27. Freud, "Inhibitions, Symptoms, and Anxiety," in *The Standard Edition*, 20:152.

28. Lacan, *The Seminar of Jacques Lacan: Book I, Freud's Papers on Technique*, ed. Jacques-Alain Miller, trans. John Forrester (London: Norton, 1988), 149.

29. Freud, "Project for a Scientific Psychology," in *The Standard Edition*, 1:318.

30. Levinas, *Existence and Existents*, 9.

31. Jacques Derrida, "Violence and Metaphysics," in *Writing and Difference*, trans. Alan Bass (Chicago: University of Chicago Press, 1978), 136.

32. Jacques Lacan, "Presentation on Psychical Causality," in *Écrits*, trans. Bruce Fink (New York: W. W. Norton, 2006), 144.

33. I have altered the relation between death and fatigue proposed by Roland Barthes; see his book, *The Neutral: Lecture Course at the College de France (1977–1978)*, trans. Rosalind Krauss and Denis Hollier (New York: Columbia University Press, 2007), 20.

34. Levinas, *Existence and Existents*, 25.

35. Lacan also somewhere characterizes the real as "teeming with nothingness."

36. Levinas, *Existence and Existents*, 59.

37. See Derrida's *Aporia* for a discussion of the German term, *Ableben* ("demising"), a medico-legal term that declares, or makes official, the death of human subjects, exclusively.

38. In *Jacques Lacan Speaks* (directed by Francoise Wolff, 1972), a documentary video of a lecture he gave at the University of Louvain, Lacan tells us that death is not a certainty but "belongs to the realm of faith. You're right to believe you'll die; it sustains you. Otherwise you couldn't bear life. . . . The worst thing is that you're not sure."

39. Gilles Deleuze, *Difference and Repetition*, trans. Paul Paton (New York: Columbia University Press, 1994), 112.

40. Deleuze, *Difference and Repetition*, 113.

41. Deleuze, *Difference and Repetition*, 112.

42. Deleuze, *Difference and Repetition*.

43. Gilles Deleuze, *The Logic of Sense*, ed. Constantin V. Boundas, trans. Mark Lester (New York: Columbia University Press, 1990), 152.

44. Deleuze, *Difference and Repetition*, 113.

45. Another question raised by the film concerns its own escape from censorship. Suicide is strictly prohibited in Islam, which surely made it a controversial film, but how is it that it was allowed to be made in the first place? This question is indirectly answered in Stefania Pandolfo's remarkable essay, "'The Burning': Finitude and the Politico-Theological Imagination of Illegal Migration," *Anthropological Theory* no. 3 (2007): 329–363. Based on Pandolfo's ethnographic research with young Moroccan's living in deplorable conditions not unlike those of the day workers in *Taste of Cherry*, the essay examines the risks of heresy associated with suicide and despair alongside Islamic ethical-political conceptions such as *jihad an-nafs*, the struggle of and against the self. Despair, Pandolfo tells us, is not summarily condemned in Islam but rather regarded as a trial that must be undergone insofar as belief is assumed to be "an open ethical work" rather than a given. Despair thrusts the subject into a battle in which they are forced to struggle "against an internal other, impossible to eliminate, and [yet] necessary for life" (348).

46. Freud, "Project for a Scientific Psychology," in *The Standard Edition*, 1:307.

47. I have discussed the "flying man" experiment elsewhere; see "Cinema as Thought Experiment: On Movement and Movements."

48. Levinas, *Existence and Existents*, 66.

49. For his discussion of "inner perception" as dreaming ("eyes wide shut"), see Hamid Dabashi, "In the Absence of the Face," *Social Research* 67, no. 1 (Spring 2000): 127–185.

50. Deleuze, *Difference and Repetition*, 77 (my emphasis).

51. Deleuze, *Difference and Repetition*, 77.

52. For a discussion of Freud's term *die Not des Lebens* as "need" or "pressure" of life, see Jacques Lacan, *Seminar VII: The Ethics of Psychoanalysis*, trans. Dennis Porter, ed. Jacques-Alain Miller (London: Tavistock/Routledge, 1992), 46, 48, 49. A concise and very useful discussion of the concept of "agency/instance" by Étienne Balibar can be found in *Dictionary of Untranslatables: A Philosophical Lexicon*, ed. Barbara Cassin, trans. Emily Apter, Jacques Lezra, and Michael Wood (Princeton. NJ: Princeton University Press, 2014), 22–23.

53. Levinas, *Existence and Existents*, 66.

54. Levinas, *Existence and Existents*, 16.

55. Levinas, *Existence and Existents*, 69.

56. Levinas, *Existence and Existents*, 16. We might describe the difference this way: while Derrida contemplates the present as immediacy, Levinas sees it as mediacy, a time that opens between one moment and the next.

57. Levinas, *Existence and Existents*, 69, 70.

58. Levinas, *Existence and Existents*, 80. See also for a longer discussion Maurice Merleau-Ponty, *The Incarnate Subject: Malebranche, Biran, and Bergson on the Union of Body and Soul*, trans. Paul Milan (Amherst, NY: Humanity Books, 2001).

59. Deleuze, *Difference and Repetition*, 77.

60. Freud, "Remembering, Repeating, and Working Through," in *The Standard Edition*, 12:151.

61. Levinas, *Existence and Existents*, 70.

62. Jean Hyppolite, "Spoken Commentary on Freud's '*Verneinung*,'" in *Écrits*, trans. Bruce Fink (New York: W. W. Norton, 2006), 753.

63. Freud, "Negation," in *The Standard Edition*, 19:239.

64. Levinas, *Existence and Existents*, 52.

65. Levinas, *Existence and Existents*, 63. This remark about the close-up is not made by Levinas apropos of the concept of fatigue.

66. Levinas, *Existence and Existents*, 49.

CHAPTER 5

1. Jacques Lacan, *Seminaire XVII: L'envers de la psychanalyse*, text established by Jacques-Alain Miller (Paris: Seuil, 1991).

2. Lacan borrows the concept of the "quarter-turn" from the mathematical theory of groups. It is interesting to note that there are eight such turns possible in group theory since the four terms can be "flipped" or "reversed," like a sheet of paper. Lacan develops only half of the possibilities. Perhaps one of his followers will develop the remaining ones one day.

3. Shame, and the blush to the face that is its most persistent sign, must be distinguished from the other passions that reddened the faces and rhetoric of those who participated in the events of May '68. Long before Lacan, Charles Darwin had designated shame (and its accompanying blush) as the affect (and passionate sign) of the human subject as such. "Monkeys redden from passion," he noted, "but it would require an overwhelming amount of evidence to make us believe that any animal could blush." Charles Darwin, *The Expression of the Emotions in Man and Animals* (Chicago: Chicago University Press, 1965), 309.

4. Cited in Helen M. Lynd, *On Shame and the Search for Identity* (New York: Harcourt, Brace, and World, 1958), 51.

5. Gilles Deleuze, "Michael Tournier and the World without Others," published as an appendix in *The Logic of Sense*, ed. Constantin V. Boundas, trans. Mark Lester (New York: Columbia University Press, 1990), 305.

6. Brian Massumi, *Parables for the Virtual: Movement, Affect, Sensation* (Durham, NC: Duke University Press, 2002), 217.

7. Jacques Lacan, *Television: A Challenge to the Psychoanalytic Establishment*, ed. Joan Copjec, trans. Denis Hollier, Rosalind Krauss, and Annette Michelson (New York: W. W. Norton, 1990), 20. In this television interview, Lacan makes precisely the same points about the relation between affect and displacement that he makes in *Seminar SVII*. On Freud's notion of discharge as an attempt to theorize the movement of thought, see also Monique David-Menard's *Hysteria from Freud to Lacan: Body and Language in Psychoanalysis*, trans. Catherine Porter (Ithaca, NY: Cornell University Press, 1989), especially the remarkable final chapter, "Jouissance and Knowledge."

8. Lacan's description of the alethosphere, written as it was at the very end of the 1960s, sounds now a bit quainter than the description I give; think "Sputnik" rather than space probes. The myth of the alethosphere and the lathouses is presented in the May 20, 1970, seminar, titled "Les sillons de l'elethosphere" in the book published from the seminar.

9. Sigmund Freud, "Civilization and Its Discontents," in *The Standard Edition of the Complete Psychological Works of Sigmund Freud*, trans. James Strachey (London: The Hogarth Press and the Institute of Psycho-Analysis, 1953–1974), 21:92.

10. Jacques Lacan, *Seminaire X: L'angoisse* (unpublished), June 26, 1963.

11. Jacques Lacan, *Seminar XI: The Four Fundamental Concepts of Psychoanalysis*, ed. Jacques-Alain Miller, trans. Alan Sheridan (London: Hogarth Press and the Institute of Psychoanalysis, 1977), 71.

12. Feminists have always noticed that there is something suspicious, a little too empirical, in the way Freud relates the story of the boy's sudden anxiety at the sight of the mother's missing genitals. Everything depends on a simple, naked perception without symbolic mediation of her missing penis. In *Seminaire X*, Lacan already employs the phrase "not without object" to rethink this notorious scenario. He adds the necessary element of mediation by contending that the whole scene plays out against the backdrop of a universal proposition, "No human being is without a penis." If a woman, then, becomes a source of anxiety, it is not because she gives direct evidence of a particular exception to a universal rule but because she is, for the boy, "not without a penis." What is affirmed is nothing visible. The important point is that the negation of the contrary does not attack the universal from without, providing contradictory evidence of what falls out or escapes from it; it attacks it from within, serving as evidence of the universal's inconsistency, its lack of self-identity. The form of negation to be found in the rhetorical figure of litotes is clearly the same as that which Kant calls "indefinite judgment."

13. In his superb book, *Truth and Singularity: Taking Foucault into Phenomenology* (Dordrecht, the Netherlands: Kluwer Academic Publishers, 1999), Rudi Visker uses the phrase "not without roots" several times to describe this same notion of an ungrounded grounding but without excavating the Lacanian background, which we obviously share. My own thesis is very similar to Visker's; I want to thank Jill Robbins for recognizing this similarity and recommending this book to me while I was writing this paper.

14. Emmanuel Levinas, *On Escape*, trans. Bettina Bergo (Redwood City, CA: Stanford University Press, 2003), 65.

15. Levinas, *On Escape*, 52.

16. Levinas, *On Escape*, 66.

17. Jean-Paul Sartre, *Being and Nothingness*, trans. Hazel Barnes (New York: Washington Square Press, 1992).

18. Sigmund Freud, "A Case of Paranoia Running Counter to the Psycho-Analytic Theory of the Disease," in *The Standard Edition*, 14:269–270.

19. Jacques Lacan, "The Function and Field of Speech and Language in Psychoanalysis," in *Écrits*, trans. Alain Sheridan, ed. Jacques-Alain Miller (New York: W. W. Norton, 1977), 47. This essay, commonly known as "The Rome Discourse," was delivered at Rome Congress in 1953; Lacan's phrase "the powers of the past" later becomes Deleuze's "powers of the false."

20. Sartre, *Being and Nothingness*, 359.

21. Levinas, *On Escape*, 66.

22. Levinas, *On Escape*, 64.

23. Levinas, *On Escape*, 67–68.

24. Levinas, *On Escape*, 67.

25. Lacan, "The Rome Discourse," 47.

26. Levinas, *On Escape*, 67.

27. Levinas, *On Escape*, 75.

28. Freud, "Notes upon a Case of Obsessional Neurosis," in *The Standard Edition*, 10:204.

29. Freud, *The Standard Edition*, 10:271.

30. "The Impromptu at Vincennes" was translated into English by Jeffrey Mehlman and published in Lacan, *Television*. It appears also as Annex A, "Analyticon," in Lacan, *Seminaire XVII*.

31. Steven Connor, "The Shame of Being a Man," paper given in the Gender and Sexuality seminar series, Institute of English Studies, November 30, 2000, https://stevenconnor.com/shame.html. This is an expanded version of the essay published in *Textual Practice* 15 (2001). It is interesting to note that in *Seminaire X*, Lacan similarly explicates the concept of the object-cause of desire by critiquing those conceptions of cause that resort to images of a will exercising itself on some part of the body, such as an arm, conceived as external to will. This reduces the arm, Lacan argues, to something as forgettable as an umbrella. In other words, one exercises one's arm only at a gym, where—it can be argued—one treats one's own body as an object external to oneself; one raises one's arm, however, through the exertion or force inconceivable as an external power.

32. Juliet F. MacCannell highlights the counterfeit nature of capitalist or superegoic jouissance in her excellent reading of the seminar; see "More Thoughts on War and Death:

Lacan's Critique of Capitalism in *Seminar SXVII*," forthcoming in *Reading Seminar SXVII*, ed. Russell Grigg.

33. The 1967 reference is to Jacques Lacan, "Proposition of 9 October 1967 on the Psychoanalyst of the School," trans. Russell Grigg, *Analysis*, no. 6 (1995): 257. The 1968 quotation is translated from Jacques Lacan, "Nota sul padre e l'universalisimo," *La Psicoanalisi*, no. 33 (2003). Both citations are borrowed from Marie-Helene Brousse, "Common Markets and Segregation," in *Jacques Lacan and the Other Side of Psychoanalysis: Reflections on Seminar XVI*, ed. Justin Clemens and Russel Grigg (Durham, NC: Duke University Press, 2006).

34. See Jacques Rancière, *Dis-Agreements: Politics and Philosophy*, trans. Julie Rose (Minneapolis: University of Minnesota Press, 1999).

35. Friedrich Nietzsche, *Beyond Good and Evil*, trans. Walter Kaufman (New York: Random House, 1966), section 263, 213.

36. Sigmund Freud, "Three Essays on the Theory of Sexuality," in *The Standard Edition*, 7:178.

CHAPTER 6

1. Imam Khomeini, "Address at Bihisht-i Zahra," in *Islam and Revolution: The Writings and Declarations of Imam Khomeini*, trans. Hamid Algar (Berkeley, CA: Mizan Press, 1981), 254–260. This speech, delivered on February 2, 1979, at a cemetery outside Tehran where martyrs of the Islamic Revolution were buried, occurred the day after Khomeini arrived in Tehran from his exile in Paris.

2. The regulations aimed at "Islamicizing" Iranian cinema were ratified, and the Ministry of Culture and Islamic Guidance instituted them in February 1983. Hamid Naficy provides the most comprehensive and cogent analysis of the impact of these regulations on Iranian films; I rely heavily on his account. See, in particular, his "Veiled Vision/Powerful Presences: Women in Post-Revolutionary Iranian Cinema," in *Life and Art: The New Iranian Cinema*, ed. Rose Issa and Sheila Whitaker (London: National Film Theater/British Film Institute, 1999).

3. The source of my information about the relation between Raphael Patai's *The Arab Mind* and the strategy of "shaming" adopted by the US at Abu Ghraib is Seymour M. Hersh, "The Gray Zone: How a Secret Pentagon Program Came to Abu Ghraib," *New Yorker*, May 24, 2004, 38. All quotations in this paragraph are from Hersh's essay.

4. In *Touching Feeling: Affect, Pedagogy, Performativity* (Durham, NC: Duke University Press, 2003), Eve Sedgwick offers an alternative to the neoconservative view of shame as she reflects on her own experience of it in the aftermath of another violent confrontation between America and Islam, the attack of September 11. Witnessing the absence of the Towers, Sedgwick experiences a loss of familiar coordinates, a fundamental disorientation. Yet what is odd is that this wound is not accompanied by a simple feeling of isolation, of being separated from society. Sedgwick describes the paradox of shame as a simultaneous movement "toward . . . individuation" and "toward uncontrollable relationality" or social contagion (31). The difference between this passage, which appears to overlap with my own, is that I am presenting an intransitive notion of shame, while she speaks in this passage of her shame "for the Towers." She points to an object of shame.

5. Giorgio Agamben, *Remnants of Auschwitz: The Witness and the Archive*, trans. Daniel Heller-Roazen (New York: Zone Books, 1999), 110, 107.

6. Hamid Dabashi's otherwise highly informative *Close-Up* (1990) explodes in its final chapter into an unfair (to my mind) rant against *The Wind Will Carry Us*.

7. Emmanuel Levinas, *On Escape*, trans. Bettina Bergo (Redwood City, CA: Stanford University Press, 2003), 52. For further discussion of Levinas and shame, see chapter 5, "May '68, the Emotional Month," above.

8. My implication is that we should also look to Islamic philosophy for a theory of the "unfinished past." See, for example, Henry Corbin's "Prologue" to his study of Islamic philosophy in *Spiritual Body and Celestial Earth: From Mazdean Iran to Shi'ite Iran*, trans. Nancy Pearson (Princeton, NJ: Princeton University Press, 1955): "Our authors suggest that if our past were really what we believe it to be, that is, completed and closed, it would not be the grounds of such vehement discussions. They suggest that all our acts of understanding are so many recommencements, reiterations of events still unconcluded" (xv).

9. In *Truth and Singularity: Taking Foucault into Phenomenology* (Dordrecht, the Netherlands: Kluwer Academic Publishers, 1999), Rudi Visker adopts this same phrase in conformity with Lacan's definition of anxiety as "not without object." Arriving at shame through anxiety, Visker offers a theory of the former similar to my own even though he does not focus on the question of jouissance. The idea of a paradoxical, rootless root can be traced backed to Heidegger's discussion of imagination in his Kantbook.

10. Jacques Lacan, *Seminar VII: The Ethics of Psychoanalysis*, trans. Dennis Porter, ed. Jacques-Alain Miller (London: Tavistock/Routledge, 1992), 71.

11. Soren Kierkegaard, *The Concept of Anxiety: A Simple Psychologically Orienting Deliberation on the Dogmatic Issue of Hereditary Sin* (Princeton, NJ: Princeton University Press, 1980), 155.

12. Jacques Lacan, *Le Seminaire de Jacques Lacan, livre VIII: Le transfert*, ed. Jacques-Alain Miller (Paris: Seuil, 1991), 155.

13. Sigmund Freud, "Inhibitions, Symptoms, and Anxiety," in *The Standard Edition of the Complete Psychological Works of Sigmund Freud*, trans. James Strachey (London: The Hogarth Press and the Institute of Psycho-Analysis, 1953–1974), 20:77–174. Freud says that "analysis shows that when activities like . . . writing . . . are subjected to neurotic inhibitions it is because . . . the fingers . . . have become too strongly eroticized. It has been discovered as a general fact that the ego-function of an organ is impaired if its erotogenicity—its sexual significance—is increased. It behaves, if I may be allowed a rather absurd analogy, like a maid-servant who refuses to go on cooking because her master has started a love-affair with her" (89–90).

14. Freud, *Inhibitions, Symptoms, and Anxiety*, 84.

15. Jean-Luc Nancy notes the instability of the earth in Kiarostami's films in his excellent study, *The Evidence of Film: Abbas Kiarostami* (Brussels: Yves Gevaert, 2001).

16. David Sterritt, "Taste of Kiarostami," *Senses of Cinema*, September 2000, https://www.sensesofcinema.com/2000/abbas-kiarostami-remembered/kiarostami-2/.

17. Michel Ciment and Stéphane Goudet, "Une approche existentialiste de la vie," *Positif* 442 (December 1997): 85; also cited in Stéphane Goudet, "Le Goût de la cerise . . . et la saveur de la mure," *L'Avant Scene* no. 471 (April 1998): 1.

18. See Lacan, *Seminar VI*.

19. Qur'an, 50:6. For a fascinating discussion of the way Ibn 'Arabi interprets this notion, see Henry Corbin, *Alone with the Alone: Creative Imagination in the Sufism of Ibn 'Arabi* (Princeton, NJ: Princeton University Press, 1990).

20. Friedrich Nietzsche, *Beyond Good and Evil*, trans. Walter Kaufman (New York: Random House, 1966), 213.

21. Nietzsche, *Beyond Good and Evil*.

22. Giorgio Agamben, *Homo Sacer: Sovereign Power and Bare Life*, trans. Daniel Heller-Roazen (Redwood City, CA: Stanford University Press, 1998), 26–27.

23. Freud, "The Ego and the Id," in *The Standard Edition*, 19:38; my emphasis.

24. Quoted in Carl D. Schneider, *Shame, Exposure, and Privacy* (New York: W. W. Norton, 1977), 38.

25. See Corbin, *Spiritual Body and Celestial Earth* for a discussion of this idea in medieval Islamic philosophy.

26. Sartre, *Being and Nothingness*, 369.

27. Jacques Lacan, *Seminar XI: The Four Fundamental Concepts of Psychoanalysis*, ed. Jacques-Alain Miller, trans. Alan Sheridan (London: Hogarth Press and the Institute of Psychoanalysis, 1977), 182.

28. Lacan, *Seminar XI*, 84–85; my emphasis.

29. Again, see above, "May '68, the Emotional Month."

30. Agamben, *Remnants of Auschwitz*, 103–104.

31. This is obviously a description of a scene from the film *Stella Dallas* (directed by King Vidor, 1937).

32. Joan Riviere, "Womanliness as a Masquerade," in *Formations of Fantasy*, ed. Victor Burgin, James Donald, and Cora Kaplan (London: Routledge, 1986), 37. All subsequent quotations in this paragraph can be found on page 37 of Riviere's essay.

33. I have used the translation of Forough's poem by Ahmad Karimi-Hakkak, which is cited in Mehrnaz Saeed-Vafa and Jonathan Rosenbaum, *Abbas Kiarostami* (Urbana: University of Illinois Press, 2003), 33–34.

34. Havelock Ellis, quoted in Schneider, *Shame, Exposure, and Privacy*, 60.

35. Nietzsche, *Beyond Good and Evil*, 50.

CHAPTER 7

1. Teresa de Lauretis, *Technologies of Gender: Essays in Theory, Film, and Fiction* (Bloomington: Indiana University Press, 1987), x.

2. Shulamith Firestone, *The Dialectic of Sex* (New York: Bantam, 1972), 10–11.

3. For a thorough analysis of these questions see, Gilbert Simondon, "The Genesis of the Individual," in *Incorporations*, ed. Jonathan Crary and Sanford Kwinter (New York: Zone Books, 1992).

4. For more on this debate, see, for example, *Individuation in Scholasticism: The Later Middle Ages and the Counter-Reformation*, ed. Jorge Gracia (Albany: SUNY Press, 1994). My own interest in the question of individuation was ignited by the defense of the medieval Islamic philosophers' position on this subject mounted by Henry Corbin; see his "Apophatic Theology as Antidote to Nihilism," trans. Roland Vegso, *Umbr(a)* (2007): 59–83. Working from a different set of sources and questions, Mladen Dolar has begun a similar exploration of sexual difference, based on a more sophisticated notion of the One, in an excellent unpublished manuscript, "One Splits into Two." See also the fine work of our colleague, Alenka Zupančič, on the problematic nature of the two in *The Shortest Shadow: Nietzsche's Philosophy of the Two* (Cambridge, MA: MIT Press, 2003).

5. Christian Jambet discusses the Islamic concept of the "unity of God" (tawhid in Arabic), which this formulation expresses, in his remarkable essay "The Stranger and Theophany," trans. Roland Vegso, Umbr(a) (2005): 27–41. This essay was originally published in Jambet's Le cache et l'apparent (Paris: Editions de l'Herne, 2003). Lacan—not coincidentally—employs the Islamic formula "There is no other God but God" in his reading of the "specimen dream" of psychoanalysis, the dream of Irma's injection. He uses this formula to drain trimethylamine (a product of the decomposition of sperm) of its sexual substance and reconstitute it as an empty signifier, one that, because it means nothing, can indicate the excess in language that gives rise to sex. See Jacques Lacan, The Seminar of Jacques Lacan, Book II. The Ego in Freud's Theory and in the Technique of Psychoanalysis, ed. Jacques-Alain Miller, trans. Sylvana Tomaselli (New York: Norton, 1988), 158.

6. See Henry Corbin, Alone with the Alone: Creative Imagination in the Sufism of Ibn 'Arabi (Princeton, NJ: Princeton University Press, 1990), 210. In Arabic the phrase "eternal haecceity" is 'ayn thabita; it means eternal "essence" or quiddity, but no mere translation does the term—which requires considerable theoretical unpacking—justice.

7. Lacan, The Seminar of Jacques Lacan: Book XX, Encore, ed. Jacques-Alain Miller, trans. Bruce Fink (New York: Norton, 1998), 3.

8. For a lucid discussion of failed versus real repetition, I recommend Alenka Zupančič, The Odd One In: On Comedy (Cambridge, MA: MIT Press, 2008), 149–182.

9. Soren Kierkegaard, Fear and Trembling/Repetition, ed. and trans. Howard Hong and Edna Hong (Princeton, NJ: Princeton University Press. 1983), 123.

10. Kierkegaard, Fear and Trembling/Repetition, 131; Sigmund Freud, "Project for a Scientific Psychology," in The Standard Edition of the Complete Psychological Works of Sigmund Freud, trans. James Strachey (London: The Hogarth Press and the Institute of Psycho-Analysis, 1953–1974), 356.

11. Gilles Deleuze, Cinema 1: The Movement-Image, trans. Hugh Habberjam and Barbara Habberjam (Minneapolis: University of Minnesota Press, 1986), 6.

12. Freud, "A Note upon the 'Mystic Writing-Pad,'" in The Standard Edition, 19:231.

13. Juliet Mitchell, "Introduction 1," Feminine Sexuality: Jacques Lacan and the ecole freudienne, ed. Juliet Mitchell and Jacqueline Rose (New York: W. W. Norton, 1982), 20.

14. Fethi Benslama uses the term monotheistic in relation to sex in the title of his interesting essay, "Le sexuel monotheiste et sa traduction scientifique," without, however, telling us what this adjective means in this context. I was happy to come upon this text in the midst of writing my argument here since Benslama confirms my own regional tale of a Western retiring of the term sexual difference in favor of gender during the 1980s. As it turns out—Benslama recounts—the Arabo-Islamic world—once thought by Foucault, among others, to be the last bastion of an ars poetica against the scientia sexualis that steadily took over the West since the nineteenth century—became subject in the 1980s to this particular form of "Westoxification." At this point, what had been the most common Arabic word for sex, farj, was rapidly replaced by the term jins, from the Latin genus or gender. And as jins, or gender, usurped the place of farj, the word that had for centuries been used for men and women, farj simultaneously became restricted in scope and began to designate the sexual organ of women only. At the same time, jins, which carried with it scientific, specifically biomedical connotations absent from farj, narrowed the sense of sexual relations or affairs to the genital register.

15. Jacques Lacan, Le séminaire, livre XVII, D'un autre à l'autre (Paris: Seuil, 2006), 144.

16. Lacan, *Le séminaire, livre XVII*, 208.

17. Michel Foucault, *The History of Sexuality, Volume I*, trans. Robert Hurley (New York: Pantheon, 1978), 143.

18. Michel Foucault and Ludwig Binswanger, *Dream and Existence*, ed. Keith Hoeller (Atlantic Highlands, NJ: Humanities Press International, 1993), 102.

19. Foucault and Binswanger, *Dream and Existence*.

20. Foucault, *The History of Sexuality*, 141.

21. Foucault, *The History of Sexuality*, 157; Foucault also calls sex a "fictitious point" (156) and an "imaginary point" (155).

22. Foucault, *The History of Sexuality*, 154.

23. Foucault, *The History of Sexuality*.

24. Jacques Lacan, *Television: A Challenge to the Psychoanalytic Establishment*, ed. Joan Copjec, trans., Denis Hollier, Rosalind Krauss, and Annette Michelson (New York: W. W. Norton, 1990), 30.

25. Jacques Lacan, *The Seminar of Jacques Lacan: Book XX, Encore*, ed. Jacques-Alain Miller, trans. Bruce Fink (New York: W. W. Norton, 1998), 11.

26. Henry Corbin, "Prophetic Philosophy and the Metaphysics of Being," in *The Voyage and the Messenger: Iran and Philosophy*, trans. Joseph Rowe (Berkeley, CA: North Atlantic Books), 208.

27. Sigmund Freud, "New Introductory Lectures on Psychoanalysis. XXXIII Femininity," *The Standard Edition*, 22:116 (my emphasis).

28. Lacan, *Encore*, 21.

29. Sigmund Freud, "Civilization and Its Discontents," in *The Standard Edition*, 22:114.

30. Freud, "Instincts and Their Vicissitudes," in *The Standard Edition*, 14:122.

31. Freud, "Project for a Scientific Psychology," in *The Standard Edition*, 1:331. This comparison between Descartes and Freud is made by Monique David-Menard in "Sexual Alterity and the Alterity of the Real for Thought," *Angelaki* 8, no. 2 (2003): 137–150.

32. Lacan, *Encore*, 112.

33. Lacan, *Encore*, 23.

34. Freud, "Civilization and Its Discontents," 21:65.

35. Freud, "Civilization and Its Discontents," 21:66.

36. Freud, "Civilization and Its Discontents," 21.

37. Gilles Deleuze, *The Fold: Leibniz and the Baroque*, trans. Tom Conley (Minneapolis: University of Minnesota Press, 1993), 47.

38. Lacan, *Encore*, 9.

39. Lacan, *Encore*, 10.

40. Lacan, *Encore*, 3.

41. Freud, "On the Universal Tendency to Debasement in the Sphere of Love," in *The Standard Edition*, 11:187 (my emphasis).

42. Deleuze, 85.

43. Corbin, *Alone with the Alone*, 155.

44. Corbin, *Alone with the Alone*, 154.

45. Corbin, *Alone with the Alone*, 156.

46. Jacques Derrida, "Sexual Difference, Ontological Difference," in *A Derrida Reader*, ed. Peggy Kamuf (New York: Columbia University Press, 1991), 386.

47. Derrida, "Sexual Difference, Ontological Difference," 387–388.

48. Derrida, "Sexual Difference, Ontological Difference," 393.

49. Lacan, *Encore*, 49: "In other words, there are three of them, but in reality, there are two plus *a*. This two plus *a*, can be reduced, not only to the two others, but to a one plus *a*." My entire essay may be summarized as an attempt to spell out the meaning of these brief sentences.

INDEX

Agamben, Giorgio
  the echo in Liebniz, 178n43
  Homo Sacer, 130–131
  profanation, 176n8 (*see also* Corbin, on secularization and sacralization)
  Remnants of Auschwitz, 123, 135–137
Al-haqq (the real), 67–72
Angel-being, 65, 147–149, 170n10
Apophatic, 36–39, 53–56, 61–66, 69–72, 76–77, 147–149, 170n10, 186n4
Aristotle
  and *barzakh*, 40–43
  on finalism, 84
  and Heidegger, 92
  Lacan on, 40, 149–150
  Levinas on, 84–85, 91–96
  "On the Soul," 27–28
  on the question of the One, 149–150
  on touch, 27–28, 40–43
Averroes
  and the rationalists, 19–20, 65
  Ernest Renan on, 50
Avicenna
  pace Aristotle, 27–28, 92
  pace Averroes, 19, 64–65
  on *barzakh*, 165–166
  "Flying Man" experiment, 27–28, 92, 94–96, 181n47
  and Lacan, 66–67
  "visionary recital," 10–11, 12

Badiou, Alain
  "covering over," 176n11
  "passion for the real," 119–120

Balázs, Béla, 38
Barzakh (limit, opening), 40–44, 165–166
Benjamin, Walter
  on aura and capitalism, 107–108
  on language, 60–61
Benslama, Fethi, 187n10
Bloom, Harold
  Omens of Millennium, 176n16
  "Preface," *Alone with the Alone*, 173n2
Blumenberg, Hans
  on the close-up, 38
  on lumen and lux, 34–35, 38
Boehme, Jacob, 53–54
Bread and Alley (1970), 1–3

Cheetam, Tom, *After Prophecy*, 171n14
Chittick, William C.
  on Corbin, 174n18
  on imagination, 172n41
  The Sufi Path of Knowledge, 171n15
Chodkiewicz, Michel, *An Ocean without a Shore*, 170n12
Close-Up (1990), 8–9, 11–12, 31–36, 38–39
Cloud, 13, 45–49, 54–56, 61–63, 76–77, 176n11
Coleridge, Samuel Taylor, 52
Connor, Steven, 117–119
Corbin, Henry
  "Apophatic Theology as Antidote to Nihilism," 61–66, 69–72, 170n10, 175n26
  Avicenna and the Visionary Recital, 10–12, 17, 54–55, 64–65

Corbin, Henry (cont.)
   on the dogma of incarnation in Christianity, 19–28
   Epiphany, 54–56
   on Heidegger, 80–81
   imaginal world, 17–19, 80–81, 86 (see also Imaginal world)
   "The Imago Templi in Confrontation with Secular Norms," 175n24
   "I was a hidden Treasure," 37–40, 54–56, 69–72
   and Khomeini, 49–50, 59–60, 66
   and Lacan, 40, 49–50, 71
   and Levinas, 80–84
   and the neo-Gnostics, 63–65, 75–77 (see also Gnosticism; Neo-Gnosticism)
   "Prophetic Philosophy and the Metaphysics of Being," 188n26
   and Schelling, 50–54
   on secularization and sacralization, 59–60, 62–64
   Spiritual Body and Celestial Earth, 17–24, 26–27, 185n8
   tautegory, 51–53
   "Theophanies and Mirrors: Idols or Icons?," 171n13
   The Voyage and the Messenger: Iran and Philosophy, 170n5
Cow, The (1969), 73–74
Crary, Jonathan, *24/7: Late Capitalism and the Ends of Sleep*, 82–84

Dabashi, Hamid
   on *The House Is Black*, 75
   "nominalism of the image," 67
   on *The Wind Will Carry Us*, 124–125, 132, 142–143
Damisch, Hubert, 10
de Lauretis, Teresa, 145
Deleuze, Gilles
   on affect, 104–105
   Cinema 1: The Movement-Image, 38
   on the close-up, 38
   on the death drive and repetition, 90–95
   Difference and Repetition, 90–95
   on Leibniz and the body, 164–165
   "Michael Tournier and the World without Others," 104–105
   "Phantasm and Modern Literature," 53–54
Derrida, Jacques
   critique of presence, 94
   "Geschlecht: Sexual Difference, Ontological Difference," 166–167
   on Heidegger's notion of death, 83–84
   on Levinas's critique of Heidegger, 88
Docetism, 22–26, 29–40, 171n28
Dolar, Mladen, 186n148

Eighth Climate, 81–82, 86. See also Imaginal world
Elena, Alberto, 169n5
Epiphany (and epiphanic form), 9–11, 24–27, 54–58, 69–71, 169n6

Farrokhzad, Forough, 74–75, 139, 141. See also *The House Is Black*
Fellow Citizen (1983), 29–31
Firestone, Shulamith, 145
First Case, Second Case (1979), 11, 59–60, 66–69, 73–78
Freud, Sigmund
   on anxiety, 109–111, 115–116, 126–127, 138, 141
   on the body, 43–44, 73, 77–78
   Civilization and Its Discontents, 107–111
   on daydreams, 32
   death drive, 90–91, 93, 95–96
   die Not des Lebens, 73
   drive, 43–44, 77–78, 81, 87–91, 146, 161–166
   fort/da, 39–40
   Group Psychology and the Analysis of the Ego, 149–150
   on guilt, 131–132
   Hilflosigkeit, 87–88
   hysteria, 43–44, 114
   The Interpretation of Dreams, 81–84
   the myth of the father, 117–118
   Nachtraglichkeit, 48–49, 57, 151–153
   "Negation," 96
   "A Note upon the 'Mystic Writing-Pad,'" 153
   Oneness, 164–167
   "On Narcissism," 112–113
   "On Psychotherapy," 5–6

The Project for a Scientific Psychology, 73, 92, 151–153, 161–162, 164–165
Rat Man, 115–116
"Remembering, Repeating, and Working Through," 95–96, 151–152
"repressive hypothesis," 155–156, 158
on shame, 120
on subtraction, 5–6
the uncanny, 10–11
"The Unconscious," 162–163
Vorstellungrepräsentanz, 105–106
"wish to sleep," 82–84
Wo es war, soll Ich werden, 56–58
Foucault, Michel
on bio-power, 83
The History of Sexuality, Volume 1, 154–162
on the Iranian revolution, 69

Gnosticism (and Gnosis), 11–13, 46–47, 64–65, 67, 69–71, 75–77, 98, 176n1, 177n35. *See also* Neo-Gnosticism

Heidegger, Martin
on anxiety, 126
and Aristotle, 92
Being and Time, 82–84, 88–89, 91–92
"being-toward-death," 82–84, 88–89, 91
Corbin on, 64, 80–84
Derrida on, 166–167
Levinas on, 80–84, 88–89, 91–92, 114
and sexual difference, 166–167
Homework (1989), 78
House Is Black, The (1962), 74–75
Hyppolite, Jean, on Freud's "Negation," 96

Ibn ʿArabi
on *barzakh*, 41–42
The Book of Unity, 36–39
and the Cloud, 45–47
"I was a hidden Treasure," 36–39, 45–47, 57–58, 69–72
Lacan's familiarity with, 49–50
on the Law, 51
on love, 8–9, 12, 165–166
"seeing with two eyes," 172n47
Ishaghpour, Youssef
Le reel, face et pile: Le cinema d'Abbas Kiarostami, 2–4
"The True and False in Art," 7–8

Imaginal world, 13, 17–20, 27, 30–33, 40–44, 51–56, 59–65, 69–70, 76–78, 79–82, 86, 139. *See also* Eighth Climate

Jalal-e-Ahmad, 176n12
Jambet, Christian
The Act of Being, 170n6, 174n6, 176n5
on the act of being, 56–58, 76
"The Constitution of the Subject and Spiritual Practice," 69, 175n9
on Corbin, 18, 48, 49, 50–51, 53, 56
"The Death of Epiphany," 175n42
"Four Discourses on Authority in Islam," 176n10
La logique des orientaux, 172n39
"The Paradoxical One," 175n27
"A Philosophical Commentary," 178n44
"The Stranger and Theophany," 187n5
on truth, 47–48, 51, 72–73

Khomeini, Imam
in relation to *First Case, Second Case*, 65–69
and the Iranian Revolution, 48–51, 59–60, 65–67, 73–74, 121
public address at Bihishti-i-Zahra, 65–67
Kierkegaard, Soren
on anxiety, 126–127
on repetition, 151

Lacan, Jacques
affect, 101–106
"alethosphere," 13, 106–111, 118–119
après-coup, 48–49, 57–58
on capitalism, 108–111, 129, 158
and Corbin, 47–50
drive, 43–44, 77–78, 146–150, 161–162, 165–166
Encore, 49–50, 150, 159–166
"extimacy," 108–110
fort/da, 39–40
on the gaze, 28, 40, 97, 104–105, 111–113, 133–142
impossibility, 6–7, 74, 164–165
"Impromptu at Vincennes," 116
limit, 164
May '68, 13, 101–104, 155–156
myth of the lamella, 106–111
myth of the lathouses, 106–107, 110–111

Lacan, Jacques (cont.)
   myth of the primordial father, 113–118
   on nominalism, 67
   the real, 33, 57–58, 67, 71–73, 105–106, 119–120, 149–150
   on Sartre, 102–103, 111–113, 135–142
   Séminaire XVII: L'envers de la psychanalyse, 101–103
   on shame, 101–103, 119–120, 130, 135–137
   The Sinthome: Book XXIII, 76–78
   unborn, 57–58, 71–73, 76–78
   on universalism, 119
   "University Discourse," 101–104, 107–108, 115, 118–120
   Wo es war, soll Ich werden, 56–58
   y a d'l'Un, 162–163
Laplanche, Jean, 48–49, 57–58
Levinas, Emmanuel
   on anxiety and shame, 110–111, 113–118, 129, 131, 135–136
   on capitalism, 110–111, 116–118
   Existence and Existents, 80, 82–85, 88–89, 91–96
   on fatigue, 80, 82–85, 91–96
   on freedom, 88
   on Heidegger, 82–85, 88–89
   "il y a," 91–96
   "Meaning and Sense," 174n8
   On Escape, 110–136
   on the present, 86, 88–89, 91–96
Life and Nothing More (1992), 17–18, 90, 130
Like Someone in Love (2012), 8–13

Massumi, Brian, 105
Mitchell, Juliet, 145, 155
Metz, Christian, 4–5
Modesty system, 7–8, 35–36, 67, 121–124, 132–135, 141–143
Mondzain, Marie-José, 172n36
Mottahedeh, Negar, 177n22
Mulvey, Laura, 11–12

Nancy, Jean-Luc, *The Evidence of Film*, 5–7
Neo-Gnosticism, 67, 69–71, 73, 77. *See also* Gnosticism
Nietzsche, Friedrich, 119–120, 130, 132, 139
Nominalism, 60–61, 67, 149–150

Occidentosis. *See* Westoxification

Pandolfo, Stefania, 180n45

Rabinbach, Anson, 81–82
Riviere, Joan, 138

Sadra, Mulla
   "existential revolution," 66–67
   Jambet on, 48
Sartre, Jean-Paul
   Deleuze and, 105
   on the gaze, 102, 105, 111–113, 133–135, 140–142
   Lacan on, 102, 105, 133–135, 140–142
   on shame, 133–136, 140–142
Schelling, F. W. J., 106
   on contingency, 56–57
   Deleuze on, 53–54
   on emanation, 53–54
   "non-unilateral monotheism," 12–13
   tautegory, 51–52
   Žižek on, 56
Shariati, Ali, 176n12
Sohravardi
   and Corbin, 50, 80
   the visionary recital, 10–12
Steinberg, Leo
   and Corbin on docetism, 23–24
   "incarnational realism," 25–26
   The Sexuality of Christ in Renaissance Art and in Modern Oblivion, 22–28
St. John of Damascus, 20, 42

Taslim (submission), 61–62, 76–77, 137–143
Taste of Cherry (1997), 79–81, 84–91, 96–98, 128–129
Tawhid (oneness of God), 46–48, 61, 75–76
Ta'wil (exegesis), 81–85
Theophany (and theophanic form), 36–38, 40–42, 54–56, 69–73
Through the Olive Trees (1994), 17
Traveller, The (1974), 2–5
24 Frames (2017), 11

Unborn, 57–58, 71–77

Varzi, Roxanne, 176n3
Veiling. *See* Modesty system
Visker, Rudi, 183n13

Wasserstrom, Steven
   Eranos, 49–50, 61, 75
   Religion after Religion, 49–55, 59–61, 64–65, 67, 70, 75
Westoxification, 62–67, 187n14
Where Is the Friend's House? (1987), 2–5, 17–18, 128
Wind Will Carry Us, The (1999), 8–9, 63, 89–90, 123–143

Žižek, Slavoj, 56
Zupančič, Alenka, 177n17, 186n4, 187n8